;EVALUATE A FORMULA

;GET VALUE TYPE INTO [A]
;SAVE THE VALUE TYPE ON THE STACK
;GET TERMINATING CHARACTER OF FORMULA

;ONTO THE STACK
;KEEPS RELATIONAL OPERATOR MEMORIES
;LESS THAN =4
;EQUAL   =2
;GREATER THAN =1
;CHECK FOR A RELATIONAL OPERATOR
;NOPE
;NUMBER OF RELATIONAL OPERATORS
;IS THIS ONE OF THEM?
;NO SEE WHAT WE HAVE
;SETUP BITS BY MAPPING
;0 TO 1, 1 TO 2 AND 2 TO 4
;OR WITH EARLIER BITS
;STORE NEW BITS
;GET NEW CHARACTER
;SEE IF RELATIONAL
;GET REALTIONAL MEMORIES
;SEE IF THERE ARE ANY
;NO RELATIONAL OPERATORS!
;SAVE RELATIONAL MEMORIES
;PICK UP FIRST NON-RELATIONAL
;CHARACTER AGAIN AND INTERPRET FORMULA
;ANSWER LEFT IN FAC
44   ;A COMMA?

;IF SO SKIP IT

;ALLOW "GOTO" AS WELL

;MUST HAVE A THEN

;POP OFF NUMBER

;COMPARE FORMULA TYPES

Source Code

Bill Gates

Source Code

My Beginnings

Alfred A. Knopf · *New York 2025*

A BORZOI BOOK
FIRST HARDCOVER EDITION
PUBLISHED BY ALFRED A. KNOPF 2025

Published by Alfred A. Knopf, a division of Penguin Random House LLC, 1745 Broadway, New York, NY 10019.

Knopf, Borzoi Books, and the colophon are registered trademarks of Penguin Random House LLC.

Library of Congress Control Number: 2024943843
ISBN 978-0-593-80158-1 (hardcover)
ISBN 978-0-593-80159-8 (ebook)

penguinrandomhouse.com | aaknopf.com

Manufactured in the United States of America

The authorized representative in the EU for product safety and compliance is Penguin Random House Ireland, Morrison Chambers, 32 Nassau Street, Dublin D02 YH68, Ireland, https://eu-contact.penguin.ie.

In memory of my parents
Bill Gates and Mary Maxwell Gates

And to my sisters
Kristi and Libby

The prize is the pleasure of finding the thing out.

—Richard P. Feynman

Contents

Source Code

Prologue

When I was around thirteen, I started hanging out with a group of boys who met up for regular long hikes in the mountains around Seattle. We got to know each other as Boy Scouts. We did plenty of hiking and camping with our troop, but very quickly we formed a sort of splinter group that went on our own expeditions—and that's how we thought of them, as expeditions. We wanted more freedom and more risk than the trips the Scouts offered.

There were usually five of us—Mike, Rocky, Reilly, Danny, and me. Mike was the leader; he was a few years older than the rest of us and had vastly more outdoor experience. Over the course of three years or so, we hiked hundreds of miles together. We covered the Olympic National Forest west of Seattle and Glacier Peak Wilderness to the northeast and did hikes along the Pacific Coast. We'd often go for seven days or more at a stretch, guided only by topographic maps through old-growth forests and rocky beaches where we tried to time the tides as we hustled around points. During school breaks, we'd take off on extended trips, hiking and camping in all weather, which in the Pacific Northwest often meant a week of soaked, itchy Army surplus wool pants and pruney toes. We weren't doing technical climbing. No ropes or slings or sheer rock faces. Just long, hard hikes. It wasn't dangerous beyond the fact that we were teenagers deep in the mountains, many hours from help and well before cell phones were a thing.

Over time we grew into a confident, tight-knit team. We'd finish a full day of hiking, decide upon a place to camp, and with hardly a word we'd all fall into our jobs. Mike and Rocky might tie up the tarp that would be our roof for the night. Danny foraged the undergrowth for dry wood, and Reilly and I coaxed a starter stick and twigs into our fire for the night.

And then we ate. Cheap food that was light in our packs but substantial enough to fuel us through the trip. Nothing ever tasted better. For dinner we'd chop up a brick of Spam and mix it with Hamburger Helper or a packet of beef Stroganoff mix. In the morning, we might have Carnation Instant Breakfast mix or a powder that with water transformed into a western omelet, at least according to the package. My morning favorite: Oscar Mayer Smokie Links, a sausage billed as "all meat," now extinct. We used a single frying pan to prepare most of the food, and we ate out of empty #10 coffee cans we each carried. Those cans were our water pails, our saucepans, our oatmeal bowls. I don't know who among us invented the hot raspberry drink. Not that it was a great culinary innovation: just add instant Jell-O mix to boiling water and drink. It worked as dessert or as a morning sugar boost before a day of hiking.

We were away from our parents and the control of any adults, making our own decisions about where to go, what to eat, when we slept, judging for ourselves what risks to take. At school, none of us were the cool kids. Only Danny played an organized sport—basketball—and he soon quit that to make time for our hikes. I was the skinniest of the group and usually the coldest, and I always felt like I was weaker than the others. Still, I liked the physical challenge, and the feeling of autonomy. While hiking was becoming popular in our part of the country, not a lot of teenagers were traipsing off in the woods for eight days on their own.

That said, it was the 1970s, and attitudes toward parenting were looser than they are today. Kids generally had more freedom. And by the time I was in my early teens, my parents had accepted that I was different from many of my peers and had come to terms with the fact that I needed a certain amount of independence in making my way through the world. That acceptance had been hard-won— especially for my mother—but it would play a defining part in who I was to become.

Looking back on it now, I'm sure all of us were searching for something on those trips beyond camaraderie and a sense of accomplishment. We were at that age when kids test their limits, experiment with different identities—and also sometimes feel a yearning for bigger, even transcendent experiences. I had started to feel a clear longing to figure out what my path would be. I wasn't sure what direction it would take, but it had to be something interesting and consequential.

Also in those years, I was spending a lot of time with a different group of boys. Kent, Paul, Ric, and I all went to the same school, Lakeside, which had set up a way for students to connect with a big mainframe computer over a phone line. It was incredibly rare back then for teenagers to have access to a computer in any form. The four of us really took to it, devoting all our free time to writing increasingly more sophisticated programs and exploring what we could do with that electronic machine.

On the surface, the difference between hiking and programming couldn't have been greater. But they each felt like an adventure. With both sets of friends I was exploring new worlds, traveling to places even most adults couldn't reach. Like hiking, programming fit me because it allowed me to define my own measure of success and it seemed limitless, not determined by how fast I could run or how far I could throw. The logic, focus, and stamina needed to write long, complicated programs came naturally to me. Unlike in hiking, among that group of friends, I was the leader.

—

Toward the end of my sophomore year, in June 1971, Mike called me with our next trip: fifty miles in the Olympic Mountains. The route he chose was called the Press Expedition Trail, after a group sponsored by a newspaper that had explored the area in 1890. Did he mean the same trip on which the men nearly starved to death and their clothes rotted on their bodies? Yes, but that was a long time ago, he said.

Eight decades later it would still be a tough hike; that year had brought a lot of snow, so it was a particularly daunting proposition. But since everyone else—Rocky, Reilly, and Danny—was up for it, there was no way I was going to wimp out. Plus, a younger scout, a guy named Chip, was game. I had to go.

The plan was to climb the Low Divide pass, descend to the Quinault River, and then hike the same trail back, staying each night in log shelters along the way. Six or seven days total. The first day was easy and we spent the night in a beautiful snow-covered meadow. Over the next day or two, as we climbed the Low Divide, the snow got deeper. When we reached the spot where we planned to spend the night, the shelter was buried in snow. I enjoyed a moment of private elation. Surely, I thought, we'd backtrack, head down to a far more welcoming shelter we had passed earlier in the day. We'd make a fire, get warm, and eat.

Mike said we'd take a vote: head back or push on to our final destination. Either choice meant a several-hour hike. "We passed a shelter at the bottom; it's eighteen hundred feet down. We could go back down and stay there, or we could continue on to the Quinault River," Mike said. He didn't need to spell out that going back meant aborting our mission to reach the river.

"What do you think, Dan?" Mike asked. Danny was the unofficial second in command in our little group. He was taller than everyone else, and a very capable hiker with long legs that never seemed to tire. Whatever he said would sway the vote.

"Well, we're almost there, maybe we should just go on," Danny said. As the hands went up, it was clear I was in the minority. We'd push on.

A few minutes down the trail I said, "Danny, I'm not happy with you. You could have stopped this." I was joking—sort of.

I remember this trip for how cold and miserable I felt that day. I also remember it for what I did next. I retreated into my own thoughts.

I pictured computer code.

Around that time, someone had loaned Lakeside a computer called a PDP-8, made by Digital Equipment Corp. This was 1971, and while I was deep into the nascent world of computers, I had never seen anything like it. Up until then, my friends and I had used only huge mainframe computers that were simultaneously shared with other people. We usually connected to them over a phone line or else they were locked in a separate room. But the PDP-8 was designed to be used directly by one person and was small enough to sit on the desk next to you. It was probably the closest thing in its day to the personal computers that would be common a decade or so later—though one that weighed eighty pounds and cost $8,500. For a challenge, I decided I would try to write a version of the BASIC programming language for the new computer.

Before the hike I was working on the part of the program that would tell the computer the order in which it should perform operations when someone inputs an expression such as $3(2 + 5) \times 8 - 3$, or wants to create a game that requires complex math. In programming that feature is called a formula evaluator. Trudging along with my eyes on the ground in front of me, I worked on my evaluator, puzzling through the steps needed to perform the operations. Small was key. Computers back then had very little memory, which meant programs had to be lean, written using as little code as possible so as not to hog memory. The PDP-8 had just 6 kilobytes of the memory a computer uses to store data that it's working on. I'd picture the code and then try to trace how the computer would follow my commands. The rhythm of walking helped me think, much like a habit I had of rocking in place. For the rest of that day my mind was immersed in my coding puzzle. As we descended to the valley floor, the snow gave way to a gently sloping trail through an old forest of spruce and fir trees until we reached the river, set up camp, ate our Spam Stroganoff, and finally slept.

By early the next morning we were climbing back up the Low Divide in heavy wind and sleet that whipped sideways in our faces. We stopped under a tree long enough to share a sleeve of Ritz crackers and continued. Every camp we found was full of other hikers waiting out the storm. So we just kept going, adding more hours to an interminable day. Crossing a stream, Chip fell and gashed his knee. Mike cleaned the wound and applied butterfly bandages; now we moved only as fast as Chip limped. All the while, I silently honed my code. I hardly spoke a word during the twenty miles we hiked that day. Eventually we came to a shelter that had room for us and set up camp.

Like the famous line "I would have written a shorter letter, but I did not have the time," it's easier to write a program in sloppy code that goes on for pages than to write the same program on a single page. The sloppy version may also run more slowly and use more memory. Over the course of that hike, I had the time to write short. On that long day I slimmed it down more, like whittling little pieces off a stick to sharpen the point. What I made seemed efficient and pleasingly simple. It was by far the best code I had ever written.

As we made our way back to the trailhead the next afternoon, the rain finally gave way to clear skies and the warmth of sunlight. I felt the elation that always hit me *after* a hike, when all the hard work was behind me.

—

By the time school started again in the fall, whoever had lent us the PDP-8 had reclaimed it. I never finished my BASIC project. But the code I wrote on that hike, my formula evaluator, and its beauty stayed with me.

Three and a half years later, I was a sophomore in college not sure of my path in life when Paul, one of my Lakeside friends, burst into my dorm room with news of a groundbreaking computer. I knew we could write a BASIC language for it; we had a head start. The first thing I did was to think back to that miserable day on the Low Divide and retrieve from my memory the evaluator code I had written. I typed it into a computer, and with that planted the seed of what would become one of the world's largest companies and the beginning of a new industry.

CHAPTER ONE

Trey

In time there would be a big company. And in time there would be software programs millions of lines long at the core of billions of computers used around the world. There would be riches and rivals and constant worry about how to stay at the forefront of a technological revolution.

Before all of that, there was a pack of cards and a single goal: beat my grandmother.

In my family there was no faster way to win favor than to be good at games, especially card games. If you were confident in rummy or bridge or canasta, you had our respect, which made my maternal grandmother, Adelle Thompson, a household legend. "Gami's the best at cards" was something I heard a lot as a kid.

Gami had grown up in rural Washington, in the railroad town of Enumclaw. It's less than fifty miles from Seattle, but it was a world away in 1902, the year she was born. Her dad worked as a railroad telegraph operator and her mother, Ida Thompson—we called her Lala—would eventually earn a modest income by baking cakes and selling war bonds at the local lumber mill. Lala also played a lot of bridge. Her partners and opponents were the society people in town, the wives of bankers and the owner of the mill. These people may have had more money or higher social standing, but Lala leveled some of the difference by handily beating them at cards. This talent got passed on to Gami and to a degree to my mom, her only child.

My initiation into this family culture started early. When I was still in diapers, Lala started calling me "Trey," the card player's lingo for three. It was a play on the fact that I was the family's third living Bill Gates, after my dad and grandfather. (I am actually number four, but my dad chose to go by "junior" and in turn I got called Bill Gates III.) Gami started me off at age five with Go Fish. In the coming years we would play thousands of hands of cards. We played for fun, and we played to tease each other and pass the time. But my grandmother also played to win—and she always did.

Her mastery fascinated me back then. How did she get so good? Was she born that way? She was religious, so maybe it was a gift from above? For a long time, I didn't have an answer. All I knew was that every time we played, she won. No matter the game. No matter how hard I tried.

When Christian Science rapidly expanded across the West Coast in the early 1900s, both my mother's and father's families became devout followers. I think my mother's parents drew strength from Christian Science, embracing its belief that a person's true identity is found in the spiritual and not the material. They were strict adherents. Because Christian Scientists don't track chronological age, Gami never celebrated her birthday, never disclosed her age or even the year she was born. Despite her own convictions, Gami never imposed her views on others. My mom didn't follow the faith, nor did our family. Gami never tried to persuade us to do otherwise.

Her faith probably had a role in shaping her into an extremely principled person. Even back then, I could grasp that Gami followed a strict personal code of fairness and justice and integrity. A life well-lived meant living simply, giving your time and money to others, and, most of all, using your brain—staying engaged with the world. She never lost her temper, never gossiped, or criticized. She was incapable of guile. Often she was the smartest person in the room, but she was careful to let others shine. She was basically a shy person, but she had an inner confidence that presented as a Zen-like calm.

Two months before my fifth birthday my grandfather, J. W. Maxwell Jr., died of cancer. He was only fifty-nine years old. Following his Christian Science beliefs, he had declined modern medical interventions. His last years were filled with pain, and Gami suffered as his caregiver. I learned later that my grandfather believed his sickness was somehow the result of something Gami had done, some unknown sin in the eyes of God, who was now punishing him. Still, she stoically stood by his side, supporting him until the end. One of my sharpest memories from childhood was how my parents wouldn't let me attend his funeral. I was hardly aware of what was going on, other than the fact that my mother, father, and older sister got to see him off while I stayed behind with a babysitter. A year later, my great-grandmother Lala died while visiting Gami at her home.

From that point on, Gami channeled all her love and attention into me and my older sister, Kristi—and later my sister Libby. She would be a constant presence in our young lives and have a profound effect on who we would become. She read to me before I could hold a book and for years after, covering the classics like *The Wind in the Willows*, *The Adventures of Tom Sawyer*, and *Charlotte's Web*. After my grandfather died, Gami started to teach me to read for myself, helping me sound out the words in *The Nine Friendly Dogs*, *It's a Lovely Day*, and other books in our house. When we had worked through all of those, she drove me to the Northeast Seattle

Library to load up on more books. I was aware that she read a lot and seemed to know something about everything.

My grandparents had built a house in the upscale Seattle neighborhood of Windermere big enough to accommodate grandkids and family gatherings. Gami continued to live there after my grandfather died. On some weekends Kristi and I would stay over, alternating who got the privilege of sleeping in Gami's room. The other one slept in a nearby bedroom where everything from walls to curtains was pale blue. Light from the street and passing cars painted eerie shadows in that blue room. I got scared sleeping there and was always glad when it was my turn to stay in Gami's room.

Those weekend visits were special. Her house was just a couple of miles from ours, but spending time there felt like a vacation. She had a pool and compact mini golf course we'd play in the side yard, set up by my grandfather. She also allowed us the treat of television—a tightly controlled substance at our own house. Gami was up for anything; thanks to her, my sisters and I became avid game players who made anything—Monopoly, Risk, Concentration—into a competitive sport. We'd buy two copies of a jigsaw puzzle so we could race to see who finished first. But we knew her preference. Most nights after dinner, she dealt the cards and then proceeded to kick our butts.

I was about eight when I got my first glimmer of how she did it. I still remember the day: I'm sitting across from my grandmother at the dining room table, Kristi next to me. The room has one of those huge old wooden radios that even then was a relic of the past. Along another wall is a big cabinet where Gami stored the special dishes that we used every Sunday for dinner.

It's quiet, except for the slapping of cards on the table, a frenzy of drawing and matching cards in rapid fire. We're playing Pounce, a fast-paced, group form of solitaire. A serial Pounce winner can keep track of what's in their hand, what cards are showing in all the players' individual piles, and what's in the communal piles on the table.

It rewards a strong working memory and the pattern-matching ability to instantly recognize how a card that comes up on the table fits into what you hold in your hand. But I don't know any of this. All I know is that whatever it is that's needed to turn luck in your favor, Gami has it.

I am staring at my cards, my head racing to find matches. Then I hear Gami say: "Your six card plays." And then, "Your nine card plays." She's coaching my sister and me while also playing her own hand. She somehow grasps everything happening at the table and even seems to know the cards we're each holding—and it's not magic. How is she doing it? To anyone who plays cards, this is basic stuff. The more closely you can track your opponent's hand, the better your chances of winning. Still, to me at that age, it's a revelation. I see for the first time that for all the mystery and luck in a game of cards, there are things that I can learn to increase my chances of winning. I realize Gami isn't just lucky or talented. She's trained her brain. And I can too.

From that time on, I would sit down to a game of cards with an awareness that each hand dealt offered the chance to learn—if only I would take it. She knew it too. That didn't mean she made the path easy. She could have sat me down and walked me through the do's and don'ts, the strategies and tactics of various games. That wasn't Gami's way. She wasn't didactic. She led by example. So we played and played.

We played Pounce, gin rummy, hearts, and my favorite, sevens. We played her favorite, a complicated form of gin she called Coast Guard rummy. We played a little bridge. We played our way through a volume of Hoyle's, front to back, dealing games popular and not— even pinochle.

All the while, I studied her. In computer science there's a thing called a state machine, a part of a program that receives an input and, based on the state of a set of conditions, takes the optimal action. My grandmother had a finely tuned state machine for cards;

her mental algorithm methodically worked through probabilities, decision trees, and game theory. I couldn't have articulated these concepts, but slowly I started to intuit them. I noticed that even at unique moments in a game—a combination of possible moves and odds she probably had never seen before—she usually made the optimal move. If she lost a good card at some point, later in the game I'd see she had sacrificed it for a reason: to set herself up for a win down the road.

We played and played and I lost and lost. But I was watching, and improving. All along, Gami continued to gently encourage me. "Think smart, Trey. Think smart," she'd say as I weighed my next move. Implicit was the idea that if I used my brain, stayed focused, I could figure out the right card to play. I could win.

One day I did.

There was no fanfare. No grand prize. No high fives. I don't even remember what game we were playing the first time I won more games in a day than she did. I do know my grandmother was pleased. I'm pretty sure she smiled, an acknowledgment that I was growing.

Eventually—it took about five years—I was winning consistently. By that point I was almost a teenager, naturally competitive. I enjoyed the mental wrestling, as well as the deeply satisfying feeling you get from learning a new skill. Card playing taught me that no matter how complex or even mysterious something seems, you often can figure it out. The world can be understood.

I was born on October 28, 1955, the second of three kids. Kristi, born in 1954, was twenty-one months older; my sister Libby wouldn't appear on the scene for nearly another decade. As a baby, I was dubbed "Happy Boy" for the wide grin I seemed to always display. It wasn't that I didn't cry, but the joy I apparently felt seemed to override all other emotions. My other notable early trait might be described as excess energy. I rocked. At first on a rubber hobby horse, for hours on hours. And as I grew older, I kept it up without the horse, rocking while seated, while standing, anytime I got to really thinking about something. Rocking was like a metronome for my brain. It still is.

Early on, my parents knew that the rhythm of my mind was different from that of other kids. Kristi, for one, did what she was told, played easily with other kids, and from the start got great grades. I did none of those things. My mother worried about me and warned my preschool teachers at Acorn Academy what to expect. At the end of my first year, the director of the school wrote: "His mother had prepared us for him for she seemed to feel that he was a great contrast to his sister. We heartily concurred with her in this conclusion, for he seemed determined to impress us with his complete lack of concern for any phase of school life. He did not know or care to know how to cut, put on his own coat, and was completely happy thus." (It's funny now that one of Kristi's earliest memories of me includes the frustration of always being the one who had to wrestle me into my coat and then get me to lie on the floor so I was still enough for her to zip it up.)

In my second year at Acorn Academy, I arrived "a newly aggressive, rebellious child," a four-year-old who liked singing solo and taking imaginary trips. I scuffled with other kids, and was "frustrated and unhappy much of the time," the director reported. Fortunately, my teachers were heartened by my long-term plans: "We feel very accepted by him since he is including us as passengers on his proposed moon shot," they wrote. (I was ahead of Kennedy by a few years.)

What educators and my parents noted at an early age were hints of what would come. I channeled the same intensity that drew me into solving the puzzle of Gami's card skill into anything that interested me—and nothing that didn't. The things that interested me included reading, math, and being alone in my own head. The things that didn't were the daily rituals of life and school, handwriting, art, and sports. Also, mostly everything my mother told me to do.

My parents' struggle with their hyperkinetic, brainy, often contrarian, tempestuous son would absorb much of their energy as I grew up and would indelibly shape our family. As I've grown older, I better understand just how instrumental they were in helping chart my unconventional path to adulthood.

My father was known as a gentle giant, six-feet-seven-inches tall with a calm politeness you might not expect from a man who was often the biggest guy in the room. He had a direct, purposeful way of dealing with people that defined him and suited his career as a lawyer advising businesses and boards (and later as the first head of our philanthropic foundation). Though polite, he wasn't shy to ask for what he wanted. As a college student, what he wanted was a dance partner.

In the fall of 1946, he was part of a wave of veterans on the G.I. Bill, the generous government program that gave millions of people an education they might not have afforded otherwise. The one downside, in my father's estimation, was that the number of men on the University of Washington campus far surpassed the number of women. That meant the chances of finding a dance partner were low. At some point he asked a friend for help. Her name was Mary Maxwell.

He knew she was an officer at a sorority, Kappa Kappa Gamma, so he asked: Did she know someone who might be interested in meeting a tall guy who liked to dance? She said she'd check. Time went by. No introduction came. One day while walking together just outside the sorority house, my dad asked her again if she knew someone suitable.

"I have someone in mind," she said. "Me."

My mother was five-foot-seven, and my dad told her that, literally, she didn't measure up. "Mary," he replied, "you're too short."

My mom sidled up next him, stood on her tiptoes, put her hand atop her head, and retorted, "I am not! I'm tall."

My father always claimed his request for an introduction wasn't a tricky way of getting my mom to go out with him. But that's what happened. "By golly," he said, "let's have a date." Then, as the story goes, two years later they got married.

I always loved hearing this story because it so perfectly captures my parents' personalities. My dad: deliberate and unapologetically pragmatic, sometimes even in matters of the heart. My mom: gregarious, and also not shy about getting what she wanted. It was a neat story, a distillation of the full story, one of differences that went beyond height, and which would ultimately play into who I became.

My mom was meticulous about keeping records of her life, photo albums of family trips and school musicals, scrapbooks of newspaper clippings and telegrams. I recently found a set of letters that she and my father traded in the year leading up to their marriage in the spring of 1951. Six months before the wedding, my father was in his hometown working as an attorney, his first job after earning his law degree earlier that year. My mother was back at the university finishing her last year. A letter she wrote in October begins with her hope that in the pages that follow she would avoid the "emotional unbalance" she felt in a conversation they had a day earlier. She didn't elaborate, but it seems like there were some pre-wedding worries about their union and how to bridge certain differences between them. She explained:

> My objective <u>conclusion</u> about our relationship is that we
> have much in common and a very fine thing. We want
> much the same social life and home life. I think it's true that

we both want a very close marriage—that is, we want we two to be one. Although our social and family backgrounds are different, I think that we are able to be understanding about problems evolving from this, because as individuals we are much the same. We do both like to be dealing with ideas—to be continually thinking and learning . . . We both want the same—all the success in the world that can be gotten honestly and fairly. Even though we prize success highly, neither of us would consider it being worth it to be unjust so to push another man down. We would like our children to have the same basic values. Perhaps our "means" would be somewhat different but I am inclined to think we could present a solid front that would complement both of our points of view . . . You know Bill that if you truly loved me always, I would do anything in the world for you.

    I love you Bill

                                              Mary

    In the letter I glimpsed the private negotiations that surely continued all though my childhood and beyond. They nearly always maintained their solid front, in private working out their differences, most of which stemmed from how each was raised.

    My mom, Mary Maxwell, grew up in the embrace of a family culture set by her grandfather J. W. Maxwell, a banker who doted on my mom and was a model for a life of constant self-improvement. As a boy in Nebraska, J.W. quit school and talked himself into a job digging out the basement of a house owned by a local banker in return for money and room and board. When J.W. put down his shovel two months later, the man offered him a job at his bank. He was fifteen. After a few years learning the banking business, he moved to Washington state to carve out a new life. The 1893 depression wiped out his fledgling bank, and the coastal town he bet would boom instead went bust. He eventually took a steady job as a federal bank examiner, work that had him away from his family for months on end traveling on horseback, wagon, and train around the West measuring the health of small banks. Eventually he succeeded in starting his own bank. By the time he died in 1951 at age eighty-six, my great-grandfather was chairman of a major bank in Seattle and an active civic leader. He had also served as a mayor, a state legislator, a school board member, and a director of the Federal Reserve.

The platform of wealth and opportunity set by J.W. and furthered by my grandfather, also a banker, meant that my mom would want for nothing as a child. She was a great student with a full slate of sports and activities with family and a wide circle of friends. Sundays were for family picnics and summer days for swimming at her grandparents' beach house on Puget Sound. Sports and games were an essential part of any gathering—croquet, shuffleboard, and horseshoes were mainstays—and there was no question that my mom would learn to play tennis, ride horses, and become a graceful skier. In the Maxwell family, games held larger lessons. Golf, for instance, was a proxy for banking, both of which, her grandfather wrote, require "skill, continued practice, sobriety, patience, endurance and alertness."

In one of my mother's albums is a photo from when she was three or four years old. A group of neighborhood parents assembled their kids for the snapshot, each with their tricycles. On the back, Gami wrote the story of the picture. One boy had the biggest tricycle. My mom wanted him to trade with her so *she* could have the biggest trike. Somehow, she got him to agree. In the resulting photo, she's beaming, sitting a full head taller than everyone else. She was never afraid to be strong, to occupy space.

Where my mom got her confidence and ambition was probably equal parts the Maxwell side and Gami, who, beyond her card-table acuity, was valedictorian of her high school class, a gifted basketball player, widely read, and aimed for a bigger life outside of her hometown. It was at the University of Washington that she met my grandfather. My mom followed, entering UW in 1946 with the full support of two ambitious parents and a family-wide expectation that she would excel.

Across Puget Sound from Seattle, my father's hometown of Bremerton was best known for its Navy shipyard, celebrated as the place where battle-weary ships came to be fixed. Not too many years earlier it had a reputation as a town of gamblers and more saloons than anyone could stagger to in one day.

Growing up, Kristi and I would ride the ferry to Bremerton to visit my father's parents. From the ferry we'd walk a short distance up the hill to the house where my dad grew up. It was a small blue Craftsman on a quiet street. We'd stay with my grandparents for a night or two. If the TV was on, my grandfather would be watching boxing, which was pretty much the one diversion he allowed himself. My paternal grandmother, Lillian Elizabeth Gates, had the same spark for cards that Gami did, so we would often get a few games in. Like my maternal grandparents, my dad's parents were Christian Scientists. One memory I have from those visits is of Grandma Gates in the kitchen every morning with a cup of coffee, quietly reading Mary Baker Eddy's Daily Bible Lesson to my grandfather.

When my dad talked about his childhood, he always seemed wistful about his father. He described him as a workaholic who left little time for much else in his life. He owned a furniture store, passed down from my great-grandfather, that had survived the Great Depression, but just barely. Constant anxiety about the family finances made my grandfather a hostage to the business. Behind the little blue house was an alley that in an earlier time my grandfather would pass through on his way home from work so that he could pick up bits of coal dropped by delivery trucks. My father said his dad never went to movies or took his son to baseball games; he saw such things as distractions that robbed time from the store. He always seemed to be running scared, my father said.

In a way, you couldn't blame him. My grandfather had known poverty as a kid in Nome, Alaska, where his family scraped by while my great-grandfather, the first Bill Gates in our family, sought his fortune in the Gold Rush of the late 1800s. Bill Jr. had to quit school in the eighth grade to support the family. He sold newspapers in the icy streets of Nome and picked up whatever jobs he could while his dad was off prospecting. Eventually they would move back to Seattle, settling into the furniture business. Times got better for the family, but the anxieties of those early experiences never disappeared.

My grandfather also maintained what my dad called a very narrow view of the world. Dad attributed this partially to insecurities. Lacking a full education, my grandfather clung to what my dad called his axioms, rigid rules about the world and life. "Learn to earn, son, learn to earn," he would tell my father. Education was about gaining the skills you needed to get a job. Nothing more.

My grandmother, proud salutatorian of her high school class, had an axiom of her own, one that influenced my dad's view on self-improvement: "The more you know, the more you don't know." But it wasn't always easy for her at home. Even as women were starting to forge new paths in society, my dad's father was stuck in a bygone time. He wouldn't allow my father's older sister, Merridy, to get her driver's license. He wouldn't consider sending her to college. The skills a woman needed were around the house.

My father was very aware of the intellectual gap between himself and his father. Though not illiterate, his dad could hardly read, while my father wanted to use his head, wanted to go to college. He didn't want to knuckle under to his father's plan for him to join the furniture business.

Next door to my dad's family home was something seemingly out of a fairy tale: a Norman-style brick-and-stucco house with

stained-glass windows and a tower topped by a conical roof. It
looked so different from the Craftsman bungalows around it that
locals dubbed it the "castle." My father's journey to a bigger life
began when he started hanging at the castle with the Braman family.
Jimmy, the oldest of the sons, was my dad's inseparable best friend
growing up. My dad said he marveled at Jimmy's ability to turn a
crazy idea into reality, and the two spent their days dreaming up all
kinds of schemes and businesses. They ran a hamburger stand in the
front yard, started a circus in the backyard. It's funny to think that
kids paid to watch my shirtless dad lie on a bed of nails. They also
published a newspaper—*The Weekly Receiver*—where for a few cents
their seventy subscribers got news picked off the radio and scores
from local school football and baseball games.

My dad became a surrogate son in the Braman family. In Jimmy's
father, he found a mentor and a model for the type of person
he could become. A high school dropout, Dorm Braman started
Bremerton's largest millworks, would later become an officer in the
Navy, get elected mayor of Seattle, and eventually serve as deputy
transportation secretary in the Nixon administration. He designed
and built that distinctive home with his own hands.

Dorm had "no sense of personal limitations whatsoever," my dad
said admiringly. That was an ethos Dorm passed on to the boys in
his family and his scout troop, which my father joined as soon as he
turned twelve.

Both my grandfather and Dorm had dropped out of school, but
they handled that challenge in completely different ways, and life's
opportunities followed suit. My grandfather lived in a state of anxiety and clung to his rigid rules. Dorm didn't dwell on what he lacked
but focused on what he could become. My dad preferred Dorm's
way of seeing the world.

In the fall of his junior year in high school, he took eighty-five
dollars from his bedroom dresser, walked four blocks to a used-car
dealer, and bought a 1939 old Model A Ford coupe with bubble tires.

His father wouldn't let him drive the family car—too much risk for a teenager. My dad wasn't yet old enough to legally buy the car, so his sister signed the title. (Sometimes when he told the story, my father said she even bought the car for him as a birthday present.)

He did this knowing his father would be angry—and not just at him. He would never have spent money on a car for his son. And now his sister, forbidden from driving, owned a car.

My father drove home and nonchalantly announced that he was the proud owner of a beat-up light green coupe. Alarmed by the shouting in front of the house, my grandmother yanked father and son inside, sat them down, and forced them to make peace. My dad maintained that keeping the car running wouldn't cost much and finally persuaded his dad to go for a drive with him. I like to imagine the two of them together, the unyielding older man finally giving in to his son's elation. That night, my dad got out of bed twice just to peek at his new purchase. "I was about to bust a button—independence at last!" my dad wrote in a college paper.

My father named his car Clarabelle, which he thought fit its middle-aged persona. Clarabelle brought him freedom, carrying him on dates, to football games, and on fishing trips. At times as many as ten people squeezed into the rumble seat and hung off the fenders as it rattled down the Bremerton streets and the rutted Forest Service roads outside of town.

By then my father had started to drift away from Christian Science, and to question religion broadly. In his last year of high school, my dad and two friends started spending their Sunday nights at the home of their school's basketball coach, Ken Wills, a revered leader at the school. On Sundays he opened his gym for anyone who'd rather play basketball than go to church. In the evening my dad and his friends listened to his arguments for why they should question the Old Testament and the existence of God.

The United States was nearly two years into the Second World War, and many of my father's friends and most men under age forty-five who weren't already fighting were preparing themselves for war. In the sky above Bremerton floated huge barrage balloons aimed at foiling an attack from Japanese dive-bombers. Down the hill at the Bremerton shipyard the USS *Tennessee* and surviving ships from Pearl Harbor were repaired. After graduating from high school, my dad joined the Army Reserves, which allowed him to go to the University of Washington until he was called up for active duty. That call came at the end of his freshman year. In June 1944, a week after hundreds of thousands of U.S. troops pushed their way onto the beaches of Normandy, my dad reported to basic training in Arkansas.

This is when my father decided to change his name. His birth certificate read "William Henry Gates III," which to him sounded too posh for the son of a furniture seller. Convinced that the implied status of "the third" would invite ridicule and abuse by drill sergeants and Army peers, he legally stripped off the suffix and replaced it with "Junior."

I recognize my dad in the nineteen-year-old who wrote frequent letters home from basic training and later Officer Candidate School. He is humorous, self-aware, talks of how hard he's working, shows deep feelings for his family back home. Woven throughout his letters is frustration over how difficult the Army's uncertain schedule makes it for him to arrange a home visit. He's playful, apologetic for needing extra money from home for small purchases (underwear) and because he loaned another recruit fifteen dollars. Mostly he is thoughtful about his life. The military is hard, he reports. But he focuses on how he is growing, striving to be better. He marvels at the new world he's exposed to, young men from all walks of life, poor, rich, and people of color. With a group of Southerners, my dad argues about the Civil War.

Officer's school had regular reviews: if you didn't pass, you got booted. With each review, my dad saw his class get smaller and smaller. Even as he survived, he worried about the next review, particularly the push-ups, chin-ups, 100-yard chest crawl, and other physical tests. He entered the service as "more or less a weakling," he wrote. "I sort of get the feeling of becoming a man instead of just a boy now. If I flunk out of here, I know I'll never recover. If I make it I believe I'll tackle everything in life more confidently and with more spirit. I'm sure it will make me. Besides the mental side of it I have never been in better shape physically."

He did make it—graduating a second lieutenant—and was on a ship to the Philippines on August 15, 1945, when Japan surrendered. My dad spent most of his deployment as part of the first group of GIs in Tokyo. His letters are full of dizzying contrasts: the beauty of climbing Mount Fuji early one morning, and the shocking state of Tokyo after America's firebombing—burned homes and buildings that were nothing more than concrete shells.

My dad rarely talked about his experience in the Army. He knew he was lucky. Officer's school kept him from battle for a half a year, and then the atomic bomb ended the war. Many of his friends were not so lucky, and those who made it back brought the war home with them. A friend of my parents who lived near us in Seattle had been shot in the head and survived. He kept his mangled helmet and Purple Heart on display at his house. If asked, my father would say military service was extremely valuable for him and leave it at that.

When he returned to the U.S., Dad was in a hurry to get his degree, start a career, and, well, go dancing.

My parents had become friends while they were both student government volunteers. The Associated Students of the University of Washington was as much a social club as it was a governing body, and so my parents had many chances to spend time together. At that point the ASUW fought the university's Board of Regents' long-held policy that banned political speeches. I know the policy angered my father and he worked to reverse the ban—though he ultimately failed.

Unlike her soon-to-be boyfriend, who liked to work behind the scenes, my mom thrived at the center, and even more so if she had been chosen for that place by her peers. With typical determination, in her junior year she ran a highly organized campaign for secretary of the student government. She wrote a campaign song (it helped that "Mary" rhymes with "secretary") and a script for supporters to follow when they phoned students asking for their vote. On election day she meticulously tracked how the five thousand voting students cast their ballots. My mother beat her rivals by a wide margin.

In one scrapbook, she saved congratulatory telegrams from friends and family, along with a handwritten note from her sorority sisters. She also kept a letter from her grandfather. He listed her big wins that spring: elected both to the secretary post and president of her sorority plus placing first in a ski race. As reward for those three wins, he enclosed $75 (about $1,000 today) and congratulated her for "coming out into the limelight."

It's easy for me to picture my parents' early friendship. My mom had a warmth and grace of manner that imbued her with an almost magical ability to connect. If you showed up to a party and didn't know anyone, my mother was the first person to extend her hand, welcome you, and smooth your way into the group in a room. The minister of our church once said that my mother "never met an unimportant person."

I imagine her compelled to try to draw out tall, skinny Bill Gates Jr. She sees he's reserved, and she tries to figure out his story, where he's from, who his friends are, and what makes him tick. She quickly finds common ground: the people and issues of student government. She does this without flirting. He's two years older, is already thinning up top. Not classically handsome. Her boyfriend at the time was. In photos he looks more chiseled. More middle-of-the-road.

Still, she's intrigued. When Bill Gates speaks, there are no wasted words. He's logical, clear, analytical. There are people who think out loud—her best friend, Dorothy, is like that—but this young man speaks from a place of wisdom that seems older, more thoughtful than the people around him. Plus, he's fun. He's got a big smile and is a joyous person.

My dad, for his part, is drawn to my mom's energy, her quick mind and fearlessness about saying how she feels, even when it comes to telling other people what's best for them. "Bill, I think it would be a fine idea if you were to . . ." is probably something he heard soon after getting to know her.

Plus, they danced well together.

Mary Maxwell's photo collection tells the rest of the origin story. From the spring of 1948 pictures show her at dances, parties, and other college events with the chiseled guy. But by early 1950 she must have moved on, no more of that other guy, just a picture from the Dreamer's Holiday Semi-formal in early 1950: my future mom and dad, seated at a table, beaming at the camera. My dad graduated that spring, with both an undergraduate and a law degree, thanks to an accelerated program offered to veterans. My mom graduated a year later with a degree in education.

They must have resolved whatever differences their letters hinted at, because in May 1951 they were married. My mom soon joined my father in Bremerton, where he was working for a local lawyer who doubled as the city attorney. The job had my dad helping people through divorce proceedings and prosecuting the city's police court cases. My mom, meanwhile, started teaching at the same junior high school my father had attended.

After two years in Bremerton, the prospects of a better job and a more vibrant life lured them back to Seattle, and within months of my birth we moved again, to a newly built house in View Ridge, an area in North Seattle with an elementary school, kids' park, and library all within walking distance. The whole neighborhood was still under construction when we arrived. I have a film my dad took right after we moved: You can see a dirt yard where our grass hadn't been planted yet. My sister rides her tricycle on a sidewalk so clean the cement looks almost liquid. Across the street is the wood frame of an unfinished house. I watch the film and am struck by how everything was so new, as if the whole neighborhood had been freshly built for kids like us.

CHAPTER TWO

View Ridge

I t started with a *BOOM,* then the house shook. My mom had just said goodbye to Kristi, me, and the babysitter as she headed out to meet my father for dinner. When the shaking started, she froze, her hand on the doorknob. At that moment we watched out the back window as the carport roof flew over our house and slammed into our backyard, crushing our neighbor's fence.

My mother ushered us into the basement, where we huddled near our stash of canned food and other nuclear attack supplies. In 1962, a bomb seemed far more likely than what did disrupt that Friday evening: a tornado, the first in Seattle's recorded history. It formed in our View Ridge neighborhood, touched down on our street, and shot through our yard before advancing across Lake Washington, where it pulled a hundred-foot plume of water skyward. It was over in fifteen minutes. Miraculously, no one was hurt.

Aside from uprooted trees and broken windows, most of the damage in our neighborhood was confined to our carport. The *Seattle Post-Intelligencer* sent over a reporter and photographer. My mother pasted the photo that accompanied the piece—a neighborhood kid posing on the flattened structure—into the scrapbook with the rest of my childhood memories.

My father wanted to host a barbecue, invite friends over, and let them check out the mass of splintered wood, metal poles, and tar shingles that was once our carport. No, my mother said. She was still shaken. Had she opened that door seconds earlier, who knows what could have happened to her, to us. Plus, no respectable family would celebrate such a thing. It would be unseemly. It didn't fit my mother's image of how the Gates family should present itself.

My sister Kristi and I (and later Libby) were part of the huge cohort of kids—baby boomers—born in the period of prosperity and optimism that followed World War II. The Cold War was in full swing and the civil rights movement had started. Weeks after the tornado hit, Kennedy locked horns with Khrushchev over Soviet missiles in Cuba. On the last day of that crisis, as the world avoided nuclear conflagration, I was in our living room opening presents on my seventh birthday. Within a year, a quarter million people marched on Washington, D.C., where Martin Luther King Jr. said he dreamed that one day our country would be a place where all men are created equal.

Awareness of these historic events came to me in snippets, just names and words overheard as my parents watched the *CBS Evening News* and talked over stories in *The Seattle Times*. At school, teachers showed us hair-raising films with footage of Hiroshima and mushroom clouds. We practiced duck-and-cover. But to a young kid in View Ridge that wider world felt abstract. A flattened carport was pretty much the most dramatic event in our lives. The overwhelming feeling in families like ours was confidence. Our parents and all the parents around us had been through the Great Depression and World War II. Anyone could see that America was booming.

As with the rest of the country, Seattle was rapidly expanding into its suburbs. Fields and forests were bulldozed to make space for homes and shopping centers. That transformation had started in our city during the war, as local company Boeing grew into a major warplane manufacturer. I was born just as Boeing launched the first viable passenger jet, and in coming years the act of traveling by plane went from rarefied to routine.

From my bedroom window I could hear the crack of baseball bats from View Ridge Playfield on the other side of our neighbor's house. When I started at View Ridge Elementary in 1960, the school had just added a new wing to accommodate over one thousand students; soon the city would need to build a second elementary school nearby. Ten blocks up the hill from our house, the Northeast Branch of the Seattle Public Library boasted the largest selection of children's books in the city's library system. When the library opened the year before I was born, a line of kids snaked out the door to the street. It would become a sort of clubhouse all through my youth and for a long time was my favorite place in the world.

It was a community of families of businessmen, doctors, engineers, and lawyers like my father, veterans of World War II, who thanks to the G.I. Bill had found their way to college and North Seattle, where they lived better lives than their parents had. It was white and middle-class. If I had been born Black in Seattle in 1955, I wouldn't have lived in View Ridge. Our neighborhood and the others around it had racial covenants enacted in the 1930s that forbade anyone who was "non-white" from "inhabiting" homes there (save for domestic help). Though such horrible restrictions were technically ended by the Supreme Court in 1948, Seattle continued to be segregated for a long time, with people of color forced to live mostly in the industrial south part of the city.

Russia's 1957 *Sputnik* launch jolted the United States into pouring money into science and technology, giving birth to NASA and what was then called the Advanced Research Projects Agency. Some of that money found its way into downtown Seattle, where the city was planning to host the next World's Fair, dubbed "Century 21." The exposition quickly morphed into a retort to Russia, a showcase of America's scientific prowess and vision for its future in space, transportation, computing, medicine, and its role as a global peacemaker. Bulldozers knocked down whole streets of low-income houses to make room for the fairgrounds. From a sketch on a napkin sprang the six-hundred-foot Space Needle.

"What we show is achieved with great effort in the fields of science, technology, and industry," President Kennedy pronounced over satellite link as he opened the exposition from Florida. "This exemplifies the spirit of peace and cooperation with which we approach the decades ahead."

Days later, my mom put me in a button-down shirt and blue blazer, and with my similarly overdressed family we set off for Century 21. We saw the Mercury capsule that had just carried the first American into space. At the Spacearium we toured the solar system and the Milky Way. We saw Ford's vision of the future in a six-wheeled nuclear-powered car, the "Seattle-ite XXI," and IBM's idea of a cheap computer, the $100,000 IBM 1620. A short film we watched, titled *The House of Science,* depicted the advances of human thought from the earliest mathematicians to the men (it would be a long while before the contributions of women scientists got even a nod) on the cutting edge of biology, physics, earth science, and computers. "The scientist views nature as a system of puzzles!" the over-the-top narrator declared. "He holds faith in the underlying order of the universe." Though I didn't really understand the specifics, I got the general idea: scientists know important things. Over the four months the fair ran, we returned again and again. We went to every pavilion, rode every ride. I tried Belgian waffles, introduced to the United States at the fair. They were delicious.

Here's how the Hollywood version of my story would go: entranced by the IBM Pavilion, nearly age seven, I fell in love with computers and never looked back. That may well have been the case with other kids. Paul Allen, my partner in starting Microsoft, credited the fair with hooking him on computers the way some musicians grab the violin at that age and never let go. Not me. I fell in love with the daredevil tandem water-skiers, and I marveled at the view of our city from the Space Needle. Best of all, at least in my opinion, was the Wild Mouse Ride, a roller-coaster-like contraption that sent little steel two-seater cars and your body snapping around turns. I remember huge smiles and a lot of laughing. It felt risky and it stoked my lifelong love of roller coasters.

Still, the fair's techno-optimistic vision must have affected me. At that impressionable age, the message in 1962 was so clear: We would explore space, stop disease, travel faster and easier. Technology was progress and, in the right hands, it would bring peace. My family watched Kennedy give his "we choose to go to the moon" speech that fall, all of us gathered around the television as the president told America that we needed to harness the best of our energies and skills for a bold future. Days later we watched the debut of *The Jetsons,* offering the cartoon version of that future, with flying cars and robot dogs. From Walter Cronkite and *Life* we were treated to a steady flow of new wonders: the first laser, first cassette tape, first factory robot, and first silicon chip. You couldn't be a kid back then and not feel the excitement of this.

This climate of limitless potential was the backdrop for my early life and the ambitions my mom held for us. I was equally raised by my parents, but it was my mother who set our clocks ahead by eight minutes so we would be on mom time.

From the start, she had a grand vision for our family. She wanted my father to be highly successful, with success defined less by money and more by reputation and his role helping our community and a wider circle of civic and nonprofit organizations. She envisioned kids who excelled in school and sports, were socially active, and pursued everything they did fully and completely. That her kids would all go to college was a given. Her role in this vision was that of supportive partner and mother, as well as a force in the community who would eventually build her own career. Though she never said it explicitly, I suspect her model for the Gates family was informed by one of the most famous families of the day: the Kennedys. In the early 1960s, before all the tragedy and troubles that would befall the famous clan, they were the model of a handsome, successful, active, athletic, and well-appointed American family. (More than one of her friends compared Mary Maxwell Gates to Jackie Lee Kennedy.)

We lived by the structure of routines, traditions, and rules my mother established. She ran, as my father would say, "a well-organized household." She had a clear sense of a right way and a wrong way that applied to all parts of life, from the most quotidian matters to the biggest decisions and plans. Mundane daily chores— making our beds, cleaning our rooms, being dressed, pressed, and ready for your day—were sacrosanct rituals. You did not leave the house with an unmade bed, uncombed hair, or a wrinkled shirt. Her edicts, repeated through my youth, are now part of me, even if I still don't abide by them: "No eating in front of the television." "Don't put your elbows on the table." "Don't bring the ketchup bottle to the table." (It would be unseemly to serve condiments out of anything but little dishes with little spoons.) For my mom these small things were the bedrock of a well-ordered life.

As a first- and then second-grader in 1962, I would walk with

Kristi up a short hill to View Ridge Elementary, where my sister had set the mold for what teachers expected from me. Kristi was a rule follower. She monitored the speedometer from the backseat of our car, letting my father know any time he exceeded the speed limit. At school she was a careful student, easy on teachers, completed her assignments on time, and, most important, she got great grades.

I was different, as my mother had previously warned my pre-school teachers. By early elementary school I was reading a lot on my own at home. I was learning how to learn by myself, and I liked the feeling of being able to quickly absorb new facts and entertain myself with chapter books. School, however, felt slow. I found it hard to stay interested in what we were learning; my thoughts wandered. When something did catch my attention, I might leap up from my seat, frantically raise my hand, or shout out an answer. I wasn't trying to be disruptive; my mind simply shifted easily into a state of unrestrained exuberance. At the same time, I also felt like I didn't fit in with the other kids. My late-October birthday meant that I was younger than most of my classmates, and I really looked it. I was small and skinny and had an unusually high-pitched, squeaky voice. I was shy around other kids. And I had that rocking habit.

I got the sense that my parents were in close touch with my teachers, more than other parents were. Did other families have their kids' teachers over for dinner at the start of the school year? I didn't think they did. To my parents this was only natural, a sign of their commitment to our education. To Kristi and me it was nothing but embarrassing. It felt unnatural to see your teacher eating at your dining room table. Over the years, only one teacher declined the invitation, fearing that being plied with tuna casserole was a conflict of interest. (She waited until school ended before accepting.)

My parents didn't hound us about grades. Their expectations were communicated mainly in how my mom talked about other families. If the son or daughter of a family friend wasn't doing well in school, or got in trouble for one thing or another, my mom would speculate about the disappointment her friends must feel. She never said, don't be like those kids. But given her tragic tone in relaying the story, we understood the unspoken message: Don't goof off. Excel. Don't let us down. They also subscribed to a rewards system: the going rate for an A was a quarter; all As earned you dinner at the restaurant of your choice, which was usually six hundred feet in the air at the Eye of the Needle, the spinning dining room at the top of the shiny new Space Needle. It was always Kristi's grades that got us there, but as her brother I got to tag along no matter my performance.

My mom by then was starting to spend more time volunteering at community nonprofits like the Junior League and what later would be called the United Way. Often she'd be out in the afternoon, so my sister and I would arrive home from school to find Gami waiting for us. I loved seeing her at the door. It meant she'd usher us inside, feed us Ritz crackers with peanut butter or some other kid snack, and ask us all about school. Then, for the rest of the day, we'd read or play games together until my mother got home. Gami was like a third parent. She joined us on vacations, Christmas skating parties, summer retreats, and pretty much every other family event. Other families knew that if they met up with the Gateses, that would often include the grandmother who would be the best dressed of the group, with a string of pearls and perfectly coiffed hair. Still, she didn't see herself as a parent proxy; she was our friend and patient teacher. She wanted to give my mom and dad space to raise us their own way. There was a clear line between roles that she respected by saying good night and heading to her own house just before my father got home from work.

Soon after he walked in the door, we'd sit down to eat. My mother would typically tell me to put my book down: reading at the table wasn't allowed. Dinner with family was a time for sharing. My mom heard that JFK's father, Joseph Kennedy, expected each of his kids to arrive at dinner ready to explain some topic that he had assigned them. The future president might have to give an overview of Algeria between bites of his carrots. We discussed this Kennedy ritual at dinner, and the important things you could learn in that hour together. My parents didn't expect us to give a recitation on any topic, but we talked about our days, and they shared theirs. Through these conversations I started to form a picture in my head of the lives of adults and what went on in the wider world they inhabited.

It was over dinner that I first heard terms like "matching funds" or "conflict resolution" as my mother described campaigns at the Junior League or some challenge at the United Way. I detected the serious tone of my mom's voice. Every person should be treated fairly. Every issue carefully considered. Every dollar wisely spent. My mother shorthanded her philosophy with a phrase we heard a lot: one should be "a good steward." Her definition was right in line with Merriam-Webster: the careful and responsible management of something entrusted to one's care. That was my mother to a T.

My father at the time worked for Skeel, McKelvey, Henke, Evenson & Uhlmann, a firm mainly known for tough and thorough litigation. I don't think being a courtroom bulldog fit my dad's temperament but, as with the Army, I'm sure he saw it as good training. I didn't understand the details of his cases, but I had a clear sense that companies paid my father to do important things. The name Van Waters & Rogers, a growing local chemical company and one of my father's largest clients, was always in the air.

Before I could have told you what a lawyer actually did, I had a sense from my father that the law was something to revere. Stories he told hinted at the roots of his highly developed sense of justice. We heard about the Canwell Committee, an anticommunist witch hunt that swept through the University of Washington when my parents were students. Albert Canwell—the state legislator who chaired the committee—prohibited cross-examining and objections, and flouted other elements of fairness. A precursor to the nation-wide McCarthy hearings a few years later, the committee ruined the careers of innocent people, including two professors who taught my dad. My father was transfixed by the coverage of the hearings, and he despised the committee's flagrant abuse of justice.

My parents on occasion let us watch *Perry Mason,* the hugely popular TV drama that centered on the trials of a masterful criminal defense attorney. Just before the end credits rolled, the details of some bewildering case would magically snap into place, and everything would be resolved. Listening to my dad, I learned the law (and life) wasn't like that. His cases seemed super complicated. After dinner he'd typically be up late, bent over a stack of papers at the dining room table preparing for the next day's case. It was far less glamorous than the TV version but way more interesting to me.

If my parents sound a little virtuous and resolute about volunteering, giving back, and all that, I can't help it. That's really who they were. They spent a lot of their waking hours planning and meeting, calling and campaigning, and whatever else was needed to help their community. My father could happily spend a morning on a street corner wearing a sandwich sign promoting the school levy and that night be at the board meeting of the University YMCA, where he once served as president. When I was three years old my mother chaired a Junior League program to show off museum artifacts to fourth-graders in their classrooms. I know this because we made the newspaper; the caption below the photo of the two of us and a box of doctor's instruments read, "Mrs. William Gates, Jr. watches as her three and a half year old son William Gates III examines an old medical kit included in a 'Tillicum Box.'"

My parents' friends were the same way. These weren't people who felt a longing to leave their hometown for more exciting lives in New York or Los Angeles. They graduated from the University of Washington with degrees in law, engineering, and business, then settled down within miles of their alma mater and their old friends. They had kids, set up businesses, joined firms, ran for office, and spent their free time on their own versions of the school levy and

YMCA board. Many of my father's friends were members of the Municipal League. No, not bowling, but an organization of young nonpartisan reformers—most of the people were like my parents, in their thirties—who were determined to upend what they saw was a hidebound Seattle government. My dad explained to us how the league evaluated the qualifications of political candidates and publicized their ratings during election years. In the early 1960s, we had dinner conversations on how the league hoped to clean up Lake Washington. Years of sewage drain-off and industrial waste left the lake water toxic. By the mid-1960s, the "Polluted Water Unsafe for Bathing" signs came down.

How much did all of this exposure to adults affect me? In time it obviously would, but as a young kid it mainly left me with the impression that to be an adult was to be busy. My parents were busy people, their friends were all busy people.

When my parents' friends came to the house, my sisters and I were expected to engage with them. Often that meant my mom gave us a job to do. Mine was pouring coffee while they played bridge. I felt proud as Mom watched me circling the table, carefully tilting the coffeepot over the porcelain cups, just as she had shown me. This is a memory that I go to even now when I want to sense my mom near me. I felt important, included in this adult ritual, essential to their fun.

On a map, Hood Canal looks like a jagged fishhook. It's not in fact a canal—those are man-made—but a glacier-formed fjord southeast of Seattle on the Olympic Peninsula. As a kid, my father caught his first fish there (a salmon nearly as long as he was tall) and as a Boy Scout he camped along its shores. My mom had attended a camp there owned by two leaders of the Soroptimists, a volunteer group of girls and women. After they married, my parents began spending time out at the canal every summer. In one of the earliest photographs I have of myself, I'm about nine months old, my dad is holding me on his lap, sitting on a bench with my grandfather squeezed in next to us—the three Bill Gateses, Hood Canal, 1956.

In the early 1960s, my parents and a group of their friends started renting Cheerio Lodge Cottages every July. I can still see the blue-and-white sign—"Cheerio"—on the side of North Shore Road as we turned in to the group of cottages that would be our home for the next two weeks. The place wasn't fancy, just a cluster of ten small cottages next to a tennis court and a center area with a campfire pit. Nearby were woods, open fields, and those pebbly beaches. For a kid, it was paradise. We'd swim, splash around in little boats, hunt for oysters, run in the woods, and play Capture the Flag. I'd eat tons of hamburgers and Popsicles. It was usually the same ten families, which between kids and adults meant about fifty other people. These were my parents' closest friends, many from their college days. My dad shed his reserved serious-lawyer face and turned into what we called "the Mayor of Cheerio," a sort of director of fun and wrangler of children. Each night as the campfire dimmed, we kids knew that when my father stood up it was the signal to join behind him, a train of kids that he led to our respective cabins for bedtime. Marching behind, we'd sing made-up lyrics to the tune of "Colonel Bogey March," from the movie *The Bridge Over the River Kwai*. (Only later when I saw the movie did I realize that the song is a rallying song for prisoners of war. To my sisters and me, it always brings forth memories of my father dancing with a line of kids trailing behind. "March on, the road to Cheerio . . .")

As mayor, my dad presided over the opening ceremony of the Cheerio Olympics. We'd kick off the whole extravaganza with a torch-lighting ceremony, where one of us kids, wearing a leafy crown, would run with a flaming torch (it was the 1960s) to mark the opening of the days-long competition. The events were more tests of dexterity and drive than athleticism: a gunnysack race, a running race, a three-legged race, an obstacle course through auto-mobile inner tubes, and the egg-on-a-spoon race. I have memories of my father holding my legs for the wheelbarrow race. Whatever the event, I'd push myself with abandon to get on the podium at the end of the day. I was low on dexterity but high on drive.

About a week into Cheerio, the adults wrote the name of each family on a piece of paper and had each kid draw one name out of a little blue box. Whatever name you got—Baugh, Berg, Capeloto, Merritt, or one of the others—you had to go to that family's cottage and eat dinner with the parents. Their kids, meanwhile, went to din-ner with the parents of whatever name they drew. My mother came up with this scheme. When I look back on my childhood, it fit a pat-tern of pushing my sisters and me into situations that would force us to socialize, particularly with adults. To my mom, her friends were role models, the type of people that she hoped we would become. All went to college. All were ambitious. The men had management jobs in insurance and finance and timber companies. One father worked for Ford and one was a U.S. attorney. One owned a big garden store, another had kicked the winning field goal in the Rose Bowl. Most, like my dad, had served in World War II. Many of the women were like my mom, juggling family and nonprofit work at places like Planned Parenthood. For me, those dinners made it impossible to fade into the woodwork or disappear into a book. At six or seven years old, this was still hard, but over time, my mother's plan would pay off, and I would come to feel nearly as comfortable with those Cheerio families as I did with my own.

Japanese automakers are known for kaizen, the philosophy of continuous improvement they followed after the Second World War to up the quality of their cars year after year. Toyota had nothing on my mom, at least when it came to the holidays. Take Christ-mas, which started in the early fall in our household. That's when my mom read her notes from the previous year's holiday to review what went wrong the last year and improve upon it. One entry: "Bill [my father] has grave doubts about using snow on tree again— a miss." I'm sure we didn't make that mistake again. At some point her Christmas kaizen sent my father into our basement, where with his jigsaw and plywood he crafted a life-sized Santa Claus. "Big Santa," as we called him, took his place next to our front door every holiday season for decades.

Not long after Halloween, after soliciting our input, my mother designed that year's Christmas card. With pens, felt, colored paper, family photos, even a silk-screen press, and whatever witty poem she'd composed, we'd form an assembly line on a foldout table, handcrafting hundreds of cards to send to my parents' vast universe of friends and family members. Gami, meanwhile, worked on her own handmade cards, a tradition she had probably inherited from her own mother in an era when store-bought cards would have been too pricey. In the year of the tornado, 1962, our Christmas card poked fun at how hard-core my family was about outdoing ourselves every year in a comic strip, each panel depicting my mom and dad ginning up outrageous schemes for delivering our Christmas message. Included was a plan to hire a plane to sky-write "Happy Holidays" in Old English letters. In one panel my father muses that we could send out debris from our carport inscribed with "Just blew in to wish you Happy Holidays."

Once the Christmas cards were in the mail, we started on the invites for the annual holiday roller-skating party we hosted with two other families. Those cards always incorporated some customized presentation or puzzle: a wooden skate my father cut with his jigsaw, or a crossword puzzle with answers revealing the party's date and the time. Guests knew that when they arrived at Ridge Rink they'd find my father circling the floor, his six-seven frame squeezed into a rented Santa suit, while my mother served guests powdered sugar donuts and cider, as Christmas songs played on the rink's old Wurlitzer.

The days that followed played out in exactly the same fashion, year after year. On Christmas Eve my mom presented everyone in the family with matching pajamas she had chosen for that year. The next morning we all assembled in the hallway wearing our new pajamas, and then we marched into the living room one by one according to age. (Doing things in order of age was a hard-and-fast family tradition.) Then, oldest to youngest, we opened our stockings. We always knew what we'd find: one orange and one silver dollar for us kids, and for my mom, always a bouquet of red carnations from my dad. Next, even with a pile of presents begging to be opened, we'd pause for breakfast: scrambled eggs and ham with a Danish Kringle from the nearby bakery. At last, we'd get to open the presents. After Kristi, I'd open one with everyone looking on, then back around, Gami on down, oldest to youngest. Presents tended toward the practical and the playful and were never expensive. You could always count on things like socks and shirts, and maybe the latest bestseller.

As the holidays wound down, the last ornament packed, the last thank-you note sent, my mother took out her pen and paper and started preparing for next Christmas. Even if on occasion my sisters and I rolled our eyes at these traditions—we never finished the presents until deep into the afternoon, still in our pajamas—to skip any one of them would have felt like a loss. Christmas is still one of the things my sisters and I like to reminisce about the most.

CHAPTER THREE

Rational

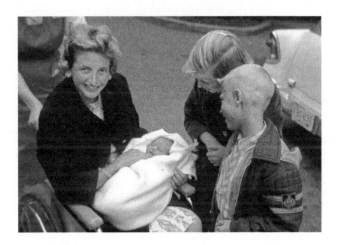

A few days after I finished second grade, my mother and grandmother packed my sister and me into the car and we headed out on our first big vacation. Kristi and I always refer to it as the Disneyland trip, but in fact it was far more. For my mom, the thousand miles we were about to drive meant a thousand chances for her kids to learn.

On that June morning in 1963, we left according to mom time at exactly 8:15—Mom timed it—for the first leg of the trip that in four days would land us in Los Angeles. My dad had to work that week; he would fly down to meet us for the Disneyland leg of the trip and the drive home.

Mom had recently bought what was then the absolute state-of-the-art in typewriter technology. Her IBM Selectric used a golf-ball-sized metal ball that was available in different fonts and scripts. You could swap the balls in and out based on the font and style you wanted—even cursive, which I thought was the coolest thing. In advance of the trip, my mom put together a travel log for my sister and me, two pages per day on which we were to record what we saw. Using that mechanical cursive, she provided headings for us to list the cities we traveled between and the approximate number of miles we drove each day. Below that, she typed categories to fill in. It looked like this:

1. *Land forms*
2. *Weather*
3. *Population Distribution*
4. *Land Use*
5. *Products*
6. *Historical or other Interesting sights*
7. *Miscellaneous*

At the bottom she put a section for Written Descriptions of the day's travel. We'd have no shortage of data for this exercise. With her usual energy, Mom had set a detailed itinerary for each day that took us through two state capitol buildings, Oregon's Lava Cast Forest, a couple of universities, the Golden Gate Bridge, Hearst Castle, San Quentin Prison, the San Diego Zoo, a beeswax-making demonstration, and a bunch of other stops.

When my mom was at the wheel, Gami read to us, a novel about Man o' War, the thoroughbred horse who broke speed and endurance records and was one of the winningest horses in history. While listening, my sister and I kept watch out the car window, mentally noting things to fill our travel log: apple orchards, adobe buildings, trucks with huge Douglas fir logs, oil wells. Every night in the motel, Kristi recorded what we had seen under the categories. She wrote carefully, knowing that my mom would look through it later to correct grammar and spelling with a red pen. In a smaller notebook, I jotted down my extra observations, writing them as neatly as my hand was able.

Through our daily entries my mother ensured we were giving ourselves lessons in geography, geology, economics, history, and even math . . . and, in the thrill of noticing things, the art of paying attention. These journals are why I know that stalactites hang down and stalagmites point up and, for anyone who cares, that it takes 262 steps to reach the top of the Washington State Capitol Rotunda.

When my father met us in Los Angeles, we regaled him with the story of the book we had just finished about the amazing horse bred and raised to win. In time it would feel like my mom was on a similar mission with her children.

By the summer of that road trip, I was vaguely aware of Gami's dedication to Christian Science. It seemed to me the faith was about structure and discipline. Like my Gates-side grandparents, she started each day with a short Daily Bible Lesson from church founder Mary Baker Eddy, the framing for a daily routine that hardly wavered. She had breakfast at 8:00, lunch at 12:00, nap at 1:30. She always had dinner at 6:00 followed by exactly one See's Dark Maple Walnut candy, her single daily decadence. After dinner she played cards or a game, then read her daily lesson again before bed. In the late 1960s after she bought a vacation house on Hood Canal, Gami would add a new element to her routine: daily swims, gliding through the cold water in a gentle side stroke, in her perfectly coiffed hair, in all weather, even in the wind and icy rain as we worried that she'd be swallowed by the whitecaps.

As far as the details of Christian Science beliefs, I had little to go on. That was until one weekend when my parents were away and Gami stayed at our house. I was playing with Kristi and her friend Sue, jumping through the sprinkler in the front yard in our swimsuits. At some point someone—me?—got the idea that we should up the risk. We dragged the sprinkler into the driveway and took turns trying to jump through the spray of water on our roller skates. Some skates back then still had metal wheels. I don't remember what ours were, but whatever they were, they didn't go well with a wet driveway, as we would find out.

Kristi got a running start, clearing the sprinkler, but as she landed her skates slipped from under her. She slammed onto the asphalt, breaking her right arm above her elbow.

The next thing I remember is huddling in Kristi's room as she wailed in pain while Gami wrestled with what to do next. From the Christian Science point of view, hospitals are generally shunned. Instead, the faithful are expected to turn to professional Christian Science "practitioners," who are believed to be able to heal through prayer. I'm guessing that while we waited in Kristi's room, Gami called her practitioner, a woman we knew as Pauline, who probably told her that bone fractures are real enough to warrant fixing. Later that day Kristi had a full arm cast courtesy of the trained doctors at nearby Children's Orthopedic Hospital.

A year or two later, I was climbing on the kitchen counter, trying to reach a glass in the cabinet, when a pain shot through my abdomen. I fell onto the floor, where Gami found me delirious. This time, no delay. It turned out I had appendicitis, and she got me to the hospital, where my appendix was removed before it burst.

Beyond the feeling that bad things happened when my parents were away (something my sister and I would joke about for years), these incidents fed into questions I had at that time about the adult world. It was very confusing to me that my rational, educated grandmother never went to the hospital, didn't avail herself of modern medicines. She read the newspaper, flew on airplanes, and was one of the smartest people I knew. And yet part of her lived in the realm of faith and what seemed like superstition.

Religion as practiced by our family was more of a social, intellectual exercise. Though both had left Christian Science before I was born, my mother and father agreed that we would attend the University Congregational Church. It was a popular church in Seattle, with well over two thousand parishioners, by dint of the charismatic minister, Dale Turner, who was a minor local celebrity. Congregationalism left a lot of room for interpretation. Reverend Turner was on the liberal side of that interpretation, melding scripture with progressive views such as support for gay rights and the civil rights movement. He would become a close friend of my parents. Even if my father had rejected organized religion in high school, my mom wanted her kids to have exposure to the moral teachings of religion. It was one of their compromises.

To me, Sunday School was just something I did, one in a long list of activities that I had to get dressed up for, but I liked it. Reverend Turner had a standing offer: any kid who could recite by memory the Sermon on the Mount got a free dinner at the top of the Space Needle. Mostly older kids in confirmation class took up the challenge, but Kristi got her dinner early, around age eleven, and so sometime after that I sat with a Bible in the back of the car on a family trip to the Washington coast memorizing "Blessed are the poor in spirit, for theirs is the kingdom of heaven . . ." and the rest of Christ's moral lessons in the Book of Matthew. When Reverend Turner announced that I had won my Space Needle dinner, I felt a surge of pride as other kids looked over at me, surprised. I'm sure I internalized some of Jesus's message, but mostly my small achievement was a brain test to see if I could do it. If the wise man did indeed build his house on the rock, as Jesus said, my rock by that age was intellect, a good memory, and my own power of reason.

Reading in the back of the car—or anywhere for that matter—was my default state. When I read, hours flew by. I tuned out the world, only dimly aware of my family moving through life around me, my mother asking me to set the table, my sister playing with her friends. I was in my own head, with my door closed, or in the back of the car, at a barbecue, at church—anywhere I could steal time to dive between the covers of a book, where I could explore and soak up new facts, all on my own, without anyone else. My grandmother—my model of a learned reader—fully supported my habit. After school she'd drive me the short distance up the hill to the library, where I loaded her car with a fresh stack of books for the week. At Gami's house I'd often head to her basement, where she kept an entire wall of *Life* magazines. She must have subscribed for decades, and felt that this catalog of the world was worth keeping. When we got an Old English Sheepdog (we named her Crumpet), I scavenged the back issues for pictures of dogs, which I cut out and assembled into a book. Later, any school report or project started with a search through the stacks of *Life* for illustrations. Paging through those magazines gave me the chance to follow whatever meandering path I chose: a random tour of current affairs, celebrity, war, science, and a cross section of America and the world.

Books were the one thing my parents never questioned spending money on. One of our greatest treasures was our 1962 set of the *World Book Encyclopedia*. It amazed me how much was in those twenty red-and-blue volumes with their slick pages and bright illustrations, particularly the neat see-though plastic pages of bones, muscles, and organs that lay on top of each other to compose a complete human body. The *World Book* volumes were a door to nature, geography, science, politics, and pretty much all the knowledge of the world, from what I could tell. When I was around nine, I read through nearly every volume, A–Z. Then every January the encyclopedia's *Yearbook* arrived in the mail like a late Christmas gift, a capsule of twelve months of history in the making. I read all of those too.

Through reading I could find answers to all sorts of things. And of course, one answer often raises even more questions; the deeper you dig, the more you want to know. I got interested in penguins and could have told you how long an Adélie can hold its breath underwater (six minutes) or how tall an Emperor can grow (4.3 feet). For a while rockets and bridges captivated me. I drew endless pictures of rockets of all shapes and sizes, and long, high bridges with intricate trellises and sturdy-looking towers, page after page with what I thought were beautiful designs. At some point, I realized that however nice they looked to me, I had no idea how they worked. How do you design a bridge so it doesn't collapse? How do you make a rocket actually fly? This gap between my imagination and the real thing annoyed me. I didn't like feeling that my designs were childish ideas that could never be realized.

To the kids I knew at school, reading a lot, being smart, showing an interest in what teachers said—those were considered girl things. It's a terrible generalization, but I felt it and so did others. Somewhere around third or fourth grade, I realized that it wasn't cool to be reading the *World Book* for fun, or playing hearts with your grandmother, or wanting to talk about why bridges don't collapse. A summer reading program at our library was only me and girls. At recess other kids broke off with their cliques, and I'd be on my own. Bigger kids picked on me. Looking back, I can't say I felt lonely or even hurt. More than anything I was just kind of baffled: Why didn't kids see things my way?

I think my mom felt the same sense of bafflement about me. *Kristi cleans her room and combs her hair, does her homework, so why doesn't Trey? Other kids keep their desks clean, their pencils unchewed, their coats zipped, why doesn't Trey?* It's not that I was actively resisting; honestly, none of it simply ever registered with me. My mother's constant reminders might snap me out of my own world for a second before I returned to the book or whatever I was thinking about. I'm sure my mom hoped I would change, become responsible in the ways she expected. But I didn't, and for her, that was both maddening and worrisome.

My lack of interest in most social interactions was particularly concerning to her. My mom kept a dog-eared copy of *How to Win Friends and Influence People,* Dale Carnegie's distillation of human relations into a series of tricks and tips. (She eventually gave a copy to each of her kids for Christmas.) I'm not sure what she learned from Carnegie, because my mother seemed to have an innate ability to connect with people on an emotional level. I watched as my mom supported my father's career, taking over the responsibility to organize bar association events and becoming a welcoming committee of one for fresh hires moving into Seattle. If they needed a house, she'd know just the right real estate agent. If he was single, she'd introduce him around. I can see now that she was a student of relationships, genuinely interested in matching people's abilities with roles and always knowing exactly who to call if you asked. But back then it was a talent that was lost on me. It seemed unimportant and kind of superficial.

It's clear to me now that my mom's hopes of making me more social were at the root of many of the activities she put me in, and how I ended up in Cub Scout Pack 144. I was eight years old, joining a scout pack of sixty-five other boys run by fathers whose memories of the Army, Navy, and Marines during the Second World War were still fresh. That meant that the pack was run with order and organization. Our advancement through the ranks was required. Every year we spent a week at scout camp where we had physical tests: broad jump, push-ups, sit-ups—basically a mini boot camp.

But the big campaign that tested us was the annual nut sale. Every fall, the pack sold bags of nuts to raise the money for the next year's activities. This was our sole source of funds. The annual drive was treated like an Army mission: we had eleven days to sell as many one-, three-, and five-pound bags of nuts as possible. The pack's very survival depended on our success—or so it seemed.

We offered filberts, pecans, walnuts, Brazil nuts, almonds, and the customer favorite, mixed nuts. We each were expected to sell and deliver a minimum of one hundred pounds. Prizes were offered based on how much we sold.

This was about as daunting a challenge as I'd ever faced. One hundred pounds of nuts? I hardly weighed half of that. The sample tally sheet from the committee listed the astronomical total of 240 pounds of nuts. How would I even carry that many? But there was no way I was going to stand out for not pulling my weight.

The challenge stirred something else in me too: competitiveness. This was a race, with clearly defined parameters and a clear goal. I marked down on the prize sheet the things I wanted to win: the water pistol (for selling 10 pounds), soccer ball (65 pounds), and the battery-operated Give-A-Show slide projector (95 pounds). Those were great. Better, though, were the bragging rights for selling the most.

With (for once) my hair combed and my Cub Scout uniform pressed, I started in the neighborhood, walking house to house, and then I got my dad to drive me to wealthier areas, slowly trailing me in the car while I knocked on doors. The Nut Sale committee gave us a script of how to introduce ourselves and how to close the sale. If someone, for instance, complained that sixty-five cents for a pound of nuts was steep, we were to tell them that nuts bought in stores were often from the previous year's crop and just not as good as ours.

This is how it went for the eleven days of selling. It was hard for me to put myself out there, to pitch our product. But it was a lot like trick-or-treating, and gradually I got more comfortable with it, and I loved the feeling of ticking off another hash mark each time I made a sale.

By the end of the campaign, I'd moved 179 pounds of nuts. I was proud of that total, though I don't remember if I was the top seller that year. I would be at least once. The near-perennial winner, as I remember him, was a kid who enlisted his father, a barber, to promote his son's sales with every haircut. That seemed unfair to me.

Entering fourth grade in the fall of 1964, I was an energetic, curious kid who had zero qualms about interrupting the class with odd questions and taking up a lot of the teacher's time. That teacher, Hazel Carlson, worked with me the best she could. Unable to manage a class of thirty kids while trying to satisfy my need for constant engagement, she spent a lot of time with me after class or in quiet periods, explaining things. I had questions about books, about science—about anything, really, that popped into my head. As the teacher, she was the smartest person in the room, so I figured she had all the answers.

Mrs. Carlson had a habit of keeping her coiffed hair in order by giving it little spurts of hairspray throughout the day. As part of a writing assignment, I turned out a tale about a teacher whose hairspray had been replaced with a can of spray paint. Throughout the day, her spurts slowly turned her hair pink, unbeknownst to her but on full display to the class. Thankfully Mrs. Carlson found it amusing, and the class loved it. That might have been the beginning of my realization that humor got me attention in class. Standing out for cracking jokes or doing odd things that got attention would increasingly become part of my school identity.

Certain rules didn't make sense to me. When we started learning penmanship, Mrs. Carlson gave us wide-ruled three-lined pages to practice our cursive. It seemed to me a contest for making it pretty. But if the function of handwriting was to convey ideas, who cared if it looked nice?

This was the same with how we were graded. We had a standard A for best, followed by B and C. That made sense to me. What didn't was the need to give us a grade for effort. If you put in a lot of effort you got a 1, medium effort a 2, and no effort a 3. Of course, an A1 was considered the top score. To me, that seemed wrong. If you truly were smart, you'd be able to get an A with as little effort as possible, so A3 should be the best grade. When I told Mrs. Carlson that ratio optimization, she assumed I was joking. For every assignment, I said, "Mrs. Carlson, please give me an A3." She thought I was showboating, which I kind of was, but the combination of high grade/low effort honestly made the most sense to me.

At some point, I got interested in how our bodies work. Maybe it was those plastic illustrations in the *World Book*. I wanted to do something about physiology for show-and-tell. I think one girl brought in her flute, other kids had mementos from family trips. I wanted to show something cool and educational. It was clear I couldn't get a human body part, so I consulted with my dad. He suggested that maybe an animal organ could be a proxy for whatever I wanted to demonstrate. He offered to check with a slaughterhouse.

That's how I came to bring a cow's lung into Mrs. Carlson's classroom one morning. By the time I got to school, a little residual blood had seeped through the sheet in which it was wrapped.

I unveiled it to a mix of awe and disgust. I pressed down on the lung to show it could still push air in and out—the oxygen transfer! A girl fainted. Later someone said that she was a Christian Scientist and was appalled by my lung for religious reasons. I remember thinking that the lungs of a Christian Scientist are the same as everyone else's lungs and not that different from a cow's lung, so what was the big deal? (In the end Mrs. Carlson made me carry the organ outside, where it stayed, wrapped in its bloody sheet, until my parents picked me up at the end of the day. I don't remember what we did with it.)

Mrs. Carlson used a record player at the front of the room to quiz us on multiplication problems. Sitting at our desks, each of us head down with pencil in hand, we'd listen to a guy read out problems. "Nine times twelve," his voice crackled over the speaker.

Everyone would scribble down their answer. Then a few moments later: "eleven times six." Scribble, scribble. It wasn't long before I realized that I was finishing each problem faster than everyone else. I'd write an answer, look up, and see most of the rest of the class still scribbling. Some kids were even falling behind, calling, "Wait, I'm not done," when the guy on the record moved on to the next problem.

This was the first time I felt I was better at something than my peers. To me, math was easy, even fun. I liked its ironclad certainty. Math followed basic rules; all you had to do was remember them. It was confusing to me why some other students couldn't seem to figure that out. Four times four always equaled sixteen.

Math appealed to my growing sense that much of the world was a rational place. I started to understand that many complex questions—about bridges, card games, the human body, whatever— had answers, answers that I could find if I applied my brain to them. I can't say it was an awakening. I had always been a thinker and searcher of new information. But now I had growing confidence in the power of my own intellect. With this confidence also came a feeling that the intellectual divide between adults and me had collapsed. My father would later say that this change happened abruptly. He said I became an adult overnight—an argumentative, intellectually forceful, and sometimes not very nice adult. Most kids go through a rebellious phase when they reach adolescence. I got there a lot sooner than most. I was about nine.

At that age, kids expect their parents and teachers to have all the answers. Increasingly I felt that they didn't—or at least they couldn't provide answers that satisfied me.

My perception of adults' limitations undermined the family compact. If I could think for myself, I reasoned, why would I need my parents' input? Maybe I didn't even need them. I started to question the whole parent-child enterprise. Why did they get to call the shots? Who were they to say when I had to go to bed or what to eat or how to keep my room? Why should I have to do things that didn't matter to me? Never mind that my mom and dad provided everything I had or ever needed, from the material to the emotional; I just didn't get why they were in charge. Their power seemed arbitrary.

My mother bore the brunt of this change. As the rule setter and enforcer, she was the usual target of my recalcitrance. I rebelled against what I saw was her need to control me.

My father got stuck in the middle. If there was some stalemate with my mother, she'd eventually retreat and wait until my father came home. The lawyer by day would become family judge at night. In one of those wait-until-your-father-comes-home talks, over some transgression I don't recall, my father put it to me clearly: "You have to respect us." I didn't agree. What was respect anyway? And why did they need it so badly? In the snidest tone I could muster, I snapped back: "No, I don't!" Today, thinking back to that moment leaves a pit in my stomach. I knew I was being a bratty wiseass. But I wasn't going to back down. Instead, I retreated more deeply into my own world.

At school, I was pulling back. In class I tamped my personality down. I stopped asking questions. I became less engaged. I was very deliberate about what I put energy into and what I let slide. I continued to excel in math and reading and made almost no effort in the subjects I dismissed as uninteresting. When Mrs. Carlson wheeled in the taped Spanish lessons, I tuned out. It was unclear how we were supposed to learn from a recording. We were hardly ever quizzed. The notion that we weren't being measured didn't jibe with my sense that math was truly superior. You could always tell if you were right or wrong.

One day Mrs. Carlson led me down the hall to the library, where she told the librarian that I needed a challenge. Was there anything she could give me to do?

The library was small, typical of what you'd find at an elementary school library in the 1960s, meaning no computers, just books and periodicals. There were a lot of *National Geographics*, popular series like the *Black Stallion,* an old set of encyclopedias, and basic science books. This room, with maybe thirty ceiling-high shelves and a chest-high card catalog, was our internet. The librarian, Blanche Caffiere, had been my first-grade teacher and was famous for her energetic story times. She made these big felt boards that she used as backdrops to animate the doings of Mole and Mr. Toad in *The Wind and the Willows* or whatever story she was reading that day.

Mrs. Caffiere had already taught school for many years by the time we met. She had seen every kind of student you can name and was known at View Ridge for helping those on the extreme ends, the ones struggling and the ones excelling. Teachers graded you and administrators punished you. Mrs. Caffiere gave you a job. In her mind, a job could fix whatever problem you had.

She put me to work right away. She said there were a bunch of missing books that likely were on the shelves but in the wrong place. Could I find them? It was the typical busywork you'd give to a kid to eat up time. But I took to it. What you need is kind of like a detective, I told her. That's exactly what I need, she replied. I took the cards for the missing books and roamed the stacks until I found each one.

Where do they go? I asked, eyeing the stack of books I'd tracked down. She explained that the nonfiction books were shelved according to a numerical range from 000 to 900. To remember the Dewey Decimal system, she told me to memorize a simple story about a caveman asking progressively more sophisticated questions, starting with "Who am I?" (that's 100: philosophy and psychology) and building up to "How can I leave a record for other people?" (900: history, geography, and biography).

When Mrs. Carlson came to get me for recess, I asked her to let me stay. I liked my job. I'm pretty sure my library assistantship was supposed to be a one-time deal. I liked it so much, however, I showed up early the next day. Mrs. Caffiere seemed surprised, but agreed when I asked if I could become a regular assistant librarian.

For a kid who loved both books and numbers, it was a dream job. The library wasn't just a room of randomness. It had a logical system, an order dictated by numbers. And if you learned that system, you could be an expert, instantly able to find what you wanted in any library anywhere. You'd know a nonfiction book on dogs and cats would be under 636 (animal husbandry), and never mistake that for *The Incredible Journey* (about two dogs and a cat), which would be filed elsewhere, alphabetically, because it was a work of fiction.

I worked in the library for the rest of the year, often skipping recess to immerse myself in finding and reshelving books, not noticing other students or that it was time for lunch. I treated it like a game, one I was playing against myself. How fast could I restore a book to its rightful place? Mrs. Caffiere had a way of expressing her appreciation that made me feel valued. She'd say things like, "I don't know how I could have found those books without your sleuthing, Bill." I realize now she was doing what good teachers do: giving positive feedback to build my confidence. Back then, I took it literally. I was helping the library, and the school. I was essential.

When I finished reshelving, Mrs. Caffiere would draw me out with questions about what I was reading or found interesting. Here too she offered me affirmation, suggesting books that were a level of reading above what I knew, biographies of famous people and ideas that hadn't occurred to me. Other kids would rather be out playing. But my time at the library was special and I considered Mrs. Caffiere my friend.

In the early part of that year, after a Sunday dinner at Gami's, my parents called Kristi and me into the living room for a game of hangman. This wasn't something that we normally did, so we knew something was up. My mom drew out the gallows and pretty soon we found the answer: "A little visitor is coming soon." If there was a bigger message there, we didn't get it. My mom explained: She was pregnant. My parents hadn't planned on having another child and didn't know if it was a girl or a boy. I don't remember which I would have preferred, but I think I was happy with the news. It would be interesting to have another kid around the house. Mitigating that good news, however, was another announcement: since rambunctious dogs don't belong near fragile babies, my mom said, Crumpet would have to go.

The mix of good news/bad news continued. Now that we would be a family of five, we needed more space. My parents owned a parcel of land where they had planned to build a home one day. That day, they decided, was now. It was just a few miles away, in an area called Laurelhurst, but it meant that I would go to a different school. This floored me. I had a job at the library, I protested. Mrs. Caffiere needed me. "Who will find the lost books?" I anxiously asked my mother. My mother said that it would be proper to thank Mrs. Caffiere by inviting her to our house for dinner. She helped me write a formal invitation that I nervously presented the next day. At the dinner, I protested our move. Mrs. Caffiere suggested that I could be a library assistant at my new school.

About six months after my sister Libby was born in June 1964, we moved into our new house. By then, we were told that Crumpet was living happily ever after on a nearby farm.

The librarian at my new school said she didn't need an assistant. Eventually, my parents decided that it would be less disruptive if I finished fourth grade back at my old school and in the library. With so much change in the family, I'm sure they knew it was wise to let me stay a little longer in the comfort of books.

CHAPTER FOUR

Lucky Kid

Good morning to you, good morning to you, good morning, good morning, good morning to you!" This was the song sung by my mother every morning of my childhood from fifth grade on. The song crackled through the intercom connecting our bedrooms downstairs with the kitchen above where she was making breakfast. I'm not sure the size of our new house justified an intercom, but to my mom it was a productivity tool, allowing her to roust us in the morning, get us ready for church, call us for dinner—all without pausing whatever else she was doing. A call from the intercom meant get upstairs now.

After we moved to Laurelhurst, my mother began her steady rise from volunteer to board member of major, publicly traded companies, and was often the first woman to serve in the role. She'd blast out the front door, briefcase in hand, impeccably dressed, on the way to a meeting. Or she was on the phone ironing out the details of some fundraiser. Long after the rest of us were in bed, my mom would be at her typewriter crafting thank-you letters for the last funding drive or a proposal for the next.

My mom would never have called herself a pioneer, but she was very much on the cutting edge of what a woman could accomplish in the restrictive workplace world of her time. Today she'd be considered a feminist, but she wouldn't have liked the label, preferring to just put her head down, finding ever bigger platforms to effect the changes she thought important. She did all this while being fully engaged as a mother. Always, of course, my grandmother was there to back her up.

My sisters and I were acutely aware that our mother was unconventional. None of our friends' mothers were running off to meetings in pantsuits or asserting their views on lawyers, politicians, and businessmen in my parents' social circle. This was the mid-1960s, two or three years after Betty Friedan's *The Feminine Mystique* argued that women needed more than housework but before American women started climbing rungs on the corporate ladder. My mother wanted both. Later my sisters and I would talk about the pride we felt in how she balanced her own ambitions with being a mom—frenetic as it was. As a ten-year-old, Libby entered my mom in a local contest for "Mother of the Year." In her submission she wrote that in addition to "usually being in a cheery mood," Mom was always there to go bowling or play tennis, and on the sidelines at soccer games. When she won, my mom, of course, clipped the article and pasted it into her scrapbook.

My father, meanwhile, supported my mom's ambition to a degree that I think was rare for the time, when roles—at least in middle-class families—were sharply defined: the man was the breadwinner, the woman the homemaker. I'm sure my dad wanted to avoid his father's mistake of binding his mother and sister to strictly traditional gender roles. In the boxes of memorabilia my mother saved, I found a college essay in which my father imagined the perfect world,

a place he called Gatesland: "In Gatesland the people would understand that there are no differences between men and women except
in physical makeup. Maxims like 'a woman's place is in the home'
and expressions like 'male superiority' and 'man, the provider,' 'the
weaker sex' would have no significance. Men and women would
meet on exactly level terms in all endeavors . . . the female would
be as common in the professions and business as the male, and the
male would accept female entry into these fields as the normal rather
than abnormal event."

In the actual Gatesland, a four-bedroom mid-century-modern
house, hearing my mom's intercom reveille meant we had to get up,
get dressed, make our beds, and head upstairs, where she would have
our breakfast laid out on the kitchen bar counter, always the same
in place and order, oldest to youngest. My mom sat across from us,
using the pull-out cutting board as her makeshift breakfast table. By
that time, my dad was already at work. He liked to show up to the
firm first, read the newspaper in the temporarily quiet office, and
greet everyone as they arrived.

Starting fifth grade at Laurelhurst Elementary, I had all the typical new-kid fears and insecurities. I didn't know anyone. Can I make
friends? Will other kids pick on me? Moving just a few miles might
seem an insignificant distance, but we were newcomers to a tight
community of families whose kids had been hanging out for their
whole short lives. Two boys in my class would joke that they met
while still in the womb.

One of my first impressions inspired a mix of fear and fascination. The school had an overpass connecting us to a playground on
the other side of 45th Street. Tiffs that started in school were settled
later in the playground dirt, out of the view of teachers. Crossing the
overpass one afternoon, I froze. Two kids in front of me were punching each other, a flurry of fists to the head and face. They were both
in my grade but far bigger than the rest of us. One was muscular, the
other just big. I had never seen anything like that fight. And I had

never imagined such raw aggression at school. A couple of teachers ran up, pulled the kids apart, and it was over.

My first thought: *I better stay away from those two.* I was fifty-nine pounds, and though not the scrawniest kid in my grade, I was close. And with my Barbie-blond hair and my squeaky voice, I stuck out. I was an easy target.

Something else about those brawlers struck me: they had a social identity. Being tough, being bad, engendered a special kind of status in school. It wasn't the kind of status that I or most kids wanted, but those big guys had marked their position within the social order of the 140 or so kids in our fifth grade. At the top of the pecking order were the kids from prominent Laurelhurst families, the Timberlakes, the Storys, and others, whom everyone knew and respected. They were a class among themselves. Somewhere under that stratum were the sports kids, the brainy kids, and one or two nerds. I wasn't tough and wasn't a jock, so those positions were out of the question. I didn't yet identify as a nerd, and I was insecure about being perceived as studious. Being diligent in class was something that I assumed cool kids didn't aspire to, the type of thing I'd be teased about.

As I saw it, I had one differentiator: humor. In my old school I had discovered that the class clown held a niche position among other kids. Raising your hand to crack a joke won more popularity points than raising it with the right answer. People laughed. Hoping for the same response from a new audience, I actively carved out the joker position at Laurelhurst Elementary. I pretended I didn't care about school. I'd wallow in my messy desk and do my homework at the last minute. I'd ham it up when we had to read something aloud; I'd laugh inappropriately while the teacher was talking. If I worked hard on something, I hid my effort behind humor. Our teacher, Mrs. Hopkins, assigned a one-page essay on any topic we chose. I don't remember my topic, but I do remember taking the time to craft it using only a single continuous sentence that ran all forty lines of the page. I silently gloated when Mrs. Hopkins called me out in class for the feat, noting that my snake-long sentence, though annoying, had perfect punctuation.

My teacher, my parents, and the school principal were at a loss as to what to do with me. My grades were mixed; my attitude depended on the day and the subject. On top of everything else, someone decided that my squeaky voice needed fixing. Early in the fifth grade I started seeing the school speech expert. A few times a week, I'd go to her office to work on my "big daddy-bear voice" (ugh) and practice pronouncing the letter *r* while licking peanut butter from the end of a breadstick. It seemed stupid to me but weird enough that I went along with it. The upshot of these sessions was the speech counselor recommended that my parents hold me back a year—repeat the fifth grade. I think she said I was "retarded," now a dated and offensive word, but back then a term applied to kids who didn't seem to fit in the classroom. Fortunately, my parents didn't follow her advice. Her verdict came a year after another educator recommended that I skip ahead a year. I thought, *If these supposed experts don't know what to do with me, why should I care about their opinions?*

Mostly I was happy to do my own thing. I started to make friends and I found at least one kindred spirit in my approach to school. His name was Stan Youngs, but everyone called him Boomer, a name given by his father for his foghorn cry as a newborn. Boomer was smart and had a contrarian streak that melded well with my jokester persona.

We met in 1965 and for the next two years would be the closest of friends. Boomer fit a type of person that I would gravitate toward for the rest of my life. He was confident beyond his years and outwardly intelligent. Willing and able to argue anything at any time, even if just for the mental exercise of testing himself, like why the Green Bay Packers were the greatest football team in history.

In my basement we'd clash over epic games of Risk and who would dominate the world. He also had a physicality that I admired. Though he was a small tow-headed kid like me, he was unafraid to meet on the other side of the 45th Street overpass to settle a score—even if he knew that he'd lose. It was my mother who signed me up for football, but Boomer was the reason I stayed on for the season. Being small was actually an advantage because it meant not being put on the line, which to me seemed far less interesting than my position, center linebacker. From my spot I got to see all the action, the full offense, the ball being snapped, and even the guy running past me for a touchdown.

One day in school, our teacher announced that the class would divide into two groups to debate the war in Vietnam. Every kid chose to argue against the war. So naturally Boomer took the pro-war side just for the challenge. I joined him. We were the only two in the group. He was more politically conservative than me and even read *National Review.* (When he ordered the subscription as a Father's Day gift, he wrote the magazine a complimentary letter, and was thrilled that William F. Buckley Jr. himself wrote him back, praising my friend for being such a bright boy.) With Boomer's familiarity with the pro-Vietnam stance and a flurry of background reading I did, we armed ourselves with arguments on the domino theory and the communist threat. We won that debate hands down.

Our new house in Laurelhurst was two stories and set into a hill with a view of Mount Rainier from the back deck. The front door opened to the main floor with the living room, kitchen, and bedroom for my parents. Downstairs, in what was essentially the basement, Kristi and I had our bedrooms, and when Libby got a little older she moved into a third bedroom down there with us.

The upstairs-basement layout of the house meant that I could retreat to my room and avoid the daily traffic of home life. I had my bed and my desk, which were often the only two things visible in a sea of strewn books and clothes. It was a holy mess. My mom hated that. At one point she started confiscating any clothes I left on the floor and charging me twenty-five cents to buy them back. I started wearing fewer clothes.

Alone in my cave I'd read or just sit and think. I could lie on the bed endlessly working through some question. I'd hear a car motor rev, leaves rustling in the wind, the footsteps on the floor above me, and wonder how these sounds traveled to my ear. Mysteries like that could occupy me for hours. Later I found an article on sound in *Life,* checked the *World Book Encyclopedia,* and read library books on the subject. I was thrilled to learn that sound is a propagation of energy made by vibrations affected by many things, including the density and stiffness of the material it travels through. Eventually I turned my new knowledge into a science paper for school: "What is Sound?" The teacher marked me down for ignoring margins and writing all the way to the bottom of the page. That seemed crazy to me. There was just too much to say on the topic to bother with those kinds of boring details.

I dug deeper into math and most nights I joined Kristi in doing her seventh-grade homework. This was when I was obsessive about getting better at cards and trying the best I could to win a few hands against my grandmother.

At some point that first year at Laurelhurst, Mrs. Hopkins had students draw numbers from a hat. In the order of your number, you picked one U.S. state to profile. Everyone wanted California, Florida, or some other colorful place. My classmate Leslie drew number one. She picked Hawaii. When my number came up, I went with the small state of Delaware. It was a contrarian choice that I was sure no one wanted. I knew one thing about it thanks to my dad: it was friendly to businesses.

I inhaled everything I could find on Delaware. I trolled the stacks at the library, dug out *Delaware, a Guide to the First State,* and books on Delaware history, the state's role in the Underground Railroad. I wrote to the state of Delaware for brochures on tourism and history. At home, Gami helped me cull articles from *The Christian Science Monitor, Life, National Geographic,* and *The Seattle Times.* I wrote to Delaware companies, including self-addressed stamped envelopes, and requested their annual reports.

As I researched, I wrote. I wrote about the state's history from the Lenni Lenape to the present, including a four-hundred-year chronology. I compiled a tourist's guide to Wilmington and a history of the quaint historical town of Arden. I put together fictitious accounts of the lives of a Delawarean oyster fisherman and a granite miner. For good measure, I wrote a book report on *Elin's Amerika,* the story of a young girl in seventeenth-century Delaware.

I spent a lot of time researching the Delaware company DuPont. I wrote about the company's management structure; I noted that its board was all men and mostly insiders. I detailed DuPont's products, its overseas operations, and its research and development, and summarized the story of nylon's invention, complete with the best descriptions I could muster on the chemistry of polymerization. I wrote up an obit of a board member who had worked his way from low-level salesman to executive committee member.

By the time I was done, I had generated 177 pages on little Delaware. It's hard to describe the pride I felt in that crazy-long report. I even fabricated a cover for it out of wood. It was in every way a dream assignment. In the privacy of my room, away from the judging eyes of other kids, I could do what I liked the most: read, collect facts, and synthesize information. The class jester wasn't expected to turn in a tome. I liked seeing other kids' confusion and admiration. My teacher loved it.

Looking back at that report, I can see hints of the adult I would become, my intellectual interests starting to take root. With a little effort I could—much to my amazement—assemble in my head models of how the world operated, whether it was how sound traveled or the inner workings of the Canadian government (another report). Each bit of knowledge I accrued added to a sense of empowerment, the feeling that by applying my brain, I could solve even the world's most complex mysteries.

That school year, I filled out a one-page form indicating my interests and favorite subjects. It was something my mom had us do every year. On the line that read, "When I grow up I want to be—" I skipped over suggested answers like Cowboy and Fireman (the girls had a separate list, the options even more limited and sexist: Airline Hostess, Model, or Secretary); instead I chose Astronaut and penciled in what I really saw myself as: "Scientist." I wanted to be one of those people who spend their days trying to understand things that other people do not.

My mother's ambitions for me were more varied, and she doggedly continued her attempts to round me out by signing me up for all the usual activities. I played baseball but was so unnerved by the chance of getting hit by a wild pitch (not a rare thing in those games where kids were still learning what their arm could do) that I quit. I suited up for that single season of football with Boomer. But organized sports didn't fit me. I was still very small for my age, a short, narrow-chested stick figure even among a cohort of kids years away from their growth spurt. I generally felt inferior to other kids on teams and shy about trying hard and looking silly. I didn't move as smoothly as they did. I'd sort of galumph along at a pace not quite a walk and nothing close to a run.

Skiing and tennis were central to my mother's coming-of-age and so would they be for her kids. She started me skiing young, on family trips to local mountains, and later I joined the bus that shuttled Seattle kids up to a nearby mountain on the weekends. I liked going fast and the thrill of taking jumps, but mostly I liked the goofing around with the other kids in the back of the bus. I had a short stint on the Crystal Mountain Ski Team but never took it that seriously. Tennis lessons were the same.

My music career started with the piano, moved on to the guitar, and crashed in the brass section. I have no idea how it was decided I would pick up the trombone, but I lugged that poor instrument around in its big black case practicing my fourth position for two years before quitting.

At one point it was decided that I should take on the responsibility of my own paper route. I made a little bit of money, but it was a thankless task delivering a free circular nobody subscribed to and few people wanted. My main memory of that venture is the struggle it took to navigate my bike loaded with all those papers. More than once, I had to be rescued by Gami, who drove me along my route while I tossed papers onto porches.

The truth was, I felt most at home in my own head.

And yet despite my aspirations, my grades were still bad and my battles at home got worse. During this period, I could go days without speaking, emerging from my room only for meals and school. Call me to dinner, I ignored you. Tell me to pick up my clothes, nope. Clear the table—nothing. Get in the car to go out for dinner: silence. Years later my parents told journalists that once when my mother tried to draw me out, I snapped, "I'm thinking! Don't you ever think? You should try it sometime." Much as it pains me to say, it's a true story.

There were days when I dreaded hearing the *thump, thump, thump* of my dad's footsteps as he walked in after work to greet my mom. I'd catch the murmur of my parents talking, my mother recounting the battle we had that day, or some problem I had at school. Soon my dad would be downstairs at my door. There were times that he spanked me. Those were rare and I could tell that it hurt him to do it. I think too that he didn't always agree with my mom's disciplinarian approach. But they were partners in the venture of child raising, so he always stood by her. Usually he'd give me a talk. He didn't have to say much to have an effect. His presence, his careful choice of words, his deep voice was enough to get me to sit up straight and listen. He was intimidating but not in a physical way, despite his towering stature. It was more his intrinsically rational mind. "Son, your mother says that you talked back to her when she was on the phone. In our house, as you know, we don't do things like that. I think it's fair that you go upstairs now and apologize," he might say, with an emotional distance that showed he was serious, and that I better listen. It was no wonder that we all thought his true legal calling was as a judge.

For a short time, my parents enrolled in a class in Parent Effectiveness Training at our church. Invented in the early 1960s, P.E.T. proposed that parents listen to the needs of their kids and never use punitive discipline. It was a precursor to modern parenting approaches that put the parents on more collaborative or even equal footing with their kids. Looking back now, I realize how frustrated they must have been to have resorted to such a step, and how hard it must have been for my mom to admit that she needed outside help. I'm also ashamed to hear Kristi's memories of this time, how my behavior sucked up so much of my mother's energy, there was little left over for her.

I'm not sure how long my parents stuck with the class, but whatever they tried with me didn't work.

Our tensions came to a head one night over dinner. I got into another argument with my mother. I don't recall its source, but I do remember that as usual I was insulting and being a smart aleck. And judging by what happened next, particularly mean: from across the table, my father emptied a glass of water in my face. I paused, eyes locked on my plate. "Thanks for the shower," I snapped. I slowly put down my fork, stood up, and walked downstairs to my room.

I had never seen my gentle father lose his temper. To see how I had pushed my dad to that extreme was a shock.

By that time, I was generating so much turmoil that my parents sought the help of Dr. Charles Cressey, a social worker who ran his own therapy practice. He was known for counseling medical students on bedside manner and couples through their challenges. My whole family came to the first visit, but everyone knew that we were there because of me.

"I'm at war with my parents," I told Dr. Cressey.

Every Saturday morning my parents would drop me off at a gold-colored Victorian house near the Jack in the Box in Seattle's University District. I'd let myself in and wait in the front room while Dr. Cressey finished with other clients. As I waited, through the plaster walls I could hear tense voices of couples trying to work through their marital problems. When I first started visiting, I wondered: *These people have real problems. Why am I even here?*

In our sessions, Dr. Cressey and I would sit in chairs next to a sunny bay window and talk for an hour or so. His space seemed intentionally designed to calm you, more like a living room than my image of a therapist's office. The window looked out on a garden with a big tree with white flowers in spring.

You'd be hard-pressed to meet a more disarming and empathetic person. He had a way of drawing me out, asking intelligent and insightful questions about my week, stuff at school, and how I was handling things with my mom. Normally my tendency would be to shut out questions like that. But he seemed sincerely interested in what I had to say rather than leading up to a lesson of some kind, or something he wanted me to do. And he himself was interesting. Before getting his degree in social work, Dr. Cressey had been a fighter pilot in World War II and had a short career as a pharmaceutical salesman, during which he saved enough money to start the counseling practice. Those kinds of personal details came sparingly. He didn't talk much about himself. Instead, he'd focus on me. He just asked his questions. He never told me how I should think or what I was doing right or wrong. "You're going to win," he assured me, without further explanation. In hindsight I realized that he was guiding me to find my own conclusions.

He was an avid student of his subject, constantly reading up on psychology and therapy in search of insights he could incorporate into his practice. He shared many of these books, assigning me readings by Jung or Freud and other experts we'd discuss. I found it intriguing that there were people who attempt to understand the human brain and behavior.

Through our talks, I started to see that he was right: I was destined to win my imagined war with my parents. With each year my independence would grow. In time I would be on my own. All the while—then and into the future—my mother and father would love me. How great was that? Win the war and never lose their love. Without being prescriptive, Dr. Cressey helped me see that (A) my parents loved me; (B) I wouldn't be under their roof forever; (C) they were actually my allies in terms of what really counted; (D) it was absurd to think that they had done anything wrong.

Rather than wasting energy fighting my parents, I should focus my energies on gaining the skills I would need out in the world.

I later learned that Dr. Cressey had had a difficult childhood, one of physical abuse that left him with a lot of anger. After the war he made the decision to dispense with his anger and dedicate his life to what he called spreading love. He obviously knew that my problems were minor compared to his own as a kid, and, I'm sure, compared to those of many of his clients. Yet he never belittled what I was going through. Once he told me, "You're a lucky kid." I was gazing out the bay window and didn't respond, but I knew he was right.

I could hear the murmur of voices through the wall, but not the details of the conversation. Dr. Cressey was talking to my parents; I had left the room so the adults could confer in private. My father later shared what Dr. Cressey said. "Give it up," he told my parents. "He's going to win." I'm sure there was a lot more to it than that, but that was the gist. Ease up, don't force it, give your son more freedom.

When my father recounted the visit years later, he told me that he and my mom were stunned. The advice dashed their hopes that Dr. Cressey would share practical steps to follow that would get me on track. Easing up must have seemed like defeat, something you do when you run out of options. It must have been particularly tough for my mom, whose solution to any problem was to apply more energy. While my parents always maintained a united front, my father had a looser view of child raising. Having staked out his own independence at a young age, I think he intuitively understood the value of a kid following their own path. It just came far sooner for his son than he expected.

Things between us gradually improved. Not because my parents suddenly gave in and let me do whatever I wanted, but because the new perspective Dr. Cressey had given me allowed *me* to ease up, to change. To refocus my energy.

Many years later—in 1980, to be exact—I watched the film *Ordinary People* when it came out in the theater. I've seen it many times since, and nearly every time I get choked up. It's a great movie, nearly perfect. Stripping out the extremes—the trauma of a brother's death, a mother who can't love enough, and a son whose struggle takes him to the brink—there are elements I recognize in my own upbringing. I was young and confused and fought with a mother who wished everything to be perfect, particularly in the eyes of the outside world. I had a father—like Donald Sutherland's character, a lawyer—who did his best to stabilize the family. And like Conrad, the son in the film, I had the guidance of a gifted therapist who helped me reason through my situation and reach my own conclusions about how I could change. Over time I would have to accept my mom for who she was, as she learned that I would never fully fit the model she set for me. Increasingly, I redirected my energy from resisting her will to preparing myself for when I would be genuinely independent. That shift in perspective couldn't have come at a better time. I had a growing awareness about the wider world of adults. And I was lucky to live in a family where it was natural, even expected, that I would engage in it.

In those days, I would often visit my dad at his law firm in the busy heart of downtown Seattle. I'd take an elevator to the tenth floor of the Norton Building, the city's first modern office tower, at just twenty-one stories. Waiting in his office for him to finish for the day, I was intrigued by the people dressed up in their suits and ties, sweeping past me as I read my book. They'd be locked in silent thought or talking animatedly about some case on their way to a meeting. It was all an impressive level of seriousness, and I imagined the things they were talking about were consequential.

If it was a Saturday, the office would be empty, and I'd explore the stacks of law books and rows of Dictaphone machines. I paged through Xeroxed copies of law cases and tried to decipher the hand-writing scribbled in the margins. I peeked at the paper time logs the lawyers kept on their desks; my father explained that to get paid, everyone had to keep meticulous track of the minutes and hours they worked. I learned there was something called a deposition, dur-ing which lawyers asked witnesses detailed questions. That's what the Dictaphones were for.

These visits reinforced my sense that my dad, as a senior partner, was responsible for overseeing complex and important matters. I realized that the coolheaded sense of order and unwavering stabil-ity he brought to our family also contributed to his success in that tenth-floor office with all those nicely dressed people. Those visits colored in a mental model of work life for me and set the metrics by which I would come to measure accomplishment.

The success stories I heard at home didn't feature sports heroes or movie stars but people making things—products and policies, even buildings, as was the case with one family friend, a civil engineer who owned a local construction company. By the mid-1960s, my parents and their friends were in their late thirties and early forties and had spent years working their way into influential positions in government and business. When I was in middle school, my parents' bridge partner, Dan Evans, was our state's governor. (Later he'd serve in the U.S. Senate.) My dad's active participation in local, state, and national legal associations and my mom's local nonprofit work broadened their circle with up-and-coming professionals who shared the same, characteristically ambitious, goals for Seattle, Washington, and the country.

These people and their stories interested me, and my access to them could not have been easier. I only needed to put down whatever book I was reading and walk upstairs, where almost every week I'd find them.

My parents hosted a lot of dinners and parties. (As with their holiday cards and invitations, in the run-up to many of these parties, my mother and father would compose a clever invite with a puzzle the recipient had to solve to figure out what they were being invited to and when and where it would be held. By this time, we had our own silk-screen setup in the basement.) Often the gatherings centered on discussing an issue or recruiting for a new cause. You couldn't be invited to the Gates house to just sit and chat. Every party, every cocktail gathering was an orchestrated affair. My parents might invite members of the Seattle Bar Association to focus attention on how to give young lawyers greater power in the state bar, or fund a scholarship for Black law students at the University of Washington. Ahead of the party, we'd move furniture around and set up folding tables to accommodate small groups. My mother would introduce a question to be discussed over dinner. At dessert, she'd have everyone look under their coffee cup, where they'd find their new seat assignment at another table. The cup trick was my mother's way of encouraging cross-pollination of ideas and helping people make new connections. She was a masterful social engineer.

Before the party began, my mother would sit my sisters and me down on the sofa for a briefing. As Libby and I wrestled and horsed around, my mother would conduct a detailed run-through of the guest list, person by person. Armed with this information, we were expected to engage our guests. Kristi might have to play a piano tune; in later years, my mom would bring in Libby's choir group to sing. I usually got off the hook with shuttling drinks to people, weaving my way through discussions on how to clean up Lake Washington, find more big-name donors for the United Way, or help support Joel Pritchard's state senate bid. I liked the feeling of asking a guest a smart question and being able to hold my own in the conversation.

One regular visitor to our house was a client of my dad's, a cardiologist named Karl Edmark. In addition to having performed one of the first open-heart surgeries in Seattle, Dr. Edmark had invented an innovative defibrillator, the machine that restarts a heart with a jolt of electricity. (Early defibrillators used alternating current—think of the electricity from a wall socket—that would not only shock the heart but send the patient into violent spasms. Dr. Edmark devised one that worked on lower, direct current and was easier on patients, as well as portable.) He developed and marketed his invention through a company called Physio-Control.

I learned this story in bits and pieces, through conversations and at family dinners, as it unfolded over time. My dad told me how Dr. Edmark had nursed his company along for years, barely making any money, until he was finally faced with the possibility of having to give it up. With my dad's help, he hired a professional manager who brought a marketing mindset to the company. My father was asked to approach outside investors. Gradually sales increased, profit edged up, and the business succeeded. I was fascinated by this story of a doctor-inventor who made a machine for saving lives, but also by what my sixth-grade brain could absorb about raising capital, patents and profits, research and development.

Before long, I found myself at Physio-Control's office in downtown Seattle meeting engineers and interviewing the new president, Hunter Simpson. He lived in our neighborhood, and I had met him at one of my parents' parties.

I took what I had learned and turned it into a school report about a fictitious company—I called it Gatesway—that made a coronary care system which I invented. My report detailed factors of production, and how I hoped to raise capital from investors in order to build my products. "If my idea is good and I am able to hire good people and raise enough money I should be successful," I wrote. The teacher gave me an A/1, maximum score for maximum effort. As much as I'd griped about the grading system, this time I agreed.

It's a sign of how much more comfortable I was socially that I started a club that year, basically a junior version of my parents' gatherings. I called it the Contemporary Club and invited a group of kids in my grade to discuss the issues of the day. The Contemp Club, as we called it for short, had six members: three girls and three boys, including my buddy Boomer. Once or twice a month we met at a member's house, each taking turns as host. Over juice and cookies we'd debate—the topics escape me, but surely we covered the Vietnam War, civil rights, and other pressing issues of the day. (We also held our own Halloween party, the mom-like twist being that you had to bring a costume for someone else to wear, which is why I can say that once in my life I dressed as a Venetian gondolier, complete with blue-striped shirt and wide-brim straw hat.)

With the help of our parents, the Contemp Club organized field trips to local nonprofits and the University of Washington. We also gathered donations for Head Start, the early-childhood education program. Our biggest get, or at least it seemed so at the time, was to visit a local think tank owned by Battelle, the big nonprofit R&D company. Their office was in our neighborhood. While playing football on their grassy field, I'd always wondered what went on in their fancy buildings. Somehow, we contacted them, and incredibly, they invited us to spend an afternoon learning about the place. Battelle was most famous for inventing dry paper copying, a technology it spun out to form Xerox. We learned the story of that then-hot technology, the office copier, and how Battelle invested the money in their copy patents. I was amazed they took us seriously and gave us so much attention. Leaving Battelle I thought, *This is what smart people do. They get together with other smart people and solve really tough problems. That sounds perfect to me.*

I continued to meet with Dr. Cressey for about two and a half years. At some point, our Saturday sessions came to an end. There was peace in our house. I can't say I was an ideal son, but I was trying harder. Meanwhile, my parents also gave me a longer leash to be myself. I recognized and appreciated that my mother was trying to give me more space; at the same time, her career was taking off and she now had a toddler to look after. In retrospect, while it took some time to adjust to the idea, I think my parents had accepted that their son was a few degrees from what a lot of parents would consider normal. As Dr. Cressey said, their love would never, ever waver. And he was right.

My parents also continued to feed my need for constant intellectual stimulation. In the summer after sixth grade, they took Kristi and me (Libby, aged three, stayed home with Gami) on a trip east, starting in Montreal at Expo 67, a sort of World's Fair Canada. From there we visited Boston, New York, Washington, D.C., and Colonial Williamsburg. Every day was packed with experiences, a mix of substance and fun, a checklist of educational sites, the *Mayflower* replica, Broadway to see *Fiddler on the Roof,* and the New York Stock Exchange. On Capitol Hill we sat in on a Senate session, toured the White House, Arlington National Cemetery, roamed the Smithsonian, and visited pretty much every other major site in the nation's capital.

The trip east was a celebration of sorts, a treat for Kristi and me. My sister was starting Roosevelt High School in the fall, and

I was also headed to a new school. My parents had decided that I should go to Lakeside, an exclusive private boys' school in North Seattle. The decision wasn't easy for them. They had both attended public schools—my mom was a Roosevelt grad—and believed in supporting the public school system. And the $1,400 annual tuition would be a stretch even on my father's salary. But they could see I needed more challenges and lacked motivation. Maybe Lakeside would stimulate me, they thought. I hated the idea at first. I had heard that older students were required to wear jackets and ties and to address their teachers as "Master." When I visited the school to take an entrance exam, I considered tanking it. But once I started working through the questions, I couldn't help myself. My pride prevailed and I passed.

CHAPTER FIVE

Lakeside

The first thing that struck my seventh-grader sensibilities about Lakeside School was that it was misnamed. The place was nowhere near a lake. It was set in the woods, just off Interstate 5 on the northern edge of Seattle, a twenty-minute drive from my neighborhood. As I rode there in my mom's Ford station wagon on that first day, it seemed like a long way from home.

Lakeside was founded in 1919 as a college feeder for boys from some of Seattle's wealthier families. Originally it was on Lake Washington—hence the name—but in the 1930s it moved to land cleared to build a larger college-like campus. In the six years I would spend there, the school would shed the last of its more conservative prep school traditions, abolish its dress code, hire women faculty, and merge with a girls' school—but when I started in the fall of 1967, every teacher was male, except the librarian, and white. We had assigned seating at lunch. While at the school I would fall in love with the adolescent staples *The Catcher in the Rye* and *A Separate Peace,* books that depict iconic East Coast prep schools. Lakeside was modeled after those places, complete with clipped green lawns and columned brick buildings. It even had a bell tower.

The school was split between grades seven and eight in the lower school and ninth through twelfth in the upper school. There wasn't much mixing. We lower-school students spent most of the day in Moore Hall, one of the oldest buildings on campus, while the upperclassman had freedom to wander, and they unquestionably ruled the place. Sports were a big deal, bad news for me, I thought. The football team had had a long winning streak and the rowing team had brought Lakeside fame by beating a better-known East Coast school in a national championship.

My class had about fifty boys in it, nearly all of them white. Their fathers had the types of jobs you'd expect at a private school in the Pacific Northwest back then. They were lawyers, doctors, bankers, forestry product executives, Boeing engineers—members of Seattle's elite. One dad had started a steak restaurant that would become a national chain. Another would start a major health insurance company. We weren't a diverse mix by any stretch, yet I still felt different from a lot of the other kids. Many seemed so sure of themselves, especially those with older siblings at Lakeside, who already seemed to know the ropes. In those first few weeks I watched as others quickly found their place, signing up for football, the newspaper, drama, glee club, or various other activities. Unlike me, many arrived with social networks. They knew each other from the ski club or tennis club or through family connections.

Lost in this new place, I fell back into my well-practiced shtick playing the goof-off. That worked well in my old school, so I figured I'd keep up the act. One of the highest honors you could earn at Lakeside was a Gold Star, a medal given to students who excelled in the "five points" of the star—athletics, scholarship, fellowship, character, and effort. In my first two years, there was no chance anyone would mistake me for that breed.

I've read depictions of me at Lakeside during that time. I was called a loner, a nerd, a bit obnoxious. I was probably all of those things. With the distance of years and perspective of age, I see how hard I was searching for an identity. All the progress I thought I had made at my old school was meaningless here. I was a nonathlete in a school known for sports. In a place where people were focused, I was an avid generalist. I didn't fit in, and I didn't know how to fix that. So I pretended that I didn't want to.

My act fell flat almost immediately.

Seventh-grade geography was taught by Mr. Anderson, the head of athletics, who was mostly known for coaching Lakeside's football team through its winning streak. He looked every bit the part, with square jaw and crew cut and a football on his desk. At times he ran his class like we were on the field. Get a bad quiz grade and you might have to drop and do ten push-ups. Give a wrong answer and he might pump-fake throwing his football at you. Although I liked geography and maps and knew at some level that Mr. Anderson was a good guy, I messed around in class, skipped assignments, barely participated, and did my share of push-ups.

I was wholly self-satisfied playing the clown until it came time to work on a group project. Mr. Anderson put the best students together and paired me with the kid that everyone knew had the worst grade in the class. Through that simple action, I suddenly saw myself through a teacher's eyes: Gates isn't smart. This stung.

My one attempt to redeem myself was a report on the Black Sea. Intent on showing Anderson that I deserved recognition, I traveled to the Seattle Library and filled pages and pages with facts and history cribbed from the sources like the *Encyclopaedia Britannica,* which I thought of as the scholarly uncle to the kid-friendly *World Book* that we had at home. But while the deluge approach worked with my fifth-grade Delaware opus, the expectations had changed in the two years since. Anderson gave me a low grade (I don't recall precisely how low, but it was bad enough that it stuck with me). Despite my high opinion of myself, in the objective analysis of Anderson—and other teachers that year—I was below average.

When the school year ended, I had all my teachers sign my yearbook, marking the space where I wanted them to sign—where I also included the exhortation, "Give me an A+!" Of course, none obliged. I didn't deserve any. Back home, I got out a pencil and wrote at the bottom of the page in big bubble letters, "Wow! You Teachers are Something to Forget! Goodbye!"

Up to that point I had floated through school thanks to teachers who saw potential under my mask of indifference. At Lakeside they seemed to see only the mask. I'm sure after that first year at my new school, my parents questioned whether they'd made the right decision. I certainly did.

But if I'd been paying attention to the final issue of the Lakeside newspaper that spring, I would have noticed a two-paragraph story at the bottom of the second page. It said that starting in the fall, the math department was going to get connected to a computer. "Hopefully some students will use it to work on extensive projects," the story mused.

At the beginning of eighth grade, I started noticing this certain kid at the lower school. He was hard to miss. Tall, with unruly brown hair, Kent Evans had a deep cleft lip and spoke with a slight impediment. Later I would learn that as a baby, his lip and palate were so badly deformed Kent's parents had to feed him with an eyedropper. By the time I got to know him in our second year, Kent had endured a series of painful operations that left his mouth full of orthodontia and slackly open all the time. Looking back now, I think those earlier challenges helped seed a fearlessness that would manifest itself again and again in the too-short time I knew him.

Kent and I were both in Mr. Stocklin's eighth-grade math class. Kent was quiet, hardly ever participated, but I could tell he knew what was going on. He seemed math-smart, at least from what I could tell from across the classroom. He struck me as more serious than any other kid in class.

I learned that he was new to Seattle. He and his family had moved here only a year earlier, right before seventh grade. Due to his father's job as a Unitarian minister, they moved around, living in Victoria, British Columbia, before coming to Seattle. Like me, Kent didn't easily fit into the established cliques at Lakeside. He was far from athletic and not one of the cool kids everyone gravitated toward. Unlike me, he didn't care. Social position, and even what others thought of him, didn't seem to touch Kent. He lived for himself and his interests, which he pursued intensely, way beyond what you'd imagine for a twelve-year-old. In eighth grade, that interest was national politics.

This was the fall of 1968, the close of a year that would be remembered as one of the most tumultuous in American history. The span of just a few months brought the assassinations of Martin Luther King Jr. and Robert F. Kennedy and the televised beatings of protesters at the Democratic National Convention in Chicago and riots from Baltimore to Boston. Opposition to the Vietnam War went from heated to a full boil. President Johnson bowed out from seeking reelection, opening the field to a host of Democrats vying to keep Republican Richard Nixon from the White House.

Kent had strong and informed views on all these issues. He was vehemently against the Vietnam War, hated Nixon, loved Ted Kennedy (he devoured the senator's book on Democratic policy). He studied the latest cases being fought by the American Civil Liberties Union and decried the rise of the science-denying conspiracy theory that water fluoridation was a communist plot to poison us. He idolized Eugene McCarthy, the U.S. senator from Minnesota running for the Democratic nomination against LBJ. I'm sure Kent modeled himself a bit on McCarthy's image as the intellectual liberal, even winning a seat on the Lakeside student senate (after losing a bid for secretary-treasurer).

When McCarthy failed to win the Democratic nomination in 1968, Kent threw himself into Hubert Humphrey's presidential campaign. He carpeted his yard with red and blue Humphrey signs, canvassed door-to-door, and passed out flyers downtown for Humphrey and the Democrats running for governor and the U.S. Senate. When Humphrey visited Seattle, Kent staked out the Olympic Hotel hoping to talk to the candidate (he failed but a month later proudly reported that he shook hands with Humphrey's running mate, Edmund Muskie). If you were active in the Democratic Party in Seattle at this time, there's a good chance you saw the pudgy teenager at rallies and the local headquarters on Union Street, the lone kid among the political operators and reporters.

One of our Lakeside teachers liked to tell the story of how surprised he was to bump into Kent at a party meeting and then hear Kent's take on the group's machinations and behind-the-scenes power struggles. "He knew more about politics than I would ever know," the teacher said. So obsessed was Kent with the presidential race that year, he used initials of the candidates to mark up his quizzes in French class: Nixon's initials for wrong answers and Humphrey's for correct ones. In the 1968 presidential election, of course, Nixon won. Kent's disappointment was mitigated slightly by his belief that he helped deliver Humphrey a narrow victory in our home state of Washington.

This intensity intrigued me. If he liked something, Kent went all in. As the author of a wood-bound, 177-page disquisition on the state of Delaware, I could appreciate this. One English teacher dinged him for being too intense. "His only shortcoming at the moment is excess preparation," the teacher wrote on Kent's report card in his first year. "For a recent 40-minute paper he produced an outline for a master's thesis." Unlike me, he got good grades.

Kent and I became best friends very quickly. Not too long after we met, we joined a camping trip with a Lakeside teacher known for leading kids on long, rain-soaked slogs in the woods. The hike he chose took us along Washington's rugged coastline. At night Kent and I pitched our tent on the beach, not focusing on how close we were to the Pacific Ocean. Later that night I woke up to Kent shaking me as the seawater sloshed into our tent and inundated our sleeping bags. Laughing hysterically, we fled, dragging our tent to higher ground.

Already close, from that point on we were inseparable. Conversations that we started at school would continue that night over the phone. I'd stretch the spirals out of the phone cord down the stairs into my room and we'd talk for hours. I still remember his phone number.

Like most kids I spent almost zero time thinking about my future, aside from a vague notion that I wanted to be a scientist, or maybe a lawyer like my dad. But at that age, it's hard to envision how getting the right answers on tests translates into a life beyond school, let alone the distant horizon of a career. Kent was way ahead of us. He was always talking about where he wanted to be in ten years, in twenty years, and strategizing how to get there. He seemed certain he was destined for great things and just had to figure out the best of the many paths to achieve them.

Together we read through a stack of biographies of famous people, leaders like Franklin D. Roosevelt and Douglas MacArthur. We spent hours on the phone dissecting their lives. We analyzed the paths they followed to success with the same teenage intensity that other kids at that time spent deciphering "Lucy in the Sky with Diamonds." What about going to West Point and becoming an Army general? We learned how MacArthur was programmed from an early age to pursue a military career. We compared that path with General Patton, who sort of fell into his life as a brilliant soldier and leader. For historical perspective we read books on Napoleon, marveling at his genius and his terrible flaws. The only way to really distinguish yourself was to be a war hero, we decided. But neither of us wanted to go to war. Cross general off the list. How about the U.S. Foreign Service? We found that only political appointees seemed to get the best jobs, and based on a report Kent had ordered from some government office, the pay for embassy staff was low. Off the list. What about becoming a professor? They had clout and the freedom to research cool things, but Kent worried again that the pay might be low. Or a politician? Maybe a lawyer like my dad?

I was the kind of kid who wanted to win every game I played, yet I had no particular aim beyond victory. I was raw intelligence, an information omnivore, but I wasn't thinking about the long-term direction of my life. Kent's ambition would help spark mine and channel my prodigious competitive drive.

Even as we were imagining our futures, the road that we would ultimately follow was right in front of us.

One morning that fall of eighth grade, Mr. Stocklin led our class to McAllister House, a white clapboard building that was home to the math department. Inside we heard a *chug-chug-chug* sound echoing down the hallway—like a cog railway grinding its way up the side of a mountain. Down a hall, a group of upper-school kids were gathered in a former office hunched over what looked like a typewriter with a rotary telephone dial on one side.

Mr. Stocklin explained that it was a teletype machine. With it we could connect to a computer to play games, and even write our own computer programs. The computer itself wasn't at Lakeside, he explained, but somewhere else—it was in California—and we logged in to it over a phone line. That's why the teletype had a phone dial on it. What our teacher described, I would soon learn, was called timesharing, a method of parceling out one computer to multiple users at the same time. I had always thought of computers as big boxes run by specialists in university labs, bank basements, and other places that most people never visited. At the World's Fair I had seen a UNIVAC computer, a series of refrigerator-sized boxes taller than a person and the length of a small truck. The machine, called the "library of the future," was run by a man who took questions from the audience and fed them into the computer, which spit out answers.

It was hard to imagine that I would be able to play on a computer myself.

Dan Ayrault, who would become Lakeside's headmaster within a year, once described Lakeside as "a school of very few rules." Few rules meant that Lakeside teachers were free to experiment. If a student had a burning interest in a topic, his teacher could deviate from whatever they had planned to teach and run in a new direction. The school hired with an eye for teachers deeply interested in their fields and who had real expertise. Some had worked in industry, at places like Boeing. One was an astrophysicist. There were a few lawyers. Another, who would become my chemistry teacher senior year, had patented a method for isolating the amino acid tryptophan.

The assumption was that this caliber of instructor would be confident in giving students room to explore—even if that meant pushing boundaries. Robert Fulghum, who taught art, was an ordained minister who would go on to fame with his bestselling book, *All I Really Need to Know I Learned in Kindergarten*. This was some years after Fulghum had tested the freewheeling spirit of Lakeside by hiring nude models for his art classes. The math department's equivalent of those nude models was this computer terminal.

We had it thanks in part to Bill Dougall, the head of Lakeside's math department. Like a lot of the faculty, Bill held a broader definition of education than sitting in a classroom passively listening to a lecture. He had been a World War II Navy pilot and worked as an aeronautical engineer at Boeing. Somewhere along the way he had studied French literature at the Sorbonne in Paris on top of graduate degrees in engineering and education. An avid mountain climber and explorer who took a sabbatical to build a windmill in Kathmandu, he was the teacher who led the seawater-soaked trip where Kent and I bonded. His camping trips were a sacred tradition at Lakeside, infamous treks through whatever weather the Pacific Northwest could throw at forty boys and a few intrepid teachers.

After Bill Dougall and several other faculty members took a summer computer class, they began pushing to bring computer access to Lakeside. In 1968 that meant paying for the monthly lease of the teletype machine and the hourly rate to connect to a timeshared computer. The terminal could cost over $1,000 a year and the computer time expense, at about $8 an hour, could run thousands more. Dougall had the support of the headmaster, but it was hard to justify the expense; high schools and homes just didn't have computers. Mr. Dougall then made the connection with a group of Lakeside parents who ran an annual rummage sale to raise money for school activities. In March 1967 the Lakeside Mothers' Club, as their official organization was known, borrowed space in a downtown office building, and in three days they raised about $3,000, enough to rent a cutting-edge Teletype ASR-33 and pay for enough computer time to get started.

The amusing part of this miracle is that no one knew how to use the thing. Mr. Dougall exhausted his programming knowledge within a week. A math teacher named Fred Wright had studied programming languages but had no practical computer experience. Still, on a hunch that this terminal was a good thing, the school bet that someone would figure it out.

All these years later it still amazes me how so many disparate things had to come together for me to use a computer in 1968. Beyond the leap of faith made by those teachers and parents who got us the terminal, and beyond the stroke of luck that people were now sharing computers over phone lines, completing this miracle was the decision by two Dartmouth professors to create the BASIC programming language. Just four years old at the time, the "Beginners' All-purpose Symbolic Instruction Code" was made to help students in nontechnical fields get started with computer programming. One of its attributes was that it used commands, such as GOTO, IF, THEN, and RUN, that made sense to humans. BASIC is what hooked me and made me want to come back.

On the wall next to the terminal, a teacher had tacked up a half sheet of paper with the most rudimentary directions to get started, including how to sign in and which keys to press when something went wrong. It also warned ominously that typing " 'PRINT' WITHOUT A STATEMENT NUMBER MAY CAUSE LOSS OF CONTROL."

The page included a sample program written in BASIC telling the computer how to add two numbers.

```
Ready . . .
10 INPUT X,Y
20 LET A=X+Y
30 PRINT A
40 END
```

That was probably the first computer program I ever typed in. The elegance of the four lines of code appealed to my sense of order. Its instantaneous answer was like a jolt of electricity. From there, I wrote the first computer program of my own—a game of tic-tac-toe. Getting it to work forced me to think through for the first time the most basic elements of the game's rules. Immediately, I learned that the computer was a dumb machine that I had to tell every single step it should take, under every single circumstance that could occur. When I wrote imprecise code, the computer couldn't infer or guess what I meant. I made a lot of errors trying to figure that out. When I finally got it right, the sense of accomplishment far outstripped the result. A game of tic-tac-toe is so simple, even kids learn it quickly. But it felt like a triumph to get a machine to do it.

I loved how the computer forced me to think. It was completely unforgiving in the face of mental sloppiness. It demanded that I be logically consistent and pay attention to details. One misplaced comma or semicolon and the thing wouldn't work.

It reminded me of solving mathematical proofs. Programming doesn't require math skills (beyond the basics), but it does demand the same kind of rigorous, logical approach to problem-solving, breaking problems down into smaller, more manageable parts. And like solving a problem in algebra, there are different ways to write programs that work—some more elegant and efficient than others—but infinite ways to make a program that fails. And mine failed all the time. Only after persevering, forcing myself to think smart, could I coax a program to run flawlessly.

Another early program I wrote was a lunar lander game. The problem: safely touch down a lunar lander on the moon without crashing and before you run out of fuel. From that I had to break the problem down into steps. I had to solve how the game player moved the lander left and right, up and down, how much fuel it had, how fast it burned. I also had to describe what it looked like and how to display the ship in dashes and asterisks on the screen.

Not long after Lakeside installed the terminal, Mr. Stocklin wrote a program that contained an infinite loop, meaning it ran continuously before someone eventually stopped it—but not before it burned through over a hundred dollars of our precious rummage-sale budget. I'm not sure he showed his face again in that room. It was a lesson to all of us.

To avoid racking up charges, I'd write out as much of my program as I could with pen and paper before elbowing into my place at the machine. With the machine offline to avoid time charges, I'd type it in and the program would print on a roll of inch-wide paper tape. That was step one. Then I'd dial the phone—the rotary dial on the side of the terminal—and wait for the buzz of the modem to confirm that I'd connected. I'd then feed my tape in, and *chug-chug-chug,* the program would input at a blistering ten characters per second. Finally, I'd type "RUN." Typically there was a gaggle of other kids waiting for the computer, so if my program didn't work, I'd have to log off and find a spot to sort through where I went wrong, then wait my turn to get back on the teletype.

This feedback loop was addictive. The feeling of getting better and better was a rush. Writing programs flowed from a combination of skills that came easy to me: logical thinking and an ability to focus intensely for long periods. Programming also stoked the persistent need I had to prove myself.

The atmosphere of that computer room was a (mostly) healthy mix of cooperation and competition. We were a mosh pit of teenage boys all trying to outdo one another. A gap of only two or three years isn't much in the grand scheme of things but feels like a lot when you're thirteen, small for your age, with some indeterminate time until your growth spurt. Kent and I were among the youngest kids in that group. The assumed superiority of some of the older kids bothered us.

I was an eighth-grader confident in my brain power and convinced that my intensity meant I could do anything the older guys could do—if not better, then at least faster. I was determined to not let anyone get anything on me. Kent also hated being put-upon by someone else. Maybe even more than me.

A sophomore named Paul Allen picked this up immediately, and he exploited it beautifully. "Bill, you think you're so smart, you figure this thing out." Those are some of the first words said to me by the person who I would go on to cofound Microsoft with years later.

It was a few weeks after Lakeside opened the computer room and a group of kids were all jockeying for time on the machine. With no instruction aside from a few hand-me-down books from our teachers, everyone was trying to piece together how to write their first programs.

At fifteen, Paul was two years older than us and considered himself way cooler. His crafted social position was Renaissance Man, as able to cite the throw weight of an ICBM as he could identify the chord changes in a Jimi Hendrix song. He was a serious guitarist and looked the part too; he was the only one with muttonchops. Unlike a lot of us, Paul had been interested in computers for a while, inspired by what he saw at the World's Fair and what he read in volumes and volumes of science fiction. Two years earlier as an eighth-grader at Lakeside, Paul used his graduation speech to paint a bright future of computers woven throughout our society, even predicting that within a few decades a computer would have the ability to think.

What he hadn't done until that fall in the computer room was actually use a computer. Of course, with Paul's goading, I threw myself into figuring it out, determined to be the first to write more complex programs than the older kids.

Some form of that scenario repeated again and again, even away from the terminal. The pattern went like this: Paul would push me. "Hey Bill, I bet you can't do this math problem," and then I'd battle my way through the problem to prove I could. Other times, it was "Hey Bill, I bet you can't beat [fill in the name of anyone else in the room] at chess." Each time I took the bait. I'd throw myself at whatever dare Paul issued until I solved/won/finished it. That dynamic would come to define the broader relationship between Kent and me on one side and Paul and his friend, another sophomore named Ric Weiland, on the other. Paul and Ric shared an interest in electronic gadgets, a hobby that for Ric was probably sparked by his dad, an engineer at Boeing who had invented a critical part of a wing assembly. A few years earlier Ric had made a simple computer of electric relays that could play tic-tac-toe. Ric was quieter and cerebral, less of an antagonist than Paul. Paired by age difference, we were rivals; as a foursome, Paul, Ric, Kent, and I became friends.

As the weeks went by, a lot of the kids who'd first played around with the terminal lost interest and drifted away, leaving a smaller group of hard-core adherents. Code-writing was a social leveler. Age didn't matter if you could write good programs and figure out cool problems. A senior named Bob McCaw created a casino program from scratch. His classmate Harvey Motulsky tried to teach the computer to play Monopoly. I worked to expand the Monopoly program so that the computer could play itself. Kent modified math programs that he copied from a book by the RAND Corporation. Together he and I figured out how to combine nouns, verbs, adjectives, and syntax to make a random sentence generator, a very primitive version of the AI chatbots that would emerge decades later. We'd have it string sentences together and then laugh at the kooky stories it told.

This surge of creativity, I realize in hindsight, was the intentional outcome of brilliant guidance—or I should say lack of guidance. Fred Wright, the math teacher, was the de facto overseer of the computer room. Fred was young, in his late twenties. He had been hired at Lakeside just two years earlier. He was a perfect fit for the school, a teacher who was thrilled when kids found their own route to an answer. I would later have him as a teacher, and he watched, amused, as I powered through geometry problems using algebra, happy to let me explore that less-efficient path while intuitively knowing that I'd eventually figure out the easier, better way.

Fred ran the computer room with the same philosophy. No sign-up sheet, no locked door, no formal instruction (Lakeside didn't yet offer computer classes). He kept the room open, let us come as we pleased, trusting that without limits we'd have to be creative and find a path to teach ourselves. Occasionally Fred poked his crew-cut head in to break up a squabble or listen to an excited kid explain whatever neat program he was writing. At some point a student taped a sign above the door, "Beware of the Wrath of Fred Wright," a tongue-in-cheek nod to Fred's laissez-faire oversight. A few faculty members argued for tighter regulations over the computer room (*What are those boys doing in there?*). Fred rebuffed them every time. That left a power vacuum that we kids instantly filled. From early on it was our domain, our clubhouse. That fall we basically lived in that room in a loop of writing programs, having them fail, and trying again and again. Our grades suffered, our parents worried. But we learned and learned quickly. It was the most fun I'd ever had at school.

Every morning I commuted to Lakeside in a carpool run by the mothers of neighbor kids. Typically, the car would be silent for the twenty-minute drive, all of us still half asleep or cramming some last-minute homework. My mom split the driving with other moms, each handling a day or two of the week. Every Monday and Tuesday I knew that I'd climb into a convertible blue Chevelle, and without fail Tom Rona's mother would have way more energy than anyone should that early in the morning, except my own mom. Monique Rona was French, and in her thickly accented English she'd draw her drowsy passengers into a conversation. In the fall of 1968, we talked about computers. At Lakeside we were running out of money to pay for our computer time. Mrs. Rona would become our unlikely savior. Soon our small group would have the rarest of gifts: free access to one of the most powerful computers available.

As a child in France during World War II, Monique Rona played a role in the French Resistance, serving as a decoy to divert German soldiers away from Jewish safe houses. Later, as a student at the Sorbonne in Paris, she married an engineering student, and after the war the couple emigrated to the United States, where her husband got a degree from MIT and she studied mathematics. A job offer from Boeing brought them to Seattle, where her husband became a senior scientist; Mrs. Rona landed a job as the deputy director of the University of Washington's computer lab. (At the time, this type of job was rarely held by women.)

Mrs. Rona picked up on my enthusiasm for my new hobby and would ask me about what I was working on, jolting me out of my silent puzzling through some programming problem. With just a month or two of experience, I'm sure that I came across way more confident than I should have. Still, she was curious, interested in what I said, and never talked down to me.

As it happens, that fall Mrs. Rona was setting up one of the first computer timesharing companies in Seattle. Through the university's computer lab, she had met a salesman from Digital Equipment Corp., a Boston-area company that was then a pioneering maker of minicomputers. DEC had established itself in the early 1960s by selling powerful small computers—they were called minicomputers—to research institutions and university labs that didn't need expensive mainframe computers from IBM and other large computer vendors. Over time, DEC moved upmarket and in 1966 began selling a computer called the PDP-10 that was far more powerful than its minicomputer cousins but still more affordable than leading mainframes. And it was geared toward timesharing.

Mrs. Rona, the Digital guy, and their other cofounders (also from the UW computer lab) saw an opportunity in the Seattle area, where big companies like Boeing would likely be expanding their computer use, and smaller ones might be enticed to computerize for the first time. The team leased the latest PDP-10 machine. They called the venture Computer Center Corp., or CCC. As a math nerd, I couldn't help but call it "C-Cubed."

At Lakeside, meanwhile, our new hobby was getting expensive. The minutes added up. Aware of this, Mrs. Rona wrote a letter to

Lakeside with a surprising proposal: if some of the school's young programmers helped her venture, the company would—and this is the crazy part—give us *free access* to their new DEC computer.

On a Saturday in November 1968, my dad dropped me off at C-Cubed's new headquarters, where I met Mr. Wright, Paul, Kent, Ric, and a few Lakeside upperclassmen. The office was near the University of Washington in an old Buick dealership within earshot of Interstate 5. Across the street, a self-proclaimed anarchist would soon open Morningtown Café, a hippie hangout, where over the next twelve months I'd eat hundreds of their pepperoni pizza slices.

From the outside, C-Cubed looked every bit the car dealership it once was, with one difference: through huge windows that must have once displayed Electras and Skylarks, there was a long row of teletype terminals identical to the one we had at Lakeside. Inside, a C-Cubed engineer showed us around. He explained that the company planned to open for business at the end of the year. That gave them two months to make sure their new computer was ready for the rigors of managing perhaps hundreds of different users at the same time.

Some context: Today, any business buying a computer system can expect it to run software that's been thoroughly tested for reliability, security, and stability. Not so in 1968. Companies like DEC and its competitors, including IBM and GE, made their money on hardware—the chips, tape storage drives, and processing units that comprised the actual computer, all the stuff in the refrigerator-sized box and devices connected to it. By comparison, software was an afterthought, so low in value it was thrown in for free. Even after a customer leased or bought a computer, its operating system (the software that controls the main functions of the computer) often required a lot of extra testing and debugging before it was ready for heavy everyday use.

That's where we came in. To help improve their software, DEC struck a deal with C-Cubed. As long as the new venture found and reported bugs, DEC would waive its monthly leasing fee. In industry terms it's called assurance testing—and typically involves a set period of time for a customer to assure its new computer system performs as promised. C-Cubed saw this as an opportunity to delay paying for their usage for as long as possible.

The deal arranged by Mrs. Rona gave us kids open access to their system, the only stipulation being that when the machine crashed or did something weird, we had to document it. Paradoxically, breaking it was a good thing. They'd rather have teenagers find a problem before paying customers did. Plus, more bugs filed meant more time not paying their lease. C-Cubed needed monkeys. Monkeys with hammers.

CHAPTER SIX

Free Time

After Monique Rona asked for our help, her company's con-
verted car dealership became our second home. In December 1968, Kent, Paul, Ric, and I spent hours and hours
at C-Cubed, coding and debugging programs, writing bug reports.
The new year came and went and Saturdays turned into weekday
afternoons, which in turn bled into nights. When other kids at Lakeside were studying or playing sports, going to church or sleeping, we
were at C-Cubed, playing on a pricey, high-powered computer for
free. As luck would have it, it was one of the snowiest winters in
Seattle history—well over five feet of snow fell—giving us the gift of
days off from school, days I spent at C-Cubed.

We knew that eventually they'd kick us out. Like kids scrambling
on the ground for candy from a smashed piñata, we had to grab as
much as we could before it was gone. That's where my head was one

night that winter as I sat in my bedroom. *Why am I wasting time here when I could be at the computer?*

It was around ten o'clock. My parents were upstairs. Kristi was in her room studying. I quietly slid open my bedroom window, climbed out, crept under our deck and around the side of our house. In a few minutes I was at Children's Hospital, where I caught the No. 30 Laurelhurst-Ballard bus to Roosevelt Way. I walked four blocks down Roosevelt to C-Cubed. Twenty minutes door-to-door.

That would be the first of many nights I sneaked out that winter and for years after. I would join hospital workers taking the late-running No. 30 home. If I missed the last return bus, around two in the morning, I'd walk the forty-five minutes home, rewriting code in my head, tuning out the students spilling from the bars and coffee shops. No one seemed to wonder why a kid was out alone at that hour. Eyes on the ground in front of me, I turned right on 45th and then a long straight stretch to my neighborhood. If I wanted to take the scenic route, I'd wend through the University of Washington campus and past a massive landfill near Boomer's house and up the hill to mine. In the backyard, and through my window. A few hours of sleep and then: "Good morning to you, good morning to you, good morning, good morning, good morning to you."

Since my parents and I had reached our détente, they had grown more lenient. But they would not have allowed their thirteen-year-old son out that late at night. Kristi knew, and I'm grateful she never told on me. I was never a morning person, but I can't believe my mom didn't notice I was dragging more than usual.

It's impossible to overstate how exceptional this period with free computer time was for the four of us. We were kids: Kent and I in eighth grade and Paul and Ric, still fifteen, sophomores in high school. None of us had any real computer experience. Monique Rona's son thinks that his mom, with her unusual background as a child wartime decoy, had a lot of faith in kids, and she knew they could handle responsibility. I can imagine that as a woman in technology in the 1960s, she had been passed over plenty of times, written off, undervalued. I like to think that her support was rooted in assuring that didn't happen to us.

A lot of successful people I've met have described how after falling in love with their chosen field, they had to put in a period of hard, focused work. It's the time in which raw interest is transformed into real skill. In *Outliers,* Malcolm Gladwell describes the 10,000 hours of deliberate practice it takes to reach a high skill level—whether it's writing music or playing tennis. He included me as an example in software. I'll add my take on his rule: without that lucky break of free computer time—call it my first 500 hours—the next 9,500 hours might not have happened at all.

What C-Cubed got out of the deal I'm sure was at first pretty underwhelming. At the beginning we were blindly playing with the powerful computer to see what happened if we did something stupid. Our early bug reports read something like this: "If you spin all five tape drives at the same time, something weird happens. If you tell the computer to do ten jobs, each trying to allocate memory as fast as it can, the computer freezes." Monkeys wielding their hammers.

And we learned.

Often long after Kent and Ric went home, Paul and I would remain at the terminals, stopping only long enough to grab food or to see a movie at the Neptune Theatre up the street. This period, really just about four months, minted a work style for me that would last for decades. Unconstrained by cost or time, I'd fall into a zone of total focus. As fast as I completed a section of a program, I could ask the computer to run it, giving me an instant answer whether I was right or wrong. Try something; see if it works. If it doesn't, try again with something different. The computer worked a bit like a slot machine that sucks you in by giving little payouts at random intervals. Instead of coins, the computer kept me going by affirming that sections of my programs could work. I loved the mental game of whether I could increase the frequency of those payouts.

Once that feedback loop got going, it fed our thirst to learn more. We couldn't watch YouTube tutorials on the internet—there was no internet. Guidebooks were rare. Kent hand-copied math programs and a way to calculate state populations from the aforementioned RAND Corporation manual he had borrowed somewhere. After I got my hands on a copy of a slim paperback titled *Introduction to Programming,* I was so worried about losing it that I slid the cover into my mom's typewriter and typed, "Bill Gates owns this Book. He wants it. Give it back to him!"

The scarcity of teaching guides back then reflected the fact that there weren't that many experts. Most of the best programmers worked in government, often on secret projects, or at a few leading universities, places like Dartmouth, MIT, and Stanford. There were a handful of known names, often leaders of labs at those top university programs. One of them, a professor at Stanford named John McCarthy, had all but invented timesharing, the system we were using, and was a father of the field of artificial intelligence. His students in turn pioneered early programming techniques, languages, and tools. As luck would have it, a few of these star students found their way to Seattle and to C-Cubed, where they formed the company's technical team.

The fact that I was a degree or two of separation from the guy who pioneered timesharing and artificial intelligence was lost on me at the time. But the benefits were not. Occasionally C-Cubed programmers would show us snippets of their code, tantalizing hints of what they might have to teach us. We wanted to see more but felt shy about asking.

We stumbled upon a workaround. At the end of every day, someone would take out the trash. Included in that trash would be used computer paper—fifteen inches wide with perforations on either side and printed with lines of code, whatever the C-Cubed engineers were working on that day. The code was incomplete, just scraps of their thinking captured in dot matrix on the page, some-times crumpled, often torn. One night when the employees had all gone home, Paul and I went out to the back of the building to see what we could find in the dumpster. Paul boosted me up and held my legs as I sorted through the dregs of the day—Styrofoam cups and food scraps, all mixed with twisted stretches of paper like a dou-ble helix that had come unstrung from itself. That first dive didn't yield much, but we went back again and again. Paul was taller and stronger, so he did the boosting. I was lighter and nimbler, so I did the diving.

Looking through our dumpster quarry one night, we found a thick stack of papers filled with columns of numbers and terse com-mands such as ADD, SUB, PUSH, and POP. Taking it inside, we spread it out on the table. Jackpot! It was instructions for portions of the PDP-10's operating system. Those instructions—the source code—were off-limits to us. What we found was cryptic, just lines of code that we'd need to reverse engineer to figure out what they did. But that crumpled and coffee-stained paper was the most exciting thing we'd ever seen.

The printout was written in machine language, the most funda-mental code that a programmer can use. Machine code allows you to write programs that run far faster than anything you can create in a high-level language such as BASIC, but it's laborious, requiring users to explicitly define every step the computer must take to perform a task. For instance, in BASIC, instructing the computer to display "Hello" requires just a single command (PRINT "Hello"), whereas in machine code that same job might call for twenty-five lines of character-by-character instructions. To a novice the code was almost impenetrable, a secret language spoken only by true experts—and for that reason I wanted to learn it.

Around the same time, Paul broke the ice with Steve Russell, one of the C-Cubed programmers from MIT who was famous for developing an addictive early video game called *Spacewar!,* in which two players battle to shoot down the other's spaceship with photon torpedoes. When Paul told him we wanted to learn more advanced languages, Steve lent us PDP-10 manuals detailing the computer's machine code and the inner workings of its operating system—called TOPS-10—that we had been trying to decipher from our trash pickings. The manuals were such precious items that we were allowed to borrow them only overnight. Paul and I would sprawl on the floor at C-Cubed reading and memorizing together deep into the night.

The better I got at coding, the more I wanted to do something real—to write a program that might truly be useful to someone. It was the same urge I had a few years earlier when I'd realized that no matter how cool a picture I could draw of a bridge or a rocket, I could never build one in the real world. This was different. With a computer, I felt like anything I could imagine, I could create. At home my mom cooked from recipe cards she kept neatly categorized in a small wooden box. I borrowed four or five of those cards, brought them to C-Cubed, and designed a simple program in BASIC that, when given the prompt "meatloaf," produced my mom's meatloaf recipe. In the language of programmers, it was a trivial program, but it taught me about DATA statements and the READ command.

War was a daily part of our lives. Television news and the covers of *Life* brought home the toll of Vietnam for both sides. That's probably where I got the idea to write a program that simulated war. What I imagined wasn't like *Spacewar!,* a preprogramed game that you played for a high score. I wanted something that would be a tool, a way to model the real world and test different strategies and tactics as if you were a general leading one side of a war. I envisioned my code capturing all the factors I could think of that might come into play in a major battle. Working on paper first, I created my virtual world on a coastline and gave the opposing sides an army, a navy, and an air force. Each side had a headquarters and airfields, plus troops, artillery, tanks, and anti-aircraft guns to protect them, and fighter planes, bombers, destroyers, and aircraft carriers to launch offensives.

For data I watched old war films to gauge how fast an anti-aircraft gun could shoot, checked out library books to understand battlefield tactics, and looked back at the military histories Kent and I had read. I wanted everything to feel as realistic as possible—not like a game, but like one of the computer models people had already begun using to forecast the weather and to predict economic trends.

As I thought through how all these pieces could interact, I realized I couldn't just tell the computer, "If this happens, then always do that." To make it realistic, I'd have to give each outcome a certain probability of occurring. If a player launched fighter jets at the opponent's headquarters, each plane would have some chance of getting shot down by anti-aircraft guns, for example. But how big a chance? My library books didn't say, so I made guesses based on what I'd seen in those movies and some rough numbers I found for the number of planes that got hit or shot down in World War II.

As the weeks burned by, my plans grew. I would work in adjustments to troop effectiveness based on how long they had to recuperate between combat encounters, the number of fighters needed to escort each bomber, the increased odds of bombers getting hit by ground fire because they are bigger and slower, the effects of weather on planes, ships, and infantry . . . on and on.

With this design mapped out, I started translating these scenarios into BASIC computer code, one line at a time, on the C-Cubed PDP-10. Often Ric and then Kent would peel off—their parents were stricter about curfew—leaving Paul and me working on our projects, him learning machine code and writing his own programs and me waging war in software.

I could clearly visualize what I wanted to create. And I believed that I could achieve that result, even if I realized it was beyond what I was capable of at that moment. I was thirteen years old, learning on my own terms with a $500,000 machine as my teacher.

And then our luck ended. Late that spring, DEC started charging C-Cubed for leasing the computer, and C-Cubed decided they no longer needed us. Lakeside, meanwhile, started paying C-Cubed for access to its computer. From that point on, the four of us were demoted from test monkeys to customers. At school, Mr. Wright kept tabs on our accounts, and at the end of each month, he'd tack up a piece of paper listing in his exceptionally neat handwriting how much each of us owed. It was a mixed blessing to be at the top of the list—bragging rights for being the most hard-core, but we paid a price in real money for that status.

If you ever get banished from a castle, it helps if you've already spent a lot of time inside, rooting around, locating its hidden doors. During our time on C-Cubed's PDP-10 I had discovered a flaw. When logging in to the system there was a window of time where, if you typed "Ctrl C" twice, the computer let you log in as an administrator. Having administrator access to a computer is like having a skeleton key: It allows access to every part of a system. With it you can see each customer's account, read their files, see their passwords, delete their accounts. You can reboot the whole system or shut it down. We didn't do any of that. Instead, Paul used the trick to find some passwords, which we planned to use to access free computer time. Unfortunately, we got caught before we could put the scheme into motion. When Mr. Wright learned what we were up to, he contacted C-Cubed and the company contacted DEC. Soon DEC had another version of the log-in software.

And soon we bypassed that too.

As lenient and as trusting as Fred Wright was, the one thing he couldn't stand was dishonesty. He summoned us to his office in McAllister, where we found a very tall man with a Vandyke beard waiting for us. I thought I heard someone introduce him as Mr. So-and-So from the Federal Bureau of Investigation. In later years, Paul would describe the guy as a C-Cubed representative, but in his dark suit he looked like an FBI agent, he talked like an FBI agent, and so I was convinced he was an FBI agent. Whoever it was, he terrified me. He sternly warned that by hacking our way into C-Cubed's system, we had broken the law.

I wasn't a bad kid. I never stole things and wasn't destructive. I had never gotten into any real trouble, and I wasn't used to being berated by adults. This was the first time that I felt a bit ashamed, not to mention slightly terrified. Later, when I thought back on the situation, I saw things differently. Our whole job was to find faults with their system. Well, we'd found a big one. At the time I worried that we'd be suspended. That didn't happen, but the punishment to me felt worse: we were all banned from the C-Cubed computers.

Eight months after laying my hands on a computer for the first time, they were off-limits.

That summer I didn't see much of Paul or Ric, and I spent much less time with Kent. His family took their sailboat on a long cruise up the West Coast of Canada for part of the summer and then Kent visited Washington, D.C., with another Lakeside friend. Off computers, Kent indulged his passion for politics.

My mother's pressure on me to pursue extracurricular activities had eased a lot in the previous year, though twice a month I carpooled with a group of other kids to the Epiphany Church for ballroom dancing lessons. (The classes were awkward but had the benefit of putting me face-to-face with girls just as I was starting to find them interesting.) And I didn't need persuading to continue with the Boy Scouts, which I'd always really liked. When I was twelve, I joined Troop 186, one of the largest and most organized troops in the area. At the time, hiking, camping, and mountaineering were on the rise in the U.S. and Seattle was gaining recognition as a mecca for outdoor sports. The homegrown outdoor retailer Recreational Equipment Inc. (better known as REI) was rapidly expanding its product line, and the head of the company, Jim Whittaker, had a few years earlier become the first American to summit Mount Everest. My new scout troop was in step with the outdoor boom and made getting scouts into the mountains its main reason for existence. In our troop, you earned your merit badges and moved up the ranks as you would anywhere else, but mostly you joined 186 to hike and camp.

I had gone on that surf-soaked camping trip in eighth grade, and we had taken a few day hikes in Cub Scouts, but I didn't have much true wilderness experience when I joined my first fifty-mile hike. Right before the trek my father took me to REI and bought me a red Cruiser backpack and expensive leather hiking boots from Italy. Heading with the troop into the Glacier Peak Wilderness, I soon felt my heels rubbing against the back of my stiff new boots. Halfway through the first day, maybe four miles in, my heels burned. I pushed on. That night when I removed my boots and peeled away my socks, my chafed heels were so raw that one scout later said they looked like the inside of a jelly donut. A father on the trip, an ear surgeon, gave me codeine pills (things were looser in the 1960s). Numbed by the narcotics and helped by other scouts who carried the contents of my pack, I limped along for another two days or so to the halfway point, where my father picked me up.

I was humiliated, sure that everyone saw me as a wimp, the only kid unable to finish the hike, and the only one too stupid not to break in his boots beforehand. In my mind, the hike was a total and unmitigated disaster.

One of the leaders on the trip was a kid named Mike Collier, who was a senior scout and about five years older than me. Everyone knew that he had a lot more outdoor experience than even the adults in our troop. His parents were big hikers and Mike was a member of the Mountaineers, an old outdoor club that organized hikes and held classes on technical climbing and other outdoor skills. Around the time I joined the troop, he and his parents had started inviting a select group of scouts on their family trips. These were always far more ambitious hikes than even our troop outings.

Despite my failure on the fifty-miler—or maybe because of it, I don't know—Mike and his parents invited me to join them on their next trip, which would take place in June after school ended. The other scouts who would be joining us, Rocky, Reilly, and Danny, were thirteen, like me, and gung ho about hiking. I was happy to be included, and excited by the chance to test myself. Plus, the timing was perfect, as C-Cubed had just declared their computers off-limits and I had nothing but free time.

Mike told us that he had seen a television show about the Lifesaving Trail, which ran along the Pacific coast of Vancouver Island, an isolated area known for storms, reefs, and tricky currents—and as the graveyard of thousands of ships. Sometime in the early 1900s the Canadian government cut a trail so that shipwrecked sailors who washed up could walk their way to civilization. Over the years, the trail had fallen into disrepair. On the show, a local naturalist and her husband hiked the fifty-mile Lifesaving Trail, and Mike wanted to retrace their route. It was going to be an adventure, he told us: we'd fly on a seaplane, ford rivers, and climb cliffs. There would be caves to explore and coves to swim.

As we were unloading our packs from the seaplane on the first day, mine fell in the water. Not a great start. Once we started walking it was clear why they had built this trail for lost sailors. Even if you made it to land, the coast was so uneven and remote that your problems were far from over. Heading north that first day, we picked our way through the thickly overgrown trail and muddy bogs. The trail would suddenly end at a cliff, leaving you to climb down a long vertical ladder or go hand under hand down a rope.

Then we'd slowly pick our way across the rocky beach for a while before climbing up another set of ladders or ropes to the overgrown trail, slithering under huge and mossy fallen trees.

The one part of the trip that worried Mike was crossing the Klanawa River. It didn't flow fast, but its depth varied day to day depending on the weather: heavy rain and mountain runoff could make it impassable for hikers. Mike sent us down the pebbly shore to gather driftwood, then cut lengths of red avalanche cord and showed us how to use it to lash our driftwood into small rafts we used to ferry ourselves to the other side.

We finished the trip at the small fishing village of Bamfield the next day. As we walked into town, an elderly woman approached us: "Where are you boys coming from?" Seattle, we proudly reported; we'd just hiked up the Lifesaving Trail. "My goodness!" she said, before inviting us into her home for some fresh shrimp her husband had caught that morning.

Later, while we were waiting for a ride to the nearby ferry, another townsperson approached us.

"Are any of you Bill Gates?" he asked.

My dad, as it happens, needed to relay a change in our plans for later that day, so he'd called some random person in the town and left a message. We thought that was amazing. The closest we'd ever get to Stanley finding Dr. Livingstone on the shores of Lake Tanganyika.

I was hooked. After that first trip, Mike persuaded his parents to let him lead trips on his own. Sometimes others joined, but it was usually the five of us—Mike, Rocky, Reilly, Danny, and me. I admired Mike's natural, easy way. He seemed to know everything we needed to know in the mountains, but he didn't lecture or dictate. He quietly led by example, and if we ever had a big decision to make, he'd put it to a vote. I appreciated that democratic approach even if it usually meant that my hope for the shorter route would lose out—as it would two years later on the Press Expedition Trail.

—

After I got home from the Lifesaving hike that summer of 1969, my family and I drove to Hood Canal, where we settled into the Cheerio traditions—the same families, same Olympics, my father the mayor—that had defined our summers my whole life. But that year was special. My grandmother announced to us that she had bought a small vacation house on the canal. After decades of visiting, my family now had a place to call its own, a base where my mother and grandmother hoped we would all gather as we grew older and our lives inevitably grew busier. That summer we lugged a television set out to the canal and set it up in the main lodge to watch the Apollo 11 moon landing, along with 125 million other Americans. Generally, we didn't let the outside world interfere with canal life, but Neil Armstrong's giant leap for mankind made the cut.

Beyond the moon walk, that summer sticks in my head as a period of personal transition. Like a lot of kids around that age, I was experimenting with different identities. I remember being distinctly aware that how I was perceived by others changed with the circumstances. In organized sports I was an also-ran. On the hike that summer, I was tough, a risk-taker, able to push myself physically in a way that no one who played football with me would have recognized. I was a valued team member in our little group where the only reward was camaraderie.

At Cheerio adults saw me as a leader. I organized other kids, young and old, into a group, made a flag, and dubbed us "Club Cheerio." I didn't do much more than spearhead missions into the neighboring woods, but the club sparked a kind of excitement and team spirit among the kids. I felt this especially from Libby, who celebrated her fifth birthday that summer. I relished the role of protector and partner in crime; in her eyes I was the infallible older brother. I loved that.

It was a different story at school, though. In class I still focused most of my attention on looking for an opening to crack a joke or play the antagonist to whatever we were doing, say something I thought might elicit chuckles even if it was rude. In the school year that had just ended, we studied the Greek play *Lysistrata,* wrote papers on it, and even had visiting actors perform it for us. How did I show my appreciation? I had the gall to tell the woman who played the title role that it was a stupid play, one of several gratuitously rude comments I made that clearly betrayed more about me than anything else. That kind of bad behavior always ate at me afterward.

Every day after lunch at Lakeside, the whole lower school was given an hour to study before afternoon classes. For most students, that meant filing into the auditorium on the second floor of Moore Hall, where you had to quietly work under the watchful eye of a teacher. Study hall was for the masses, those with average or mediocre grades, or those who were disengaged in class. Meanwhile, a small group of students with the best grades, the honor students, were exempt from study hall, rewarded with what was called free study.

They got their own room on the first floor where, completely unsupervised, they were allowed to do homework or compare notes on a project or just talk. They could even go out to the quad to read or wander around campus if they felt like it. Free study was an earned right, one that could be forfeited if your grades dropped. Everyone knew that the free study kids were the best students in the class.

No surprise, I got stuck in study hall. With my mixed grades and bad attitude, I deserved it. And for a while I didn't care.

Kent, of course, had quickly earned his place among the free study elite. Off he went with the other "smart kids," while I sat slumped in the auditorium. I was sure I belonged with Kent. If my Black Sea project was my first big hint, this was my second: Lakeside had no respectable place for the joker. It started to sink in that Lakeside offered freedom to kids who deserved it. If you got good grades or were deeply interested in something, the school made space for you to learn and grow. There was probably also a passionate teacher willing to help. Kent understood that instinctively. For me it was a slow awakening.

There was another school experience that was on my mind that summer. Lakeside's upper school—our high school—had a math team that competed in an annual four-state regional exam and had won a few years in a row. Though in no way comparable to our past glory as a football powerhouse, the team scratched out a reputation for itself among a certain set at Lakeside. In 1969, a few of the better math students in the lower school had been allowed to take the test. I was one of them. I did exceptionally well, scoring higher than nearly everyone on the math team, which put me, an eighth-grader, among the best high school math students in the region. This, of course, fed my ego. Even more meaningful, though, was the recognition I received from the senior who got the highest score on the test. Aside from the computer room, where the big kids tolerated younger ones, there wasn't much interaction between the lower- and upper-school students; it just wasn't cool to acknowledge kids a whole four years younger. Still, the senior math whiz came down to the lower school and found me. Maybe, as a math weirdo, he just wanted to meet another up-and-coming math weirdo. Whatever his reasons, I was thrilled. He was super nice. Congratulations, he said, it was a rare thing for a young guy to do so well.

Beyond the math crowd, word spread that an eighth-grader had outscored nearly everyone in the school. Not only that, but—surprise—it was Gates, who was always horsing around and whom no one considered a top student. I thought a lot about that perception. And it started to bother me.

In my emerging worldview, the logic and rational thinking demanded by math were skills that could be used to master any subject. There was a hierarchy of intelligence: however good you were at math, that's how good you could be at other subjects—biology, chemistry, history, even languages. My model, as simplistic as it was, seemed to be borne out at school, where I felt I could map a student's math ability to their broader academic achievement.

That summer on Hood Canal, I decided to test my theory—on myself. For the first time in my life, I was going to apply myself to school.

CHAPTER SEVEN

Just Kids?

L akeside made you buy all your own books. The school had a little bank branch downstairs in Bliss Hall where your parents would deposit money. Throughout the year you'd write checks for books and other school expenses (like our computer time). At the bookstore—a table parked in front of a basement classroom—you'd tell Joe Nix your classes, he'd disappear into the shelves for a few minutes, return with a stack of books, and you'd write a check. Joe was the night watchman—a beloved figure always accompanied by his German shepherd—who doubled as the school's book clerk. He greeted me with a big smile as I showed him my schedule my first week back. Full of my new resolve, I'd worked up a scheme I was pretty sure would be a great success.

As he reviewed my class list—ancient and medieval history, English, Latin, biology, and honors algebra—I told him that I wanted two copies of each book. He paused for a second, clearly puzzled by the request, but then turned and gathered the books. To this day I'm not sure my parents noticed that they paid double.

My plan was to leave one copy at home and one at school. This was less about the inconvenience of carrying books back and forth than it was about appearing as if I didn't need to study at home. I'd turn myself into one of the scholarly elite—but I wasn't ready to let go of my smart-aleck, devil-may-care façade. While everyone else groaned under the weight of their heavy textbooks, I went home each day conspicuously empty-handed. At night, holed up in my bedroom with my duplicate textbooks, I solved and re-solved every quadratic equation, I memorized Latin declensions and reviewed names, dates, history of all those Greek wars and battles and gods and goddesses. The next day, I'd arrive at school fortified with all that I had learned but no indication that I had studied. I doubt anyone noticed or cared, but in my mind, they were marveling: *No books! How does he do it? He must be really smart!* Such were my lingering insecurities.

I'd always possessed the ability to hyperfocus. Now I was becoming aware of how I could harness that ability to my advantage at school. If I truly concentrated on a subject, taking in the facts and theorems, dates and names and ideas and whatever else, my mind automatically sorted the information within a framework that was structured and logical. And with that framework came a sense of control: I knew precisely where to access facts and how to synthesize what I had stored. I could instantly recognize patterns and ask better questions; any new data that came along, I could easily slot into the existing scaffolding. As goofy as it sounds, it felt like the revelation of a superpower. At the same time, my powers weren't fully developed. I was fourteen years old and didn't always have the discipline to put off reading yet another Tarzan book instead of trying to interpret the assigned history lesson.

And I still struggled to apply focus to subjects that didn't feel relevant to my larger worldview. In biology that year, we were instructed to dissect a planarian, a flatworm, but the teacher gave us no notion of why this was supposed to be important. Where did flatworms fit into the hierarchy of living things? What were we supposed to learn from this slice or that one? It felt so random. The teacher was educating us on arguably the most relevant subject of all: the science of life, the systems that determined health, sickness, species diversity, billions of years of evolution, and even the roots of consciousness. Later in life I discovered what I was missing and dove headfirst into the beauty and wonders of biology. My ninth-grade self, however, stared at the pieces of that worm and concluded that if this was all that biology was about, I didn't get it. (As it happens, the same teacher taught us sex ed, which as it was presented made it seem about as engaging as the planarians.)

I always remembered ninth grade as the year I made straight As. But recently I came across my transcript and was surprised to see a mix of As and Bs (including one in biology). Clearly, the memory of my perceived breakthrough had blotted out the fact that my mental discipline was still a work in progress. In any case, my mom, who for years worried about the amount of time I spent isolated in my room, could finally see a payoff. Those were the best grades I had ever earned, and they energized me to try even harder. I was also set free from study hall.

Once I made the decision to lower my guard and show teachers that I was curious and interested in learning, I blossomed. One root of the word "education" is the Latin word *educere,* meaning "to lead or draw out." Most of my Lakeside teachers intuited that they could draw me out further by challenging me. They saw that it mattered to me to prove that I was smart, capable of coming up with an insightful comment in class or understanding extra reading they gave me.

I pounced on every book my physics teacher, Gary Maestretti, recommended. In the many conversations we engaged in outside of class, he knew how to direct my frantic energy into questions that would expand my perspective. He blew up the notion of science as a collection of proven facts to be rotely memorized; science was a way of thinking about the world, an ongoing story of challenging long-held facts and theories. Throughout history, researchers had become famous for discovering that "facts" accepted for generations or centuries were wrong, and for coming up with better ideas.

The example Mr. Maestretti gave that made the biggest impression was how at the turn of the twentieth century, many physicists believed that most of the big questions in their field had been answered. Thanks to Newton, Maxwell, and many other pioneers, they could calculate how the forces of gravity, electricity, and magnetism work. Science also had a decent explanation for the composition of atoms. But even then, physicists had noted phenomena they couldn't fully explain, such as X-rays and Marie Curie's discovery of radioactivity. Less than a decade later, Einstein showed that Newton's laws provide the right answers for most common situations, but for the wrong reasons. The universe is much weirder than earlier scientists had realized. Matter can bend space and light. Motion and gravity can both make time slow down. Light behaves like a particle as well as like a wave. The new theories of relativity and quantum mechanics even upended scientists' understanding of the history, operation, and future of the universe.

After studying physics at Lakeside, you moved on to chemistry and into the lab of Daniel Morris. Dr. Morris, as everyone at the school knew him, was a former industrial chemist who had earned a PhD in organic chemistry from Yale. He was the teacher who had patented an improved method for isolating the amino acid tryptophan. In his signature white lab coat, sipping coffee from a glass beaker, Dr. Morris fit my image of a scientist. Something he wrote in the introduction to his own textbook sums up an idea he got across to pretty much all the kids in his classroom: "We seem to forget the true foundation stone of science: the belief that the world makes sense."

I remember being fascinated by ads claiming that super-strong glue could make anything stick together. "Why is it so incredibly sticky?" I asked Dr. Morris. He encouraged curiosity-driven questions like this and used them as teachable moments. The glue, he explained, is made from small molecules that want to link up with each other but are prevented by trace ingredients that keep the glue liquid. When squeezed between two surfaces—including your fingers, if you aren't careful—traces of water neutralize the inhibitors, freeing the glue to solidify almost instantly.

Like Mr. Maestretti, Dr. Morris emphasized the layering of knowledge that allows scientific understanding to expand and deepen over time. His favorite historical figure was a nineteenth-century French chemist named Henry Louis Le Chatelier, who devised a principle about changes in the equilibrium of a system. Dr. Morris found examples from everyday life to illustrate this, such as why soda stays fizzy if you empty half the bottle but screw the cap back on. (I never forgot the answer: Fizzy gas does bubble out of the liquid into the emptied space, but eventually enough pressure builds up again inside the bottle that the gas dissolves back into the soda just as fast as it bubbles out.)

For Dr. Morris, the principle of "dynamic equilibrium" was an elegant way to organize much of chemistry broadly, and a way to understand many chemical reactions specifically. Chemistry can be a real slog as it's often taught, a plodding set of memorization tasks. Dr. Morris's gift was to strip away the complexities to reveal simple models that made sense to young students.

Dr. Morris changed my view of what a life anchored in science could look like. The stereotype then was of someone monomaniacally devoted to a very narrow, esoteric question that barely anyone else could understand, or even want to. But Dr. Morris had deep and wide-ranging interests. He played the clarinet, directed a choir, researched the geometry of the fourth dimension, and—to the particular delight of his adolescent male students—was a licensed pyrotechnician. He helped us concoct a liquid that exploded on touch; some kids spread it on staplers and even on toilet seats. (My story then was that I wasn't one of them, and I'm sticking to it.)

Science grabbed me in part because it fit my need for order and organization and offered the kind of reassuring, satisfying framework I'd already found in math. It also appealed to my hyper-rational sense of the world. At its core, science requires a wildly curious mind that can tame itself with discipline and skepticism. I liked how scientists think, constantly asking themselves, "How do I know?" and "How might I be wrong?"

My Lakeside teachers gave me the gift of an altered perspective: To question what you know—what you think is true—is how the world advances. It was an inherently optimistic message for me at that impressionable age.

After our banishment from the C-Cubed castle, Paul had talked his way into a computer room at the University of Washington, where he spent the whole summer honing his programming skills without us. He didn't tell Kent or me about his coup, because, he confessed later, we looked too young to pass as college students, and he was afraid that if we showed up, he'd lose his privileges. He made up for it halfway through the school year when he got us back into C-Cubed. By then relations with the company had thawed and they asked Paul to help with some programming.

That's how, after a six-month hiatus from computers, I started joining Paul at C-Cubed and resumed work on my war simulation. Bit by bit I got portions of it to work. I'd print out the program and mark up where I was going wrong, punch in the new code, and print it out again. Eventually the perforated computer paper stretched to more than fifty feet. Parts of it were running pretty well when we got the bad news: C-Cubed was shutting down. Just over a year old, the venture had failed to sign up many major customers. Demand for computer time wasn't what they had forecast. Added to that, Boeing, Seattle's biggest employer, had run into deep trouble. Airline orders had dried up and Boeing had borrowed heavily to develop its first jumbo jet (the 747), leading the company to lay off tens of thousands of employees. The ripple effects dragged Seattle into economic decline and with it many businesses. (Within a year, someone would post a now famous billboard on Highway 99 that read "Will the last person leaving SEATTLE—Turn out the lights.")

On a Saturday in March, Paul and I were at C-Cubed frantically working on our projects even as movers packed up everything that wasn't nailed down. At one point they swiped the chairs from beneath us. Paul and I moved to the floor, tapping away at the terminals on our knees. A few minutes later we saw one of the chairs rolling down Roosevelt Way toward Lake Union as if trying to escape the repo man, and we burst into laughter.

The loss of free access was a problem for me. I had pitched my war program as a final project for a history class. Now, without a means to finish it, I had to pivot. Earlier that spring I had decided to read the New Testament. I had attended Sunday school since first grade and the previous year had gone through Confirmation, the ritual a young person follows to commit themselves to Christ. But I still wasn't clear about my beliefs, so as I did whenever I needed to make sense of something, I read. I calculated that if I covered 5 chapters a night, I would be done with the rest of the 252 New Testament chapters I hadn't already read in 50.4 days. I finished a little early and so I also read a few books on Christianity, including *Dear Mr. Brown,* a set of fictional letters written to a young man who, the author Harry Emerson Fosdick wrote, is "seriously trying to work out an intelligent philosophy of life." That aptly described me, and though I didn't totally buy all of Fosdick's conclusions, they factored into my exploration.

The report I handed in was half a description of the war simulation and half my analysis of the Bible. In parts I struggled to express what I felt about God and my faith. (The teacher said as much: "Extremely ambitious project + well done although I occasionally can't decipher your writing style.")

"Dear Paul, I thought you might be getting lonely without us so I decided to write," begins an unsent letter I wrote a couple of weeks after school ended that year. I had just finished another adventure with Mike Collier and three younger scouts. We hiked the Lifesaving Trail again, in the opposite direction of the trip we'd made a year earlier. The letter brought back the innocent, free-form fun of those trips. Five of us crammed into Mike's Volkswagen Beetle, our packs lashed to the roof. At some point during the four-hour drive, I battled a kid named Phil in a breath-holding contest. I lost. His remarkable two minutes and ten seconds easily bested my one minute and forty seconds, as I wrote to Paul, also relaying the important fact that Phil's younger brother scarfed down my bag of animal cookies in the first five minutes of the drive.

On the ferry that night, the younger guys giggled as they peeked over the shoulder of a man reading a *Playboy* while Mike studied maps and I read a book—probably Robert Heinlein or some other science fiction. From Port Alberni we hitched a ride on a barge carrying tons and tons of ice, where we watched agape as a group of men and women sucked down bottle after bottle of wine. We stayed up late, got lost, ate hot dogs for breakfast, and rescued a dog that had slid down a steep cliff.

I wrote the letter a few days later from the Evanses' boat, which was anchored in a place called Pirates Cove. At the end of the hike, Mike had driven me to the south part of the island, where I met Kent and his parents. They had sailed up to Victoria from Seattle the previous week and invited me to join them for the next ten days. We headed north to Princess Louisa Inlet, a strikingly beautiful narrow body of water where the mountains rise nearly eight thousand feet straight up from the water's edge. We swam and read, and at night played board games. Kent liked Stocks and Bonds, a game that mimicked what it's like to manage a portfolio through the ups and downs of the market and news events (company "president hospitalized in sanatorium for an indefinite period"). Whoever had the highest value portfolio at the end won. The companies were make-believe, but the game taught us about stuff in the real world: stock splits, bull markets, PE ratios, and bond yields. Like my hiking friends, Kent had a healthy competitive streak, but he was more into games that had a real-world application.

It was on that trip that I got to know Kent's parents. I saw how close they were to him. Just before moving to Seattle, Kent's dad, Marvin, had retired from full-time work as a Unitarian minister, thanks to a small inheritance from his mom's side of the family. Kent's parents lavished that free time on their two sons. As the one dad without a day job, Marvin was always there in his '67 Dodge Polara, ready to shuttle Kent and me around Seattle. We sat in the backseat, he in the front, but every so often, he'd cock his head in our direction and in his soothing Southern drawl ask a question about what we were discussing or pose an inquiry of his own.

Looking back, I realize how Kent's early struggles must have shaped his family. As a baby, his mouth was so disfigured that he couldn't eat. Mary and Marvin feared he'd grow up unable to form words, ostracized, his whole life a struggle. The 1950s were less accepting of disability; I think some relatives even suggested putting him up for adoption. Surgeries, therapy, and lots of metal in his mouth corrected the worst of the physical part. As for their other worries, the outcome couldn't have been better. Mary and Marvin found that as Kent grew, he was unhindered by that rough start: in fact, he possessed a level of self-confidence and maturity far beyond his years. He had no qualms about taking on new challenges; he had high expectations of himself and confidence in his abilities to succeed at them. In recognition of that self-assurance, Kent's parents treated him as an adult. By extension, I think, he assumed he was one.

By the time I met Kent, sailing, and being good at it, was a big part of his identity. One of his prized possessions was a print of Winslow Homer's *Breezing Up,* a depiction of a man and three boys in a small sailboat heeling under heavy wind, that he hung on a big cork board in his bedroom. He loved the painting so much he made a special trip to the National Gallery in D.C. just to see the original.

The boat we were on that summer, a thirty-five-foot Pearson, was a new purchase, a sloop big enough for long cruises up and down Puget Sound. They named it *Shenandoah* after the river in their native Virginia. Kent, his brother, and their mom and dad would set sail right after school ended and be away until school started again in the fall, visiting places—like Pirates Cove—that sounded straight out of the Hardy Boys: Desolation Sound, Secret Cove, the Sunshine Coast. Kent's mom carefully noted the details of each day in a big heavy record book, its cover stamped in gold: *Log Book of the Yacht Shenandoah.*

The extent of my sailing experience began and ended with a local breed of cheap plywood boat known as a Flattie. After my sister Kristi got hooked on sailing, I took lessons, in part to keep up with her. As Laurelhurst residents, we had access to the neighborhood beach club, which sounds fancier than what it was—a strip of sand with picnic tables and a few docks. The club ran Flattie races in the summer. As a team, Kristi and I relished the days of slack wind when our featherweight gave us an advantage. All this is to say that before I boarded the *Shenandoah,* the highlights of my sailing career were a few adrenaline-fueled attempts to round a marker faster than an adult in an identical eighteen-foot boat.

On our trip, Kent all but captained the boat as we sailed north. He checked tides and the depth sounder so we wouldn't run aground entering Malibu Rapids, the narrow opening to the Princess Louisa

Inlet. He monitored the apparent wind indicator so he could make adjustments to the sails and boat position. He knew how to do dead reckoning—determining the position of the boat based on charts—and what different flags meant and when and where they should be flown. In my nine days on the boat, I witnessed the same drive to master a skill that in the coming year would spark Kent's interest in learning to climb mountains.

Most of our conversation that summer revolved around computers. We'd learned a lot in the year and a half or so since we wrote our first programs. But what could we do with what we knew? Make money? Kent was convinced we could.

The career paths we talked about now focused on business. Kent's great-grandfather had made a small fortune selling fruit trees and other plants at a nursery he founded. That was the origin of the inheritance. Kent was proud of that legacy and felt that he was destined to find his own path to riches. I shared what I'd learned about the businesses of my parents' friends, like the heart defibrillator maker Physio-Control. Kent encouraged me to start reading *Fortune* magazine and *The Wall Street Journal.* He, meanwhile, adopted the look of a businessman, buying a huge briefcase more suited for a middle-aged salesman than a teenager. The "monstrosity," as he called it, was always stuffed with magazines and papers. He carried it everywhere. Pop it open: instant library.

Just as we'd plowed through biographies of generals and politicians in our earlier career explorations, we now went to the library and dug up corporate proxy statements to see what local executives got paid. Kent and I were astonished to discover that a friend of my parents, the head of the largest bank in the region, got paid about $1 million a year, which we both thought was a lot until we saw his stock options.

"The guy is worth FIF-TEEN million dollars!" Kent blurted out.

"Can you imagine if he asked for all of it in cash?!" We speculated how much space it would take up in his car.

We tried to imagine how we could ever make that much money. Clearly a career in banking was one way, or if you invented some lifesaving medical device, or reached a top position at IBM. We read a *Fortune* magazine story on the booming market in computer peripherals: the printers, tape drives, terminals, and other extras that you added onto computers, which were mostly made by IBM. (The idea that *programming* computers could lead to riches wasn't even in the cards at that point.) The big industries around us were banking, shipping, and timber. The software industry wasn't among them. Not in Seattle. Not anywhere. We had no models for that. Still, we hoped we could make a little money off our programming abilities. Like some kids do cutting lawns, but more fun.

Kent was the one who hit on the idea of pretending to be something akin to a company so we could get free product brochures mailed to his home. Back then computer magazines like *Datamation* and *Computerworld* had mailers you could send in to receive information on Sperry Rand, Control Data, and a dozen other companies that no longer exist. Kent got in the habit of mailing in any and all cards he found. I'm sure plenty of computer hardware vendors in the late 1960s thought 1515 Woodbine Way was the headquarters of a company called Lakeside Programming Group. The name was deliberately vague—calling it a club might betray that we were just kids and not a full-blown corporate entity. "Group" split the difference. In that name was a proto-company, and the kernel of a notion that someone, someday, might pay us for our skills.

My early high school years coincided with the arrival of a new headmaster at Lakeside. Dan Ayrault had been a teacher at the school before taking a sabbatical to get his master's in education. He returned as headmaster during the tumultuous close of the 1960s, when all institutions, schools, and businesses were struggling to adapt. Lakeside could have responded by doubling down on traditions that had served it so well for so long, things like uniforms and addressing teachers as "Master." Instead, it got looser. The school dropped its age-old dress code, allowing us to shed our jackets and ties for what today would be called business casual. By the standards of the day this was radical, and some parents protested that the school's reputation was deteriorating. Dan also tried to cultivate more diversity in our very white school with a program that welcomed more Black students. This was a modest attempt, to be sure, but it put Lakeside a little more in step with the times.

During his sabbatical, Dan had traveled the United States studying independent schools, concluding that students did best when they were free of constraints. He wanted to see a world with "no compulsory schooling," he told our school newspaper that fall. Kids should find their own motivations to learn. Once they did, they'd succeed. More unscheduled time, more elective classes, more nontraditional ways of learning added up to more motivated students.

That sounded good to me. And so did one of his routes to achieving that: girls. To handle more freedom, boys needed a dose of maturity, Dan believed. "Boys seem to handle themselves with more decorum, maturity, and discipline when there are girls around," he told our school paper. He admitted that might be a generalization, but "it's compelling in my mind."

Mine too, I thought.

So it was with some fascination for me and most everyone at Lakeside that Dan signed an agreement to merge with the nearby all-girls St. Nicholas School. St. Nick's was decidedly old-fashioned. Its dress code—heavy wool skirt, no makeup, no jewelry—may have suited the 1940s but had become sorely outdated in the late 1960s. With student numbers dropping, the school had approached Lakeside about a merger.

Bob Haig, one of Lakeside's lower-school math teachers, took on the task of trying to integrate the class schedules of the two schools. Lakeside decided the upcoming merger would be the perfect opportunity to computerize the scheduling of classes, a job that had always been done—ad hoc and imperfectly—by hand. Mr. Haig asked Kent and me to help. It would be a complicated program. After thinking it through, I couldn't come up with a smart way to write it. We declined.

To free up time to tackle the project himself, Mr. Haig then asked if Kent would take over his introductory computer science class. Kent conscripted the rest of the Lakeside Programming Group to assist him. Our first gig, if you could call it that, was as teachers. Well, more like unpaid tutors, really. Just kids teaching kids.

The class had never been taught before. We had no course plan, no textbook. So, we made it up. Each of us took a section to cover. Ric taught What a Computer Does; I did Assembler Language; Paul covered Memory Theory; and for one of his classes, Kent showed a movie on Shakey the Robot. (Shakey was the hottest thing in AI back then, basically a box and TV camera on wheels that could navigate its way around a room.) Teaching held surprising challenges. We could describe what a compiler does or explain a GOTO command, but what were we supposed to do when kids showed up late, or didn't pay attention, or skipped class? When students did badly on a test, was it their fault or ours? We hated the thought that bad grades might hurt kids' feelings, so we liberally handed out As and Bs.

C-Cubed's demise had left Lakeside without a computer provider. In the fall of 1970, the school contracted with another young timesharing venture. This one, in Portland, Oregon, was called Information Sciences Inc. and it charged a lot more money for time. So, of course, we poked around until we hacked a way to get free usage. And of course, we got caught before we could really take advantage of it. Kent was miffed. There was no way we should pay ISI's high prices! He had a plan. ISI soon received a letter from the very official-sounding Lakeside Programming Group, offering its services. We used my mother's cursive typewriter ball to make the letter look even slicker. We were convinced there was no way they'd see through the subterfuge. But I'm pretty sure what happened next was thanks to the friendly sales guy at ISI who knew exactly who the Lakeside programmers were and liked our work. They gave us a job.

ISI was focused on trying to entice Portland area businesses to computerize their operations just as C-Cubed had tried to do in Seattle. One ISI client, a maker of pipe organs, wanted to automate its payroll system. ISI asked us to write the program for no pay on the grounds that it would be a good educational experience. ISI drew up a contract stipulating the scope of the project, encouraging us to "exercise full creativity in program design," and set a March 1971 deadline. Our "contract" was dated November 18, 1970. That gave us just about four months, which, we quickly realized, would be barely enough time.

Our first hurdle was the fact that ISI wanted us to write the program in COBOL, a computer language none of us knew except Ric. We also lacked the necessary tools. Just as you need hammers and levels to build a house, you need an editor and debugger to write software. Ric started building us an editor while the rest of us began to learn COBOL.

Even though Paul, Ric, Kent, and I considered ourselves friends, there was a lot of competitiveness and pettiness in the ways we related, and the older-versus-younger pecking order still applied. Until now our battles had been low-stakes, though. With ISI, we were working toward something of value: free computer time.

Which may have explained why a few weeks into our ISI project, Paul decided that he and Ric would handle it on their own. "There's not enough work to go around," he told me and Kent. As the senior partners in the Lakeside Programming Group, they pulled rank and effectively fired us. Kent was outraged, which was typical of how he responded when he felt slighted. I was calmer. I was taking geometry with Fred Wright and liked spending time with him talking math; I figured I'd be happy to do more of that. Still, as we left the computer room, I told Paul: "You'll see how hard this is. You'll need us."

And I meant it. More clearly than Paul and Ric, Kent and I had gleaned early on that the project was going to be way more involved than we initially thought. Any payroll system had to be built on rules of finance, business, and government regulation. Paying employees meant adhering to laws about federal and state taxes, and Social Security deductions. It meant considering sick pay and vacation pay, unemployment insurance, check reconciliation, savings bond programs. That was all new to us.

As the weeks went by, Paul and Ric began to comprehend the complexity of the job. First, they invited Kent back in. About six weeks after firing us, Paul approached me. You were right, he said. Payroll is a lot more complicated than I thought.

By January we were back together, but the project was flagging. Ric went down a rabbit hole. The editor became his sole focus; it was so cool, he decided, he could sell it on its own. Paul, meanwhile, started to lose interest, spending time on other programs. Didn't he know a contract was *binding*? I was annoyed by what I considered their laziness and unprofessionalism. Here was this opportunity to build real software and Paul and Ric were letting it slip by. Toward the end of the month, I got everyone together and informed them that if Paul really wanted me on the project, I would need to be in charge. And if I was in charge, I would decide who got what portion of the free computer time. I devised an allocation plan based on my judgment of who was doing the most work, dividing our compensation into elevenths. I assigned Paul an insulting one-eleventh and Ric two-elevenths. Kent demanded that he and I be equal, so we each got four-elevenths. Paul and Ric shrugged and agreed. They probably thought we'd never finish the program.

In the meantime, Kent had approached the head of the University of Washington Computer Science lab, explained our project, and asked if we could use the lab. It was a perfect example of Kent acting like an adult and getting treated like one. The lab had multiple terminals, which meant we could all work simultaneously, and was a short walk from the UW library and the all-important UW food court, pizza places, and an Orange Julius. As with C-Cubed, we had found a castle where kids our age usually weren't allowed to trespass. But like C-Cubed, it wouldn't last.

For the next month and a half we worked in the lab nights after school and on weekends, banging out our program, which we'd dubbed PAYROL. The UW lab was even closer to my house than C-Cubed. By now it was routine for me to feign going to bed, then disappear through my window for a night of programming. I'm sure my parents knew, but by that point we had an unspoken pact: I kept my grades up and stayed out of trouble, and they didn't micromanage me.

Not everyone was thrilled to have high school kids camping out in the lab, tying up the terminals for hours on end, and stuffing the garbage cans with Orange Julius cups. But the administrators of the lab mostly tolerated us. That is, until the night before our deadline, when we were frantically trying to wrap things up. Paul got his hands on a keyboard that would allow him to work faster, but he needed an expensive device called an acoustic coupler to connect a terminal to a computer over a telephone line. He decided to "borrow" one from another office.

At about 9:30 that night, the owner of the device, a professor who didn't like us using the lab in the first place, stormed in, enraged that Paul had helped himself to the coupler without asking anyone's permission or leaving a note. Paul told the professor he didn't think he'd done anything wrong—and that, actually, he'd done it before, with no problem! That only stoked the professor's anger. He called in the director of the lab, who chastised Paul. The fireworks over, we went back to work.

On virtually no sleep, the four of us met the next morning at the bus terminal in a particularly gritty slice of downtown Seattle to catch a 7 a.m. Greyhound to Portland and present our work to ISI. The trip took nearly four hours. We walked from the station to ISI's office. We'd done our best to look professional and not like kids who needed permission to skip school that day. We wore blazers, ties, and carried briefcases. Following Kent's lead, I tried to project confidence and nonchalance: Yeah, we do this all the time. But inside I was nervous that the ISI executives would cast one disbelieving look at us and say, "You're just a bunch of kids. Get out of here."

Just the opposite. They took us seriously. They pored over the code on our PAYROL program, printed on a stack of computer paper we had brought. PAYROL needed more features, but apparently we had made enough of the core program to impress them.

We spent the whole afternoon at ISI, meeting all the company's top executives, including their thirtysomething president. They took us to an upscale spot called Henry's for lunch, over which our hosts told us about the growing competition between timeshared computing businesses, even though demand for their services hadn't taken off yet—the concept of switching paper-based functions like payroll and sales tracking to computers was so embryonic, few companies were even aware of it. We told him about witnessing C-Cubed go belly-up.

Back at the office, the president said he could give us more work and asked for our résumés. I scrawled one on the spot in pencil on lined paper, listing my experience at C-Cubed, the machine language I'd learned, and everything else I'd ever attempted on a computer. At some point Kent broached the issue of money. In the future, he said, we didn't want to get paid by the hour or in kind. We wanted to get paid by the job or receive royalties on the sale of whatever we created. Kent had thought through this part. As kids, we didn't need money to live on, but if one of our products went big, we could make a killing on the royalties. The president said yes to that too. But the first job was to finish PAYROL.

In my mind we were hotshots. We were good enough to be taken seriously and good enough to write the program. Looking back, I also sense the helping hand of beneficent adults. Our main proponent within ISI, for instance, a man named Bud Pembroke, had been active for years in promoting computer programming to Oregon schoolkids, writing curricula, and designing classes. His passion seemed to be education. I'm sure he viewed giving a job to four teenagers in the same spirit. At Lakeside, Fred Wright was the adult sponsor of our work. Even if he was hands-off, Fred signed our "contract" with ISI and typed an addendum at the bottom releasing Lakeside from any obligation to actually deliver the program, stipulating that he would "in every way possible encourage the students involved to follow through on this project." Whatever they did to set us up with the job, however, these adults then stood back and let us show what we could do.

Up to that point everything we had attempted with computers was practice, with no real-world results, like managing stocks and bonds in Kent's board game. Make-believe. Now we'd shown ourselves—and the world in our minds—that we could create something of value.

When we left the ISI office, Kent wanted to go to dinner at the Hilton, which he maintained was where real businesspeople would celebrate the closing of a deal. Instead, I dragged the four of us to Hamburger Train. We giddily rehashed every minute detail of the day while picking our fries and burgers off model railroad cars circling the restaurant.

Back in Seattle three days later, Kent and I arrived at the UW computer lab ready to start in on the next phase of our big project, only to find a sign on the door informing us that the Lakeside students who had been using the lab were no longer permitted entry. The woman at the front desk explained that the professor who owned the device was so miffed, he had us banned.

A graduate student watched over us as we gathered our materials, mostly printouts and yellow notepads. Kent and I then took a bus to Lakeside, hoping to get into the computer room. It was closed for the weekend. After a lot of scrambling around we borrowed a portable terminal. We set it up in my bedroom and tried dialing in to the computer, but every time someone in my family picked up the phone, our connection got cut. My dad came to the rescue by letting us use his office downtown. It was the weekend, so we had it to ourselves.

I will always remember the spring of 1971 for the growing rift— Paul and Ric on one side and Kent and me on the other—that seemed serious at the time but in retrospect reflected the natural ebb and flow of teenage friendship. Kent and I were miffed over Paul getting us banned from UW on top of the fact that Paul and Ric were steadily losing interest in our ISI deadlines. The older guys were absorbed in their own programming projects and also, I'm sure, as seniors they were enjoying their last few months of life as high school students.

Then came the DECtape scandal.

In those days, hard disk drives and floppy disk drives were available but not that common. Instead, on the computers we used—the PDP-10—the standard for storing data was a 260-foot-long magnetic tape three-quarters of an inch wide rolled onto a four-inch-diameter spool. It came in a plastic canister that you could fit in your pocket. (To store and retrieve data, the tapes needed to be threaded onto a reel-to-reel machine connected to a computer.)

At some point following C-Cubed's demise, Kent researched its bankruptcy proceedings and learned that the assets would be auctioned off at the Federal Courthouse downtown. Included in the fire sale would be over a hundred DECtapes. If we could get them cheap, Kent figured, we could sell them to businesses and computer centers at a premium and turn a profit. The tapes probably had code stored on them, but it could be overwritten by whoever bought them. What's more, before we resold the tapes, we could scour them for useful code. Kind of like dumpster diving without the grime and coffee stains.

On the day of the auction, Kent and I were stuck at school taking a standardized reading test. When we finished, we raced to the courthouse. The tapes were sold, but the clerk shared the buyer's name. I called him. He was a physics student at UW who, from what I could tell, had no plans for the tapes he had bought. Throughout the spring, I called back every few weeks, hoping he'd sell. By May he'd agreed to sell us 123 tapes. We didn't tell Paul and Ric, who by that point had all but stopped working on PAYROL. They were weeks from graduating, and dedicating all their time in the computer room to their own projects. With only two terminals for the entire school, we were constantly squabbling over turns. At least once, it escalated. Ric pinned me against the wall; Paul grabbed a fountain pen from my hand and smeared ink on my face. He was yanking me around the room when Fred Wright appeared and broke us up.

The tension between us came to a head later that same week. We had bought the tapes at this point, and Kent had about eighty of them stuffed in a paper bag. It was pouring rain that day. Worried that our precious tapes would get soaked on Kent's bus ride home from school, we stashed them in the hollow base of the teletype terminal. We could barely contain our glee at our cleverness. The next day the tapes were missing. Convinced that Paul had absconded with them, Kent went ballistic, accusing Paul of theft and threatening to call the police, sue, take him to court, and a litany of other legal measures he later spelled out in a three-page list of grievances entitled "STATEMENT OF KENT EVANS, BILL GATES ON ASSOCIATIONS WITH PAUL ALLEN AND RIC WEILAND."

The first paragraph laid out our complaint: "We have concluded that falsehoods and partial truths about us that a number of individuals have been exposed to in the past several days have significantly damaged us. This statement is an attempt to present our case so that opinions are not based on partial information or only one side of the story." On the last page Kent grandly concluded, "we were the victims of grand theft. . . . No legal action will be taken assuming the tapes are returned by tomorrow morning." We signed the document and submitted it to Mr. Wright. Eventually Paul gave the tapes back.

We were all still friends, but it was unclear whether we would see each other much once the school year ended. After graduation, Paul was set to head off to Washington State University, on the other side of the state in Pullman, while Ric would attend Oregon State University before entering Stanford the following year. Lakeside graduating seniors had a tradition of publishing mock wills in which they bequeathed joke gifts to students and teachers. In his, Ric wrote that he "willed to Kent Evans and Bill Gates a part of my supreme sense of fairness which they so dearly need for computer-room discussions." In a senior-year essay, Paul wrote about me: "Very suggestible and is ready to jump at any chance to have fun in strange ways. We fit together very well." The feeling was mutual.

As the two remaining members of the Lakeside Programming Group, Kent and I were left to finish PAYROL. We labored over it all summer, sorting through the states with income taxes and contacting the U.S. Treasury for rules on savings bond deductions. After nine months on a project we thought would take three, we finished the program in August. Best of all: it worked.

CHAPTER EIGHT

The Real World

W e gotta sue them!" Kent was pacing around my family's living room. It was a few weeks into our junior year. I was just shy of my sixteenth birthday, Kent not much older.

I kept quiet as Kent ranted to my dad about how unfairly we were being treated by ISI. After all the work we'd put in, the hundreds of hours, ISI was refusing us the free computer time it had promised. My father the lawyer listened patiently, his hands folded in front of him.

Kent was convinced that my father would bring the full weight of Shidler, McBroom, Gates & Baldwin down on the Portland company. I thought his reaction was over the top, but what the heck, it was fun to watch him in action. I had learned by then that whenever he was being put-upon or something in the universe struck him as unjust, he blew up. Sometimes he found a reasonable outlet for his ire. That month, for instance, he wrote a stern letter to our local CBS affiliate protesting its decision to drop Roger Mudd as the anchor of *Sunday Evening News*. Other times he let it fly, as he'd done the previous May when he accused Paul and Ric of grand larceny over our missing DECtapes. To Kent, ISI reneging on our computer time reached the level of grand larceny.

When Kent had exhausted himself, my father started asking questions about our program, the last time we talked with ISI, and the contract we had signed. At the end of the meeting, Dad said he'd give the company a call. And he did, right there and then.

He told the ISI president that he was Bill's father, acting on the two boys' request to see if they could reach an agreement over the owed time.

The ISI president spoke for a long time while my father just listened. When the man finished, my father simply said, "I hear you."

Those three words of my father's, and their tone, have stayed with me ever since. *I hear you.* To me, they captured the essence of my dad's quiet power. Unmoved by the man's arguments, my father simply acknowledged that he had noted them; in not saying anything else, he made clear that he did not accept them. The boys delivered, and now they were due what you had promised, was the implicit message I took away—and the ISI president seemed to get it too. With little more discussion, he agreed to give us the computer time.

My father helped us craft a letter proposing payment and other details. Within two weeks we signed an agreement to receive $5,000 in computer time, which the company stipulated had to be used by June of the following year, seven months away. My father signed the agreement "parent/advisor." As any attorney would, he billed us for his services: $11.20 to cover the cost of the fifty-five-minute long-distance call.

That's the way I remembered our tiff with ISI: the company behaved unfairly, and my father agreed with our position. Looking back at the paperwork, I realize it wasn't that straightforward. Initially, ISI executives thought they were doing a few kids a favor, giving them a rare education in business and programming. I don't think they expected us to take the job so seriously. But when we did, they decided that some payment was in order. That is, until they realized that in writing the program we'd racked up over $25,000 worth of computing time already, plus storage costs. I can also see now that my dad was partially playing a role for our benefit, a learning experience for his son and his son's friend.

I was happy we got the free computer time, but I also loved the simple fact that we had completed our first software product. We dove in with no knowledge of taxes, Social Security, or any of the other payroll essentials. A year on, any manager at a midsize company with a computer terminal could use our program to accurately cut paychecks for their two hundred or thousand employees. It wasn't perfect or polished, but it worked—that fact astounded me. And we were compensated. It wasn't cash, but it was something.

This was a start to build on. That fall we turned over every stone hunting for other opportunities.

Presenting himself in letters as "marketing manager" for Lakeside Programming Group, Kent pitched prospective customers our DECtapes. We offered free shipping and volume discounts depending on the number of tapes the customer bought. Pretty soon we'd made a few hundred dollars from a science museum and a high-tech industrial electronics company, both in the Portland area.

While he was still at Lakeside, Ric had gotten a part-time job programming for a company that studied traffic flow on Seattle-area streets. It was a high-tech job in a very low-tech business. The company, called Logic Simulation Co., collected data on traffic flows with boxes installed on the side of the road. When a car or truck rolled over a rubber hose, the box recorded the time by punching tiny holes in a paper tape. Cities and states used the data to help make decisions about things like traffic light timing and road repair.

The machines produced rolls and rolls of paper tape that had to be manually tabulated. For a little while Kent and I did this piecework, a tedious job. Kent wanted to expand, hire younger kids at Lakeside as subcontractors. He pitched Lakeside's administration, and pretty soon we had a handful of seventh- and eighth-graders working for us.

And we had our $5,000 worth of ISI computer time. Kent wanted to find a company that needed computer access and offer it a discount of what ISI would charge. I balked at that idea. Competing with ISI using their own computer seemed unethical. Fred Wright, the math teacher who oversaw the computer room, agreed. He caught wind of the scheme and wrote on Kent's report card to make sure his parents knew where the school stood. "Activities of the Lakeside Programming Group do not always seem completely above board," he noted. "I feel quite uneasy that they are going out and selling the time that ISI has finally given them to potential ISI customers. I want to be certain that you realize that the boys are on their own in this venture." Kent dropped the plan.

Lakeside that fall was chaos thanks to the merger with St. Nick's. The task of scheduling classes on a computer, which math teacher Bob Haig had been managing, was proving far more difficult than he had expected. Some students arrived on campus that September to discover they were scheduled for classes that didn't exist. Others were slotted for French I in a classroom where Latin II was underway. Kids overwhelmed their advisors with questions and formed long lines at the registrar's office. "Can you change this because I have all my classes in a row and then four free periods?"

There was also a deeper unease. For fifty years, Lakeside had been a male bastion, its students secure in its insular embrace. Some believed going coed would degrade that familiar culture. One of my classmates published a piece in the school newspaper bemoaning the decline of our football team, which he attributed to the school's increasingly free and casual atmosphere, including the "distraction" of having girls on campus. (And, God forbid, the growing popularity of soccer!) Another argued that the changes fell short, making the key point that thirty young women did not a revolution make, and Lakeside, still mostly white males, far from represented the broader society. Kent, meanwhile, was deeply concerned about our academic standards. He was convinced—incorrectly as it turned out—that St. Nick's wasn't as academically rigorous as Lakeside. In typical Kent fashion, he insinuated himself into faculty meetings to advocate his case, even helping to draw up a new plan for evaluating teacher performance.

The only issue I had with the addition of the St. Nick's students was that I had no idea how to talk to them. I had trouble even communicating with non-geeky boys my age. Girls? Apart from my sisters and some family friends, they were a foreign country. And what would they make of me? I was still skinny, with that squeaky voice, more a kid than a teen. I had started driving but didn't have a car. One way I managed my insecurities was to think of myself as an antihero, a wannabe Steve McQueen in *The Thomas Crown Affair,* minus the good looks. I had recently seen the movie and loved the actor's cool confidence; he was an irresistible mastermind. About the closest I got to that self-assurance was in the computer room. Our physics teacher had assigned a problem for his students that involved writing a short computer program. I planted myself in the computer room, knowing that most of the students had never touched a computer before and would need help. Some of those students, I reasoned, would be girls.

As the second trimester started, I took a radical step that I hoped would yield more surefire results: I joined drama class. Admittedly, the main draw for me was the higher percentage of girls in drama. And since the main activity in the class was to read lines to each other, the odds were very good that I'd actually talk to one.

While I was exploring my thespian potential, Kent dug into his own new interest: mountain climbing. That winter he was fixated on joining a Lakeside trip to climb the enormous, slumbering volcano Mount St. Helens with snowshoes, crampons, and ropes. The trip was canceled once due to bad weather, and then a second time. This was serious stuff, a far cry from the hike we had gone on together that required minimal equipment and was undertaken regardless of weather. I was surprised by Kent's drive to learn technical climbing. It was as big a stretch for him as drama was for me. Kent wasn't athletic; anything involving strength or coordination was a challenge. But he was undaunted, fully aware of his shortcomings and unabashed about trying to overcome them. He had already done this with skiing. After completing a season of lessons, he proudly reported that he won a trophy for becoming the best in the worst group of skiers. That little glint of progress was all he needed.

Despite a herculean effort in the fall by a group of teachers helping Mr. Haig, the scheduling problems persisted. By mid-January, Bob was in front of the school's board trying to explain why. In the meantime, we continued teaching Bob's computer class, and now seniors as well as middle-schoolers were sitting at the desks before us.

Another of Lakeside's former Navy pilots and Boeing engineers, Bob was a talented math teacher and dedicated crew coach but had limited exposure to computers. With everyone so up in arms over the mess, Kent and I decided we should step in to try to help. We met with Bob a few times to figure out how we might fix things for the spring trimester. In the UW library, Kent dug up years of academic literature on college scheduling programs with titles like "Construction of School Timetables by Flow Methods." Nothing in his stack of papers was useful to us.

There were so many variables to coordinate, starting with the needs and desires of hundreds of students, each taking nine classes in an eleven-period day. Throw into that mix the schedules of 70 courses, 170 sections of those courses, and a long list of special considerations: drum class couldn't be scheduled in the room above choir practice; while most classes covered just one period, some, like dance or biology lab, took up two. It was a very hard math problem.

Yet, almost without my realizing it, I had been working on the problem for the past six months. Walking to class or lying in bed at night, my mind would form different permutations of the schedule: X number of classes, Y number of students, and so on, including the many conflicts and constraints that needed to be factored into the equation.

January 1972 was one of Seattle's snowiest months on record, and that meant days off from school. On Tuesday, January 25, nearly eight inches of snow fell, all but shutting down the city. Instead of going skiing or sledding, I holed up in my bedroom, pen on yellow pad, working through what up to that point was the toughest problem I had ever attempted: how to satisfy the distinct, seemingly mutually exclusive needs of hundreds of people, and do it in a way that a computer could understand. In math it is what's called an optimization problem, the same puzzle airlines solve to seat passengers and sports leagues to schedule games. I drew a matrix of students, classes, teachers, times, and all the other variables. Gradually that week I refined my chart, and steadily it grew clearer and clearer. On Saturday I walked out of my room knowing I'd sorted through the conflicts in a systematic way—one that I knew a computer could grasp. For the first time all week, the sky was totally clear.

The next day, Sunday, January 30, Mr. Haig piloted a Cessna 150 from an airport north of Seattle. The temperature had stayed below freezing all week and sunny skies were forecast that morning. He was joined by Bruce Burgess, a Lakeside English teacher who was also the school's photography guru. Their goal that morning was to capture a perfect picture of Lakeside's snow-covered campus with Mount Rainier in the distance. A few minutes into the flight, they experienced engine problems; their plane hit a power line and crashed in a neighborhood north of Seattle. Both men died.

Lakeside was a small place. Students—as well as their families—formed tight bonds with their teachers. As middle school teachers, Bob and Bruce had gotten to know kids when they were young and seen them through their academic careers. Bob's son was in my class. Bruce was my first English teacher at Lakeside. He'd often duck into the computer room with his camera. (He took what is probably the most famous photo of Paul and me at Lakeside, looking up from our work at two teletype machines.)

Death was a constant in the news from Vietnam and in the violence of the period. The Robert Kennedy and Martin Luther King assassinations had left the country shellshocked; closer to home, Seattle civil rights leader Edwin T. Pratt had been shot on his doorstep. But in my experience, cocooned by the wealth and privilege of Laurelhurst and Lakeside, death took place at a distance. Aside from my grandfather and great-grandmother, no one close to me had ever died.

Two days after the crash, Dan Ayrault called Kent and me to a meeting with a group of teachers. The headmaster encouraged us to team up to finish the schedule. There wasn't time to rewrite a new program around the solution I'd come up with. To be ready for spring, we'd have to triage a temporary fix. Dan told us the school could pay us $2.75 an hour for the work.

For all the pressure we felt writing the payroll program, most of it was self-imposed. We had no critical deadline. The schedule program felt entirely different. A whole school, *my* whole school, expected us to fix it. And everyone would know if we failed. This was the first time I felt responsible for something larger than myself. Kent and I took to reminding ourselves: "This isn't a class project. It's the real world."

For about three weeks, Kent and I and four teachers worked twenty-hour days, trying to cobble together a schedule in time for the next trimester. We skipped school, and struggled to not make

My mother, Mary Maxwell Gates (seated on the sofa next to her grandparents, above left), grew up in a family of bankers who loved games of all kinds, sports, and community service. A natural-born leader, she rides the biggest tricycle in the childhood photo (above right).

My father, William Henry Gates Sr., grew up in Bremerton, Washington, where my grandfather ran a furniture store. Driving his Model A Ford coupe, "Clarabelle," gave my father an early taste of independence. He went on to become the first in his family to graduate college, followed by law school.

My parents met as students at the University of Washington and married two years later, in May 1951. Their contrasting personalities and backgrounds complemented each other and formed the bedrock of our family life.

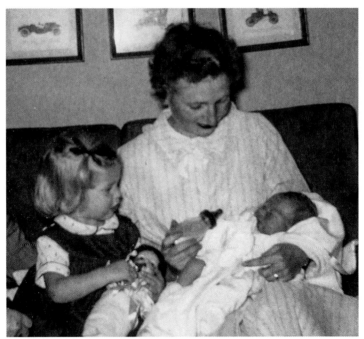

I was born on October 28, 1955, twenty-one months after my
sister Kristi. In most of my early memories, she is right by my side.

As a baby, I was dubbed "Happy Boy" for my ear-to-ear smile and ready laugh. Early on,
my parents knew that the rhythm of my mind was different from that of other kids. Kristi,
for one, did what she was told, played easily with others, and from the start got great
grades. I did none of those things. My mother worried about me and warned my preschool
teachers about what to expect.

Books were a big part of our household. By early elementary school I was reading a lot on my own at home; I liked the feeling of being able to quickly absorb new facts and could spend hours lost in books, an early sign of my ability to block out any distractions when something interests me.

My sister Libby was born in 1964 and would turn out to be the most social member of our family and the most athletic. As the youngest—I was nine years older—Libby remembers growing up in a frenetic household of busy siblings and busy parents.

When I was three, my mother and I made the local paper when she chaired a Junior League program to show off museum artifacts—in this case, an old medical kit—to elementary school students.

My mother had high aspirations for her family, and both she and my father believed in giving back to the community long before that phrase came into vogue.

WHEN I GROW UP I WANT TO BE—

BOYS		GIRLS	
☐ Fireman	■ Astronaut	☐ Mother	☐ Airline Hostess
☐ Policeman	☐ Soldier	☐ Nurse	☐ Model
☐ Cowboy	☐ Baseball Player	☐ School Teacher	☐ Secretary
■ _Scientist_		☐ _____	

SIGNATURE — *Bill Gates*

The Space Race and the promise of science were part of the climate growing up in the sixties. It's no wonder I checked "Astronaut" on the "When I Grow Up" form in fifth grade. But "Scientist" was my dream job: to be a person who spends their days studying the mysteries of the world seemed perfect to me.

My maternal grandmother, whom we called Gami, was a constant presence in our young lives. After my grandfather died, she channeled her love and attention toward me and my sisters, sometimes joining our family on vacations, like this one to Disneyland.

In the early 1960s, my parents and a group of their friends started renting Cheerio Lodge Cottages on the Hood Canal for two weeks every July. For a kid, it was paradise. My dad was the Mayor of Cheerio, a sort of director of fun and a wrangler of children who also presided over the opening ceremony of the Cheerio Olympics. The events were tests of dexterity and drive more than of athleticism, but whatever the event, I'd push myself with abandon to get on the podium at the end of the day. I was low on dexterity but high on drive.

Our family lived by the structure of routines, traditions, and rules my mother established. She ran, as my father would say, "a well-organized household." Take Christmas. Planning started in the early fall, when my mom reviewed her notes from the previous year's holiday to see where there was room for improvement. From homemade cards to the annual skating party we hosted to the matching pajamas we wore on Christmas morning, we went all out. Even if on occasion my sisters and I rolled our eyes at these traditions, to skip any one of them would have felt like a loss. Christmas is still one of the things we like to reminisce about the most.

I joined the Cub Scouts when I was eight years old. By the time I moved on to Troop 186 four years later, hiking, camping, and mountaineering were booming in the U.S. and Seattle was gaining recognition as a mecca for outdoor sports. Our troop made getting scouts into the mountains to hike and camp its main reason for existence.

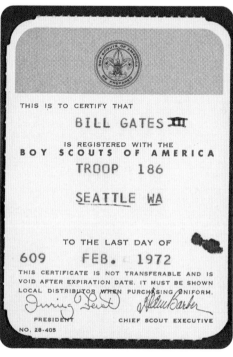

THIS IS TO CERTIFY THAT

BILL GATES III

IS REGISTERED WITH THE
BOY SCOUTS OF AMERICA
TROOP 186

SEATTLE WA

TO THE LAST DAY OF
609   FEB.   1972
THIS CERTIFICATE IS NOT TRANSFERABLE AND IS
VOID AFTER EXPIRATION DATE. IT MUST BE SHOWN
LOCAL DISTRIBUTOR WHEN PURCHASING UNIFORM.

PRESIDENT   CHIEF SCOUT EXECUTIVE
NO. 28-405

The summer following ninth grade, a senior scout invited me to join a trip hiking the Lifesaving Trail (now known as West Coast Trail), which runs along the coast of Vancouver Island, a rugged area famous for its storms, reefs, and tricky currents. The trip—which involved traveling by seaplane, fording rivers, and climbing cliffs—was more challenging than anything I had ever experienced, but also more rewarding. I was hooked.

Kent Evans (pictured below, left) and I became best friends very quickly in eighth grade at Lakeside, the private school I attended during my middle and high school years.

In the fall of 1968, Lakeside got a teletype machine. Kent and I became regular users, as did Paul Allen (above, middle) and Ric Weiland (right). Paul and Ric were two years older, but we quickly grew to be friends as we all tried to piece together how to write our first programs. We called ourselves the Lakeside Programming Group.

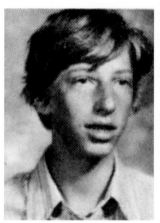

As my class photos suggest, I looked younger than my age throughout high school (and beyond). Between work with the Lakeside Programming Group, hiking, Boy Scouts, and school, I was figuring out who I was and what I wanted to become.

As a high school sophomore I served as a House page in Olympia, our state capital (above), and later spent part of the summer before my senior year working as a congressional page in Washington, D.C. It's nearly impossible to be around Congress and not get swept up by it; that experience stimulated a life-long interest in politics and government.

In my emerging worldview, I had formed a hierarchy of intelligence: however good you were at math, that's how good you'd be at other subjects—biology, chemistry, history, or even languages. After graduation from Lakeside, I was convinced that my path would be mathematics. Harvard was my next step toward that future.

In April 1975, Paul and I came up with our company name: Micro-Soft (we would eventually drop the hyphen). Our one product was 8080 BASIC, which we wrote while I was a sophomore in college. Our Lakeside friend Ric (with me in the photo below, left) soon joined us in Albuquerque, where we initially worked out of office space in an aging strip mall. As Microsoft grew, so did the amount of time I was spending on the company; I took my second leave of absence from Harvard in the winter of 1977 and never returned. We were beginning to attract media attention—in the photo at the bottom right, I'm conducting one of my first television interviews—but it wasn't until we hired our first employees from outside our circle of friends that Microsoft felt like a real company.

MICRO

January 15, 1977

Mr. George Smith
Senior Tutor
Currier House
Harvard College

Dear Mr. Smith,

This letter is to inform you I plan to take the spring semester
of this academic year off. A friend and I have a partnership,
Microsoft, which does consulting relating to microprocessor
software. The new obligations we have just taken on require
that I devote my full time efforts to working at Microsoft.
Since I have taken a semester off previously I have a full
year of school to complete and currently I plan to return in
the fall and graduate in June '78. My address and phone number
will be those given for Microsoft on this stationary.

Sincerely yours,

William H. Gates

SOFT

MICROSOFT/P.O. BOX 754
ALBUQUERQUE, NEW MEXICO 87103
(505) 256-3600

Gami remained a steadying voice in my ear throughout my growing pains both at Harvard and in the early years at Microsoft.

A constant source of support and advice, my father realized early on that Microsoft was turning into a serious business. My mom's understanding came more gradually. For a long time, she held a belief that eventually things would settle down and I would get my Harvard degree.

My mother expected me to meet her very high standards but also did all she could to support and encourage me, sometimes by example, as with her work with the United Way of America, which appointed her to their board in 1980. With wealth comes the responsibility to give it away, she would say. I regret that she didn't live long enough to see how fully I've tried to meet that expectation.

mistakes as each night wore on and we fought off fatigue. I remember a late-night rubber band shooting contest with an English teacher on our team. I remember falling asleep at the punch-card machine while typing, realizing that it was three in the morning, and not remembering what day of the week it was. I remember another teacher suggesting that we go home for a few hours to say hello to our parents—it had been a few days.

We did most of the work at University of Washington, where the school had access to a computer. Even then, the machine was a bit outdated. It performed what's called batch processing—handling one program at a time—using punch cards, the now-defunct system in which you'd type your program on a machine that punched holes into thin pieces of cardboard. When you finished punching, you had a stack of cards. At UW, the computer was in the basement. I'd grab my stack of cards, walk down the hall to the elevator, descend into the bowels of the building, and hand my deck of cards to the computer operator. Then I'd wait. Eventually the operator would load the cards into the computer, which would print the results. Any small problem in our code tripped up the computer. Something as minor as a syntax error in line 10 would derail the whole program, sending us back up the elevator to start over again, punching out new cards. Start to finish, one test run of the program could take five hours. Anytime a grad student asked if we were working on a school project, Kent and I would repeat our mantra. "It's not a class. It's the real world."

At last, we managed to coax our program to life the night before our deadline. At the start of school that spring, there was hardly a line at the registrar's office.

The program we'd built was a sort of working prototype held together with spit and glue. It melded pieces contributed by Mr. Haig—written in FORTRAN, a computer language used by scientists and technicians—and core parts that we cobbled together over those late nights. It even called for one step of the schedule-making process to be done by hand, since we didn't have time to build that part into the program. Dan, the headmaster, was so happy with it he said he could come up with funds to pay us to write a fresh version with all the features the school needed—and to do it in BASIC, our language of choice. Kent, as always, immediately saw a bigger opportunity. He was convinced that with our success at Lakeside, we could entice other schools around the country to pay us to manage their schedules using our software. He wrote up a pitch touting our various projects, including the traffic-counting venture, which was still going strong. By now we had three kids working for us and had assigned an eighth-grader named Chris Larson to manage that work. We typed up flyers and plastered them around school, announcing that we were hiring for Lakeside Programming Group and the traffic work we were doing for Logic Simulation Co.:

> LPG and LSC are two computer-oriented organizations involved in a number of attempts to make money. These include class scheduling, working on traffic volume studies, producing cookbooks and "fault-tree simulation." This spring and summer we may want to expand our workforce, which now is 5 Lakesiders! It's not just for "computer freaks." We think we'll need people that can type and/or do drafting or architectural drawing. If you're interested see Kent Evans or Bill Gates (Upper School) or Chris Larson (middle school).

On the application we noted that we were an equal opportunity employer.

That spring was busy. I had to make up for the class time I'd missed working on the scheduling program, even while starting work on its next phase. I had a full course load and was still teaching Bob's computer classes. Kent had an even heavier schedule. Alongside classwork, he was deep into his contributions to the Lakeside faculty, writing a paper for administrators on what he saw as flagging discipline among students, and planning a pilot program to teach calculus to middle-schoolers. On top of this, he started an introductory course in mountain climbing at the University of Washington. He began attending Monday-night lectures on technique, and spent weekends practicing in the mountains and outcrops in Western Washington.

As always, we talked on the phone every night, and he'd call me when he got home from his lectures and climbs. Just as he had done with sailing terms, Kent adopted climbing's lexicon, throwing around terms like crags and cruxes, belays and 'biners. He talked about overcoming fear on his first big climb—his first "Class 5," as he put it. (*Difficult, with sustained climbing, high commitment, and few bivouac sites,* according to one rating system.) I was happy for him and so were his parents. They thought it was good that he was branching out, pursuing an activity without me, making new friends among the college kids and couples in his climbing class.

On the Friday before Memorial Day, after weeks of ironing out the details, we signed the contract with Lakeside to get paid for the next phase of the schedule work. The school agreed to give us a stipend, and pay for the computer time involved.

That night Kent called me as usual. No time to work that weekend, he told me. He was headed to Mount Shuksan, a nine-thousand-foot glaciated peak a few hours north of Seattle, for the final climb of his class. His parents had been debating whether he should go; the weekend before, the group was climbing at a spot called the Tooth when a rock gave way, sending two of his classmates careening down an icy slope onto rocks. Kent had watched as helicopters airlifted them back to Seattle. Ultimately his parents decided he'd be okay. Kent had always been able to handle himself. "I'll call you when I get back," he said.

I'm not sure what I did that weekend. I was probably in the computer room at Lakeside working away on the class schedule.

On Monday, May 29, I was in my room when I heard the phone

ring and the mumble of my parents' voices through the ceiling. My father called down from the top of the stairs to say that Dan Ayrault was on the phone and wanted to talk to me. I took the stairs two by two, thinking it was weird that the headmaster was calling me at home. My father directed me into my parents' bedroom, where my mom gave me the handset.

Dan didn't waste any time. There had been an accident on the climbing trip. Kent had fallen. A helicopter search and rescue team had picked him up and transported him to a hospital.

I waited for him to tell me when I could go visit him.

"Unfortunately, Bill, he didn't make it. Kent died last night."

I have no memory of hanging up the phone, or what my parents said to comfort me. I retreated into myself, watching a slideshow in my mind's eye, ticking through images of recent days, grasping for evidence that what I had just heard wasn't true. Kent at school. Kent typing into the terminal, looking up at me. The two of us on the phone. *Call you when I get back.* I imagined the mountain and him falling. Dan had said something about a helicopter. Where was he now?

I have a vague recollection of going to see Kent's parents at their house the next day with Tim Thompson, another Lakeside friend. We returned the following day and learned that a memorial service had been planned for the next week. Kent's parents asked us to tell Paul and Ric the tragic news and see if they could come.

The clearest memory I have is of sitting on the steps of the school chapel and crying as hundreds of people filed inside for Kent's memorial service. Kent's parents and his brother, David, sat in the first row. Our art teacher, Robert Fulghum, greeted everyone as they came in. I sat with my family and stared at the floor. Robert ran the service. As friends and teachers got up and shared their memories of Kent, their words washed over me.

Kent appreciated the silly side of life . . .

He stuck up for what he thought was right . . .

A young man pushing his resources and capacities as far and as hard as he possibly could . . .

He was never so happy as when a situation got frantic or confused or complicated . . .

Intelligent, self-reliant, a juggler of honors classes, hiking, teaching . . .

A great schemer and entrepreneur, an accomplished sailor and the worst artist in Lakeside . . .

I had a piece of paper in my hand on which I had written my thoughts. I might have planned to read them in front of everyone, I'm not sure. But I couldn't move; I sat frozen in place. Outside, when the service was over, a stream of people approached to say how sorry they were for my loss. Everyone knew how close we were: the tall ungainly kid with the briefcase, the spindly showoff with the big mouth. Both with their huge ambitions for the future. I could see their sympathy was genuine. But still, they could never picture all those hours and what they contained. Our goofy inside jokes. Our intense bursts of work. It felt strange to be singled out. Then I caught a glimpse of Kent's parents. Who was *I* to feel so sorry for myself? This was the tragedy of their lives.

This realization fully sank in at the reception the family hosted after the memorial. Paul, who had driven four and a half hours from college for the service, gave me and a few others a ride. We walked in together and Kent's dad greeted us and shook our hands. Kent's mom was curled up on the sofa, sobbing. It was at that moment I understood that for all my grief, it would never run as deep as hers. He was my best friend, but he was her baby. At some level I knew she and Mr. Evans would be forever marooned in this loss. The stricken expressions on the faces of Kent's kind, gentle parents that day have never left me.

Kent's friends should feel free to take home anything of his that might have meaning, his dad told us. Entering his small room—with its familiar stacks of computer papers and books piled on the floor, the huge desk made from a door bridging two file cabinets, his print of *Breezing Up* on the corkboard—made me so sad. It felt too painful to take even the most inconsequential of his belongings. I thanked Mr. Evans and said I didn't need anything.

Over time I learned the details of what happened on the mountain the day Kent died.

The climbing class and its two instructors had made it to the peak of Shuksan late in the afternoon. As they descended, they stopped at the top of a chute above base camp, and an instructor and one student climbed down to make sure the area was safe for the rest to follow. There was a tense moment when one of the students at the top shifted his weight, setting off a small avalanche that sent the student careening down the chute, but he steadied himself and signaled to the group that he was okay.

The relief of that moment was short-lived. Kent stumbled forward, and for a split second turned to face uphill—the students had been taught that if they started to fall, they should drop facedown, uphill in the snow, and use their ice axes to stop from sliding—before tumbling backwards down the chute, into the rocks at the bottom. He was still alive when the others reached him. The group built an igloo over him to keep him warm while two members hiked out to get help. Among the students were two doctors who tended to Kent as best they could.

That night an Army helicopter lifted him to a hospital in Bellingham. He was gone by the time they got there.

I learned that he was probably the most gung ho among the student climbers but also struggled the most. He was the last one up on nearly every climb. I also learned that as the month-long course progressed, more and more people had dropped out, finding it too tough or too dangerous. But Kent was determined to go on the final climb. It was his nature to always push the limits of what was expected.

In 1973, a local climbing magazine published a short piece that declared the previous year "the worst accident year in the history of mountaineering in Washington." It included a long list of deaths and injuries that took place in the mountains, including Kent's, and blamed the rash of accidents in part on the popularity of climbing classes, which put inexperienced climbers in peril. It questioned new climbers' lack of judgment and fitness. If I'm being honest, I wondered about that too. Part of me was angry at Kent. I couldn't understand why he had to challenge himself with something as extreme as mountaineering. To some degree I still harbor that feeling.

More than anyone I'd ever met, Kent was driven by the promise of all the amazing places his life would take him, from career success to an overland trip through Peru in a Land Rover that he'd acquire somewhere, somehow. That summer he had been cooking up a plan to serve as an assistant forest ranger, even though he knew they didn't accept many high school kids. This optimism about what he—and I—could accomplish was the through line of our friendship. So was the assumption that we'd be doing it together.

When someone close to you dies, the socially expected thing to say is that from that point on, you lived your life as they lived theirs. That you found traits of theirs that guided you forward. The truth is, by this time—I was sixteen years old—Kent had already had a profound effect on who I was. When we met, I was a thirteen-year-old kid with raw IQ and a competitive streak, but little aim other than to win whatever game I was playing. Kent helped give me direction, setting me on the course of defining who I wanted to become. I didn't have an answer to that yet, but it would drive many of the decisions that followed.

I recently read through the big, gold-stamped logbook from the Evanses' boat, the *Shenandoah,* stopping on the notes his mom wrote during our trip in the summer of 1970. Her entries in the spring of 1972 recorded every time Kent chose to climb rather than sail with the family. About a third of the way through the logbook, she left two pages blank, save for the very middle of one, where she wrote:

Kent Hood Evans
born March 18, 1955
died May 28, 1972
Kent was killed in a mountain climbing
accident on Mt. Shuksan

Throughout my life, I have tended to deal with loss by avoiding it: tamping it down to make it through the early stages of grief and then quickly setting my focus on a distraction that fully engages my mind. As a family we didn't dwell on the past; we always looked forward with the expectation that something better lay ahead. And in 1972, there was much less focus on actively processing grief than there would be in the decades that followed. Counseling wasn't the norm; you just got on with things. Kent's parents grieved their unimaginable loss in their own way: Three weeks after the service they took the *Shenandoah* on a long cruise north to Kent's favorite place, Desolation Sound. They said a short prayer on the boat before they set sail.

As for myself, right after Kent died, I called Paul, who was home from college for the summer. I told him that I was going to try to finish the class schedule before the end of the month, before our free computer time was up. There was still a ton of work to be done. I didn't say so, but it mattered to me that I finish the thing I'd started with Kent—plus the school was counting on me. What I did say was, "I need help. Do you want to work with me on it?"

Within a day we were in Lakeside's computer room coding for twelve-hour stretches at a time and sleeping on old Army cots in between. The school gave us master keys to the buildings, allowing us free rein all summer on the empty campus, which to me seemed pretty cool. Paul no doubt had better things to do. Instead, he joined me in our old space and we instructed the computer how to give one kid his bio lab before lunch and another a free period on Thursdays before soccer, or whatever any of the 580 Lakeside students needed in order to squeeze all their classes into a single schedule.

For a month Paul and I lived in that room. I fell asleep at the terminal more times than I can remember, my nose gradually meeting the keys for an hour or two. Then I'd wake up with a start and immediately start coding again. We got so punchy at times we cried with laughter. The smallest thing could set us off. I don't remember specifics of those sleep-deprived nights, but Paul did. In his book, *Idea Man,* he recounts that we found a random letter *X* had somehow landed in the lines of our code, a bug. We fell into hysterics, screaming "X!" over and over like we'd unmasked our secret nemesis.

The whole crazy project, I see in retrospect, was part of our grieving, a mission built on our shared past with Kent and with each other. Paul knew more than anyone what I was going through. He knew the best way for me to cope was by losing myself in the complexity of that coding puzzle, and he wanted to be there with me. Of course, we never talked about these feelings. But they were there.

When you share so much time with one person it's impossible not to grow closer. I had never spent much time at Paul's house before, but I visited a few times that summer. His father was quiet, what you might expect from the associate director of libraries at the University of Washington. His mother, on the other hand, was very friendly—you could see that she longed to connect, and she did so through books. Over time I'd recognize her as one of the greatest readers I've ever encountered. She had read every book I knew and hundreds I hadn't even heard of, from classics to more recently published novels by authors like Chinua Achebe.

Getting to know someone's family at that age reveals so much that's hidden by the social haze of school and whatever affectations a kid puts on in public. I saw Paul's geekiness in its full glory, and parents who, like my own, knew their son didn't quite fit into the mainstream but were still deeply supportive. In the basement Paul had what you'd have to call a laboratory, including a huge chemistry set and a contraption that generated electricity between aluminum orbs—a Christmas present from his dad—with which Paul once had almost electrocuted himself. He kept boxes of spare electronics parts, soldering irons, and assorted other mysterious tools—mysterious to me at least—that he scoured thrift stores to find. Upstairs, his room was packed floor-to-ceiling with seemingly every science fiction book ever written. I liked science fiction, but Paul subsisted on a diet comprised solely of Heinlein, Asimov, Herbert, Bradbury, Dick, and many lesser-known writers of the genre.

On the intermittent breaks we took, we'd walk around the deserted Lakeside campus while he educated me on his views on sex, drugs, and rock 'n' roll. He was far more well-versed than I was in all three, which is to say that I hadn't tried the first two and knew almost nothing about the third. Paul had actually been on dates and even had a girlfriend. He was deep into music, which typically meant seminal guitarists like Procol Harum's Robin Trower, or his hero, Jimi Hendrix.

Ah, Hendrix. To Paul, Jimi Hendrix was the beginning and the end of creative genius. That summer he rhapsodized over how with six strings and a lot of distortion Jimi could take you to the cosmos and bring you home safely, all in one solo. On weekends Paul wore purple bell-bottoms and a brimmed hat. By then he had turned "Are You Experienced?" into a mantra—and a test. The question posed by the title track of Hendrix's debut album was Paul's shorthand for whether a person had attained self-awareness, and whether you had experimented with drugs. Aimed at me, the song's chorus was another goad from Paul: *"Are you experienced? Have you ever been experienced? Well, I have."*

It started with scotch. Really cheap scotch that Paul brought to the computer room. He got me drunk for the first time, so drunk I threw up and passed out that night in the Lakeside teachers' lounge. That episode was followed days later by a demonstration of how to smoke a joint. And then, of course, Paul argued, I couldn't be truly experienced without trying LSD. I declined.

I felt tremendous pressure that summer. I felt the weight of the trust the school had placed in my ability to come up with a scheduling program in time. Within a month I was supposed to go to Washington, D.C., and serve as a congressional page for part of the summer. (I had done a stint as a House of Representatives page in Olympia during sophomore year and was looking forward to seeing the U.S. Congress.) I couldn't stand the feeling that if we failed, it would be on my shoulders.

Fortunately, the round-the-clock work paid off. Paul and I finished the program on time. In the fall, it worked flawlessly and the code we wrote that summer would be used for many years to come. No longer did kids have to run to their advisors screaming for help. And we got paid.

One legacy of my friendship with Kent was the realization that another person can help you be better. That summer Paul and I forged a partnership that would define the rest of our lives, though we didn't know it at the time. A partner brings something to the relationship that you lack; they inspire you to up your own game. With Paul as my partner, I felt more assured about tackling a challenge that was on the edge of my capabilities. Having someone taking the same risky step alongside you emboldens you to take the next one.

Our work styles, Paul and I learned, were complementary. My approach was rapid-fire, in your face. I prided myself on my processing speed—that I could come up with the right answer, the best answer, on the spot. Impatient, real-time thinking. And I could work and work and work, for days on end, rarely stopping. Paul's style was quieter, calmer. He had a lot going on inside. He mulled things over. He'd listen, process on his own. His intelligence was patient. He could wait for the right answer to arise. And soon it would.

Paul had always been interested in the hardware side of computers. He read every magazine he could find on the nitty-gritty technical advances being made in labs and computer companies. That summer of 1972 he talked a lot about the innovation coming out of a little California company called Intel. I had first heard about the company from Paul in the fall of the previous year. He had shown me an advertisement in *Electronic News* in which Intel announced that it had invented "a micro-programmable computer on a chip." In short, it fit the main functions of a computer onto a single piece of silicon. They called it the 4004 microprocessor.

It was a breakthrough. Computers do what they do thanks to electrical impulses that follow a logical set of instructions. When I was born, in 1955, that job was performed by vacuum tubes (they look like little light bulbs) inside large computers. The fragile glass tubes took up a lot of space, used a lot of power, and generated a lot of heat. Around that same time, engineers invented the silicon transistor—which performed the same function as the tubes but did so via tiny electronic circuits etched onto microchips the size of a thumbnail. Intel took it a leap further by using those circuits to cram most of the brains of a computer onto a single silicon chip.

The 4004 was exciting if you were an electronics enthusiast like Paul, with his cardboard boxes full of old radios and his soldering iron. But it was very limited. Intel had developed it for a Japanese company for use in a handheld calculator. It didn't have the power to do much else.

At the time, Paul told me about a prediction made in the mid-1960s by Gordon Moore, an engineer and cofounder of Intel. Moore had studied the advances in engineering and manufacturing that semiconductor makers were using to etch smaller and smaller circuits onto their chips. The innovations were coming at a rate, Moore predicted, that would double the number of transistors on a chip every year (an estimate he later revised to every two years).

Double every two years? That was exponential growth. When Paul said it, I pictured a line on a graph that rose gradually and then shot up in the shape of a hockey stick. We tend to experience the world in a linear, incremental way: inch by inch, ounce by ounce. The computer industry was no different. For a long time, advances had been gradual, limited by constraints of size, heat generation, and power consumption of the many discrete components wired together to make the brain of a computer. Moore's prediction implied that the speed of microprocessors would increase exponentially. If that happened, a computer that now occupied a whole room would one day fit on a desk. Moore himself wrote that the trend might give birth to "such wonders as home computers."

So, even if the 4004 couldn't do much, future microprocessors might—much, much more. That is, if the prediction held. So far, it had: the latest Intel chip, the 8008, could process data at twice the speed of its predecessor.

Was this it? The brains to a home computer? I looked at the specs and told Paul no. There was no way that the new chip could handle programs that did anything interesting like play games or manage payroll. I told Paul we should wait until Intel came out with something better.

There was one possibility, he said: the traffic-counting work Kent and I had started just before he died. That could be the perfect application for the chip: imagine if we could replace the tedious hand counting and manual data entry with an 8008-based computer. The problem was simple enough that the 8008 could do it, I told him: with a tape reader and software, the machine could convert the punched holes into usable digital data. Maybe we could build the computer that rapidly turns holes on paper into usable traffic data for hundreds if not thousands of cities around the country?

The first step was to find someone to work on the hardware. We visited Paul Gilbert at the University of Washington. Back when we were at C-Cubed, Gilbert was part of a wider circle (though still very small) of kid computer enthusiasts in Seattle. A few years older than us, he was now an electrical engineering major. Through his campus job in the physics lab, he had access to all sorts of electronics tools and equipment. Based on little more than a verbal description of our idea, he agreed to help. Now, where could we get an Intel chip?

In July, Paul Allen wrote a letter to Intel asking some questions about their plans. In a sign of how small the whole industry was back then, a manager wrote back, responding that Intel aimed for a new family of chips in two years—probably by 1974. Paul had also asked where we could buy an 8008. A big electronics parts supplier called Hamilton/Avnet had signed on as Intel's first distributor, the Intel manager wrote. As luck would have it, the company was a major supplier to Boeing. It had a sales office in Seattle.

Which is how in the fall of 1972 Paul and I ended up in the industrial area of South Seattle telling a sales guy we wanted to buy a single Intel 8008 chip. Even now it makes me laugh to imagine how surprised the sales guy at the store must have been, wondering what the heck we were thinking.

I laid down $360 in cash—about $2,400 today—that I had earned from the scheduling-program job. The guy handed over a box that, had we been in a different store, might have held a nice piece of jewelry. My first thought was: *How could something so small be so expensive?*

It's incredible to look back at that moment, knowing the impact of Intel's invention. The doubling of circuits would become known as Moore's Law and the microprocessors would drive the digital revolution that would give us the personal computer and smartphones.

The invention of the microprocessor would prove to be the single most significant event in my professional life. Without it, there would be no Microsoft.

All that, of course, was far in the future for a sixteen-year-old nerd and his nineteen-year-old hippie techie pal. Excited to see what a microprocessor looked like, we ripped open the aluminum wrapper right there in the store to find what resembled a stick of chewing gum with eighteen gold legs. Paranoid that some electrical charge from our hands would fry the thing, we quickly wrapped it back up and got out of there.

CHAPTER NINE

One Act and Five Nines

I n writing my application essay to Harvard, I condensed the full
breadth of my computer background into six hundred words in
that neat cursive font on my mom's Selectric. Starting from the
"fruitful arrangement" with a local company (C-Cubed) and moving
on through payroll, class schedule, and our automatic traffic counters, I told the abridged Tales of the Lakeside Programming Group.
As for my stint teaching, I admitted, "Of all the things I've done
this is the hardest. Usually there are some students in a class who get
very interested and continue working with the computer. . . . On
the other hand, there are students who consider the computer more
of a mystery after I leave than they did when I first came in."

If the admissions officer reading my essay made it through to
the end, they might have been surprised by my conclusion: "Work
with the computer has proved to be a great opportunity to have a lot

of fun, earn some money, and learn a lot. However, I don't plan to continue concentrating in this field. Right now I am most interested in business or law."

In truth, I knew that a career in computers—specifically software—was a possible path, maybe even the most likely one if the microprocessor birthed cheap, general-purpose computers like Paul and I hoped. But in the fall of 1972 that was still a big unknown. For now, to satisfy my own curiosity and as a backup plan, I wanted to explore new worlds.

That summer I had spent a month in Washington, D.C., working as a page at the House of Representatives. It was a fantastic experience living in a boardinghouse with other pages—all high school students—and going to Capitol Hill every day. My time in D.C. coincided with the decision by Democratic vice presidential candidate Thomas Eagleton to drop out of the 1972 race after disclosing he had suffered from depression and other mental health challenges. His running mate, presidential candidate George McGovern, had stood by Eagleton for a couple of weeks but ultimately scrambled to find a replacement. I got caught up in this drama, which was the closest thing to a political thriller I'd ever witnessed. I also tried to capitalize on it. Before Eagleton quit, a friend and I snapped up as many McGovern-Eagleton campaign buttons as we could, betting that he'd resign. When he did, we sold the buttons to congressional staff and anyone else around the Capitol who wanted a collector's item from those eighteen days of history. We used part of our earnings to pay for nice meals and nights out with the other pages.

It's nearly impossible to spend time in Congress, even on that lowest level, and not get swept up by it. That month stimulated me to think more seriously about a career in government and politics, a path that would likely begin with studying law.

Though I drove my college choices and applications, I know my mother was heavily invested in the outcome. The expectation had been set that every Gates kid would attend a great college. I had seen how happy my mom and my dad were with my sister Kristi, then in her second year at the University of Washington. She was studying accounting—a practical major that would surely lead to a good, respectable job in my mom's eyes—and she was deeply involved in student government, just as our mom had been when she was a UW "Husky." I was next up. My mom never explicitly said that Harvard was the goal, but clearly it was.

That fall, my attention was focused on a new role: nervous artist. Surprised by how much I had enjoyed drama class my junior year, I had signed up again. Rather than stressing me out, acting was freeing, I found; with each reading I felt more confident. I was fully aware, though, that any objective observer at Lakeside would have very low expectations of me as an actor. I was the computer guy. And I bristled at the narrow classification. Drama was an attempt to broaden myself, to try something new and see if I could succeed.

The show we put on was *Black Comedy*, by British playwright Peter Shaffer. It's a farce centered on Brindsley, an insecure young artist, and his fiancée, Carol, the debutante daughter of a strict former Army colonel. Over the course of a single night, Brindsley will meet the colonel for the first time as well as a famous art collector, "the world's richest man." If all goes well, nervous Brindsley will win the colonel's approval and get his big break selling a sculpture to the collector. It doesn't go well. A fuse blows, the lights go out, and the characters spend most of the play groping around in what only they perceive as the dark—the audience sees them flooded in light, the better to enjoy the pratfalls and madcap mistaken identities. I had seen the play on our family trip to New York the summer before I started at Lakeside and really liked it. It was an easy play to like, as Brindsley falls over the priceless antique furniture he's "borrowed" to impress the collector and tries to shoo out an ex-girlfriend who appears at an inopportune moment.

Against all expectations, I was given the role of Brindsley. My costar was Vicki Weeks, one of the most popular girls in our senior class. Three afternoons a week, our cast would meet in the chapel to attempt to nail down the play's split-second comic timing.

As far removed as the play was from the passions that had carried me through high school, it turned out to be one of my best experiences at Lakeside. I'd walk into those rehearsals and throw myself into my character. Running around the chapel moving furniture, pretending to grope around in the dark—it was pure, antic fun, made better by the bonding among the cast and crew. It was like those early years in the computer room, but with a key difference: girls. And one girl specifically, Vicki, whose confidence boosted my own and helped me take more risks in my acting. We joked around, calling each other the stupid pet names from the play, "darling" this and "sweetie poo" that. Wrapped in the safety of my character, I got my first practice at flirting. Nervous about blowing the performance, I'd go home, close the door to my room, and run through my lines over and over again.

I hadn't anticipated how rewarding it would feel to venture out of my comfort zone. That was something I was really looking forward to about college: the chance to once again redefine myself. If I went someplace like MIT, I felt I'd be a math nerd surrounded by other math nerds. That prospect sounded too . . . narrow. (Which is why I had blown off my interview at MIT that summer and played pinball instead.) Leafing through the college course catalogs, I saw a tantalizing menu of different possibilities: pure math, cognitive psychology, the politics of war, management theory, advanced chemistry. These were the kinds of classes that could broaden me in all sorts of new ways. As I filled out the applications, I experimented with my persona. As I learned in drama class, each was a performance—one actor, three characters:

To Princeton I said I wanted to be an engineer who knew how to write software. I showed off samples of my code and emphasized my math grades. I told Yale I wanted to get into government work, maybe law. I emphasized my experience in D.C. and highlighted my love for the Boy Scouts and my pursuit of the dramatic arts. To Harvard, as I wrote in my essay, I expressed my interest in business or law.

On the November night we performed *Black Comedy,* I stumbled and sprawled, flailed around in the dark, tried to kiss two separate girls—as was scripted—and didn't miss a line. Our whole cast got kudos for its spontaneity.

From the stage after the performance, I could almost read the faces of my parents. They saw their son, the onetime class clown, surrounded by new friends, in a new realm, demonstrating his social, confident side. They knew that side privately, but like most everyone else in the room, they were taken aback to see it displayed in public. For my part, I felt good. I had set a high bar for myself, and I had cleared it with room to spare. As we took our final curtain call, I committed to a new challenge: at some point, when the time was right, I was going to ask Vicki out.

Right after Christmas, I got a call from the executive at ISI who two years earlier helped Lakeside Programming Group land the payroll project. Bud Pembroke said he was consulting on a project for Bonneville Power Administration, the federal authority that generated and distributed electric power across Washington, Oregon, and California. It was best known for overseeing the massive Grand Coulee Dam on the Columbia River.

BPA was in the process of computerizing its power generation. The big defense and technology contractor TRW was overseeing the job, which involved turning a mostly manual system into one run on a PDP-10 computer, the same computer Lakeside Programming had used for almost all our work. Over budget and past deadline, TRW was casting around the country for PDP-10 experts. At some point their search led to Bud, who led them to Paul and Ric and me.

When the call from Bud came, I had just returned from a week with Paul at Washington State working on our traffic venture, by then called Traf-O-Data. Paul Gilbert had assembled a rough version of the hardware, a tangle of wires and chips housed in a microwave-oven-sized box. But the software wasn't done yet. While we hacked away at it on the Washington State University computer, Paul told me he was already getting tired of school. The classes weren't challenging enough for his quick mind and omnivorous curiosity. He was thinking about taking a leave to get a job.

So when I phoned to tell him about the BPA prospect, Paul didn't hesitate for a moment. He was in. Ric, an electrical engineering major at Stanford, decided to stay in school. (He would end up joining us in the summer.)

Right after Christmas, Paul and I drove his parents' '64 Chrysler New Yorker to the BPA office in Vancouver, Washington, a then somewhat rough town on the border of Oregon. In the car that day we joked how the conversation Bud had with the TRW people must have gone:

"Hey Bud, you know anyone who's any good with PDP-10?"

"Well, there's Gates and Allen."

"Who are they?"

"Couple of kids."

At the interview we made clear we knew the machines inside and out. We also brought printouts of code we had written for the scheduling program and for our traffic venture. I'm not sure how much came down to our skill versus their desperation, but we got the job.

It seemed like a great gig. We'd be paid by the hour, and as at C-Cubed and ISI, we assumed we'd have plenty of free time to work on our side projects. Paul immediately filed the paperwork to take a leave of absence from school.

The night we got back, I told my parents that we'd been offered a job at a premier company and one of the most significant utilities in the country. I explained that our expertise was needed on an important project, and it would be great exposure, and plus we would get paid. What about school? my mother asked. This was my senior year, and I needed a strong finish for college admissions. I was sure it wouldn't be a problem. She wasn't convinced. Your son abandoning his great high school to live on his own hundreds of miles from home was a big departure from the script.

So that week, my mother, my father, and I went to see Lakeside's always wise headmaster, Dan Ayrault. I made my pitch. I would miss the second trimester—just two months—and be back to finish the school year and attend graduation. I'd been pretty certain that Dan would side with me, and he delivered. Not only did Few-Rules Dan think it wouldn't be a problem, he even suggested the time could be used as an independent study and count toward graduation.

When I was a kid in the mid-1960s, I was a big fan of *The Time Tunnel,* a sci-fi show where the main characters, two scientists, traveled back and forth across time to places real and imagined. I'd stay up on Thursday nights and watch these guys try to save the *Titanic* or tangle with arrows in Sherwood Forest or outrun lava from the great Krakatoa. The show was set in a huge control room deep in the ground, where a team of scientists in white lab coats turned dials and punched commands into a computer to send their colleagues through time and into their latest sticky situation.

My very first thought when I saw our new job site: *This is the control room from* The Time Tunnel—*only better!* A wall-sized screen tracked the state of the power grid and every dam and power facility in the Northwest. There were rows and rows of computer terminals, each with the latest cathode-ray tube monitors—with color graphic screens! The ceiling was so high, guys scrambled up and down long ladders to adjust lights and fine-tune displays.

The control room was the heart of an electrical system serving the West. It took power from the Grand Coulee and other dams throughout the Northwest, along with additional sources such as coal plants, and channeled it to millions of homes and businesses. Bonneville generated that power mostly through hydroelectric dams. The trick was to match fluctuating power supply with fluctuating demand. The company had always done that by hand—workers calling each other and saying "turn up power from this dam" or "turn back power from that dam," then literally turning dials. Our job was to computerize that process.

That was simple to say, but not to do. DEC had engineered the PDP-10 and its TOPS-10 operating system to handle advanced, real-time tasks in which every microsecond counted, such as controlling production on an automobile factory floor. But even that was a straightforward job compared to the challenge facing TRW. They had to program the computer to sift through a deluge of data—on power usage, dam capacity, and anything that affected supply and demand of electricity—and flawlessly make instantaneous decisions about balancing the supply and demand.

At first, I didn't grasp the weight of this task. Early on we were sitting in a meeting when one of the programmers said something about "five nines." I had no idea what he was talking about. As I listened, I figured out that he meant that the computer system we were building had to assure that power would be running 99.999 percent of the time—five nines. That level of efficiency would mean downtime of just 5.26 minutes a year—virtually uninterrupted power. Nothing I had ever worked on required such near perfection. I thought they were joking.

The TRW guys explained to us that the utility had to maintain uninterrupted power even as electricity supply and demand fluctuated. Typically, demand rises during the morning as people get up and turn on their appliances, then peaks in the afternoon and early evening when people get home from work, crank up the heat or air-conditioning, turn on the lights, watch TV, and so on.

Even at 2 a.m., power is needed for streetlights, hospitals, police and fire stations, and all-night diners. That baseload demand, as it's called, requires power plants that can churn out a steady supply of electricity.

The *Time Tunnel* room was a testament to that culture: Bonneville's grid displayed on a big wall in lights and screens. At any moment you could see in full color where power flowed through the grid—and if there were disruptions.

I arrived in January as confident of myself and my coding abilities as I had ever been. I had four years of computer experience, mostly on the very machines Bonneville used. I'd worked on the payroll program, the school scheduling program was a hit, and I had my own company that was going to automate traffic studies in American cities.

The first task they gave me was to document error messages, which meant writing in simple language messages that would pop up any time there was a problem with the system. It wasn't a particularly creative or interesting job. Still, I threw myself into the work. Paul and I got there early every day and put in long hours. Over time, they gave us increasingly more significant jobs.

I prided myself on writing code fast, in long stretches of intense work. I can only imagine what the seasoned professional programmers at Bonneville thought of the kid working like a maniac late into every night, burning out code and eating Tang powdered drink mix straight from the jar until his tongue turned orange. I broke my record for sustained work that spring, once not leaving the *Time Tunnel* underground for nearly a hundred hours straight. That meant not showering and hardly eating for nearly four days.

One morning I came in and saw on my desk a printout of code I had written the night before, covered in blue ink. Someone had gone through and, like a schoolteacher, corrected my work. It was more than that, actually. The person had completely torn it apart— he wasn't just fixing syntactical issues, but the whole structure and design of what I had written. Normally, my first reaction would have been to defend myself. If anyone at Lakeside tried to critique my code, I might snap: "No way. You're wrong." But this time, as I sat reading the comments, studying the code, I thought to myself, *Oh wow, this guy's so right.*

The man's name was John Norton, a programmer TRW had sent in to help save the troubled project. Tall with close-cropped black hair, John was in his late thirties and, I would find out later, had a reputation for high-quality code-writing and one catastrophic failure. In his late twenties, John oversaw the software that controlled a key part of the 1962 Mariner 1 space probe. The Venus-bound probe made history when NASA destroyed it minutes into its flight after controllers realized its radar systems weren't working. The source of the problem was a tiny glitch—likely one missing "-" in computer code John Norton oversaw. Legend has it that Norton was so haunted by the error that for years he carried a newspaper story of the Mariner fiasco in his wallet, neatly folded like a piece of origami.

I had never met anyone as vigilant and sharp about computer coding. He consistently returned my work with corrections that raised it to levels I didn't know existed. He was quiet, confident, and always focused on the job in front of him. It was never about his achievements, but about how he could channel his knowledge to make the work better and the project successful.

The axiom that you learn more from your failures than your successes is trite but absolutely true. Up to that point I had spent more time thinking about code and syntax than probably any other teenager alive. But Norton opened a completely new level to me. With his firm tutoring, I got a lesson not just in writing better code but about my self-perception. I remember thinking: *Why am I so arrogant about this programming stuff? How do I even know that I'm that good?* I started to consider what near-perfect computer code would *look* like.

In March I called home. My dad picked up the phone, and I could sense he was excited about something. "Son, we received a letter from Harvard." I heard him tear open the envelope. "This is to certify that William Henry Gates . . . is hereby admitted to Harvard College," he read. I could practically feel my mother's pride coursing through the phone cord. I had already gotten into Yale, and in a month Princeton would notify me that I was accepted. But without even having to say it, everyone in Gatesland knew I would pick Harvard.

I spent the next three months back in Seattle wrapping up my senior year and spending time with the drama crew, including Vicki, rehearsing for our final show, a bunch of short skits written by the great deadpan absurdist James Thurber. I performed "The Night the Bed Fell," a monologue that put me onstage alone for nearly ten minutes weaving Thurber's wacky tale of a family's overreaction after the narrator's bed tips over on him.

Vicki and a few others in our class decided to organize a prom, the first since Lakeside merged with St. Nick's. It was set up as a low-key affair, to include everyone in our class, without pomp or circumstance. That seemed like low-enough stakes for me to ask Vicki to go as my date. A few nights before the prom I screwed up the courage to call her. Every time I dialed her number I got a busy signal. I dialed over and over, and at one point added the challenge of dialing the phone with my foot. Finally, around ten o'clock, Vicki's brother picked up. He went to get her out of bed.

"Hello."

"Vicki, this is Bill . . . Bill Gates," I remembered to add, though I'm sure she recognized my signature high voice. I told her I'd been trying her all night but couldn't get through and had even dialed with my toes, perhaps not the best way to make the case for myself as a dashing date. I circled around my main question: "What are you doing Saturday night?"

"Oh, I thought I'd go to the prom," she said.

"Well, would you like to go with me?"

"Will you give me until tomorrow?" She explained that there was a guy she was hoping would ask her; if he didn't, she'd let me know. The next day on the Lakeside quad she broke the news: her guy came through. She couldn't have been kinder, but she made it clear she saw me as a friend. It took me a while to get over the rejection; I shied away from making myself vulnerable for a while after that. I did go to the prom, though, and I had a great time with a very cool junior, even though I suspect we were each other's backup dates.

As is tradition at many high schools in America, Lakeside seniors skip a day of school in the spring for a chance to relax together before everyone heads their separate ways. For Lakeside Class of 1973, Senior Sneak took my class on a short ferry ride to Bainbridge Island, where we all spent a night at the sprawling home of a class-mate. For a while I hung around with Vicki and the popular crowd, but eventually they went off on their own and I found a few strag-glers. I had smoked some pot earlier, so I was feeling a bit unin-hibited when a friend offered me acid. I had always resisted Paul's assertion that I needed to "be experienced" by taking LSD. This time, I decided to see what it was all about. Part of the trip was exhilarating, but I took the drug not realizing that I'd still be feeling its effects the next morning as I arrived at the orthodontist's office for some long-scheduled dental surgery. I sat gaping at my doctor's face, his drill grinding away, unsure if what I was seeing and feeling was really happening. *Am I going to jump out of this chair and just leave?* I vowed that if I ever dropped acid again, I wouldn't do it solo and I wouldn't do it when I had plans for the next day, especially a dental procedure.

After graduation I spent my summer back in Vancouver, toggling between all-nighters in the Time Tunnel coding with Paul and water-skiing on the Columbia River, where one of the Bonneville engineers kept a boat. Ric, on break from Stanford, joined us. We still sometimes referred to ourselves as the Lakeside Programming Group, but it never felt right without Kent.

The three of us lived together in a run-down Vancouver apartment. Late at night we'd use the Bonneville PDP-10 to work on our side jobs, writing software for our traffic-counting venture and helping Lakeside update the class-scheduling program. I was working crazy hours, subsisting on Tang and pizza; it felt like the most free and easy time I'd had in my life.

The TRW engineers teased me about my oddball work habits ("You are one weird dude" was something I heard a lot that summer), but they were also incredibly supportive. They overlooked my age and immaturity and let me into their circle. I felt accepted, like I belonged, the way I did with my hiking friends and the computer-room bunch at Lakeside.

The engineers got a kick out of my eagerness to take on whatever they threw at me. They'd give me an assignment just to see how fast and how well—or not—I could write it, knowing that I'd spend all night trying. Sometimes they had already written the code themselves, so when I was done, I'd compare my work to theirs, absorbing lessons from their smarter subroutines and clever algorithms.

That summer I thought a lot about how a person becomes the very best at something. Norton was such a commanding figure, peerless in his talent and professionalism. I tried to understand what he had that other programmers didn't. What does it take to be 20 percent better than everyone else? How much is that just latent talent versus dedicated effort—being relentlessly focused and deliberate about performing better today than you did the day before? And then repeating that tomorrow and the next day and the next for years and years?

I was well along that path in programming—so much so that the TRW guys tried to convince me that I should skip college. Don't bother with an undergraduate degree, they said. They prodded me to leapfrog to graduate school, study computer programming, and then get a job at Digital Equipment Corp. "You belong there," one of the programmers said. "You belong back there working with those guys, deciding what the next version of the operating system will be."

That was a wild idea. On the occasions that DEC engineers swooped into Bonneville that summer, I'd seen how the Bonneville programmers—exceptional in their own right—deferred to the specialized knowledge and clear hotshot status of the DEC guys. The notion that people thought I was talented enough to be one of them was a big boost to my confidence. DEC held an almost mythic stature in my imagination; during our career research project, Kent and I had absorbed every detail we could find about the company. I knew the story of how in 1957 the engineers Ken Olsen and Harlan Anderson left their jobs at MIT to start DEC with just a four-page business plan and a $70,000 investment. At the time, IBM was the industry giant, and its million-dollar mainframe computers were considered unbeatable. The idea that an upstart company could carve out a place for itself seemed like a pipe dream. Olsen and Anderson had started small, first making electronic testing equipment, and then steadily built a profitable business over a few years before launching DEC's first computer. Within a decade, DEC was the envy of corporate America and Olsen lauded as its visionary founder. DEC's story made the notion that we could create a successful company seem possible.

Paul was ready to get going. Early that summer, he pushed me to forgo Harvard. He said he'd extend his leave from college. We could start small, like DEC did, develop our nascent traffic venture and its single-use computer, and then expand, become consultants, work on interesting projects like Bonneville, all while writing software for that new universe of microprocessors that Intel had recently pioneered.

I played devil's advocate, and pointed out why I thought many of his ideas and technological visions didn't make business sense—at least not in the near future. I also wasn't convinced that any of the endeavors he pitched were big enough opportunities for me to drop my plans for college. I was briefly tempted by the idea of skipping right to graduate school, however, and even floated the idea by my parents. They didn't like it. The truth was that I really wanted to go to college. I wanted the chance to see how I stacked up against the other brainy kids from a much wider pool than Lakeside.

My view at the time was that advances in the world sprang from individuals. I pictured the proverbial lone genius, the solo scientist working tirelessly in their field, pushing themselves until they had a breakthrough. My small taste of that was the success we had with the scheduling program. Even months after we delivered that software, I still felt profound satisfaction with the whole project, a mathematical proof that, once translated into computer code, improved hundreds of lives. In the grand scheme of things, it was a modest achievement. But it fed my imagination of what I might be able to achieve. I thought one path could be mathematics. Did I have a brain that could find the solution to a centuries-old math theorem or hatch a scientific solution that could improve life? It seemed far-fetched, but I wanted to see how far I could go.

My solo-scientist view of the world was grist for an on-and-off debate with Paul. He saw the world advancing through collaboration, in which teams of smart people pulled together toward a common goal. Where I saw Einstein as the model, he saw the Manhattan Project. Both views were simplistic, though in time his would define both of our futures.

As the weeks passed, that philosophical debate became the backdrop for a very real argument over the Lakeside job. In our spare time at TRW, we were continuing the work updating the schedule ahead of the coming school year. Just like the previous summer, I worried that we wouldn't get it done on time. We fell into a predictable pattern: Paul came up with ideas for the schedule that I would shoot down, usually because, as the original designer of the program, I simply understood its underlying math and structure better than he did. We'd argue, and then I'd go off and code it the way I thought made sense. Our spats over the schedule weren't helped by the fact that we were spending all our time together. Every meal. Every movie. Every day at work. It was natural that we'd get on each other's nerves.

We were arguing one night as we left the Time Tunnel for dinner and headed to the parking lot. Often, like drivers at Le Mans, we'd run to our cars—me to the Mustang borrowed from my dad and Paul to his Chrysler—and then race to whatever restaurant we had decided upon. That's probably why I made a beeline for the car. Whatever the reason, I ran ahead of Paul. At some point during the day, someone had strung a rope across the entrance to the parking lot. In my haste and in the dark, I failed to notice the rope catch my waist. I also didn't notice the rope growing tighter and tighter as I ran until, *whoosh,* it slingshotted me backwards onto the pavement. Paul ambled over and stared down at me. We laughed ourselves sick.

The stress of living and working together grated particularly on Paul, who decided one day to exit both of our little ventures. In a letter he left in my bedroom, he wrote: "Recently I have had the growing conviction that our work and discussions and even living together was unsatisfactory, at least from my point of view." He said he felt that I disrespected his ideas, his intelligence, and the "time had come to sever all of our connections" related to the Lakeside schedule and Traf-O-Data. In language that read to me like a divorce settlement, Paul wrote that "I hereby void my interest in scheduling . . . I hereby void my interest in the traffic machine. It's all yours (100%)." The handwritten letter included a space for our signatures. At the very bottom he wrote: "P.S. I'm serious."

I didn't sign. I assumed that when we both settled down, our relationship would find its equilibrium. In the meantime, though,

I left. Without bothering to pack my things, I drove to Seattle and worked at Lakeside around the clock to finish the schedule just in time for the deadline. I ended up not returning to Bonneville; Ric was kind enough to bring my stuff back to Seattle.

The dynamic between Paul and me had always been complicated, a blend of love and rivalry similar to how brothers might feel. Usually our differences in temperament, style, and interests came together for the good. Those differences propelled us forward and made each other better. But that summer was an early test of a partnership that would continue to evolve. I was seventeen, Paul was twenty. We still had a long way to go.

Within a couple of months Paul and I had started speaking again. By then he was back at Washington State University, and I was starting my first year at Harvard. We made peace and resumed work on Traf-O-Data, as I reported to Ric in a letter, thanking him for his role in helping us reach a detente:

"I'm sure you know Paul and I are on the forward road again (and a long road it is proving to be) on a completely equal and somewhat enthusiastic basis. I really want to thank you for the special friendship you showed Paul and I in a particularly trying time for both of us. I really like to think we both would have realized the ridiculousness of our positions at some point anyway. Being kind enough to take all the stuff I left down in the apartment back to my house was an extension of the personal consideration you showed all summer. I wish I could have been the same, though, all in all it was a really great summer . . . your friend, Trey."

CHAPTER TEN

Precocious

I n the dark hours one Sunday morning of 1969, a U.S. Army truck rumbled onto the Harvard campus. Men in fatigues unloaded large crates containing a gift of sorts from the U.S. Department of Defense: pieces of a DEC mainframe computer that had been disassembled in Vietnam, where it had been installed as part of the war effort. The parts, big as refrigerators, were uncrated in Harvard's Aiken Computation Laboratory, where technicians connected them to form a PDP-10, just like the models I had been programming for five years by the time I arrived on campus in the fall of 1973.

The nighttime delivery successfully dodged the antiwar protesters who had been agitating against universities' participation in defense-related research. The chanting students weren't exactly wrong: the military was probably the computer industry's biggest customer back then, and Cold War fear of the Soviet Union was driving lots of public money into university work on automated systems to guide missiles, pilot submarines, and detect ICBM launches.

By the time I arrived in Cambridge for freshman orientation, years of major government investments in defense technology had remade the Boston area. DEC and dozens of other companies in the region had spun out of projects at MIT to build computers and other technologies for military use. Before Silicon Valley took its place as America's high-tech hub, the sixty-mile Route 128 around Boston held the title.

I got a window into that legacy of government money the first time I walked into Harvard's Aiken Computation Laboratory a few weeks after school started. I was there to meet the lab's director. In the lobby, I saw a hulking machine with a sign that explained it was the Mark I, a proto-computer developed by Howard Aiken, for whom the lab was named. As a Navy commander in the 1940s, Aiken worked with IBM to create the Mark I as a tool for calculating the trajectory of missiles. It was later used in the Manhattan Project. The Mark I was a breakthrough in its time, a mass of wheels and electric relays that was basically a fifty-foot-long calculator, a machine able to add, subtract, multiply, and divide faster than a human. By the time I laid eyes on the Mark I, it was just a portion of the original, a nonworking museum piece.

Across the hallway, I could see the room with the Harv-10—as Aiken Lab had dubbed its government-donated PDP-10. DARPA, the Defense Department's Advanced Research Projects Agency, was funding Aiken so that Harvard's engineering faculty and students could use the system to experiment with new ways of programming to make software faster, more reliable, and less expensive. The agency had also wired up a connection that tied Harv-10 into the ARPA Network, which became better known as ARPANET. Aiken was one of a few dozen computer centers around the country that had begun testing email and other new communications protocols, the bricks that would become the foundation of the internet.

That fall I knew nothing about the Aiken Lab's government connections. My thinking only went so far as (1) Wow, Harvard has a PDP-10!, and (2) I have to get access to it. I didn't realize at the time that the lab was largely off-limits to undergraduates. It was the domain of graduate students, most of whom were doing research under its director, Tom Cheatham. Professor Cheatham came to Harvard after stints in the computer industry and the government. He was the overseer of the Harv-10, the person who directed how it was used and who could use it. To me, he was merely the signature I needed.

In much of academia, computers were not yet a serious area of study in their own right. Computer science at most universities typically nested within more established departments, such as at Harvard, where it was part of Engineering and Applied Physics. The pride of that department was fluid dynamics, a field built on centuries of elegant math invented to describe how birds fly and blood flows. Computer science might be a nice tool to study those phenomena but was in no way seen as an equal. Typically, a student interested in computers majored in applied math or engineering. It would be another ten years before Harvard offered an undergraduate degree in computer science.

For those reasons and my own pride, I told Cheatham that I wasn't going to take any computer classes—except maybe some advanced graduate courses—but I still wanted to use his computer lab. That first meeting set the tone for our relationship for the rest of my time at Harvard. Me, the hyperkinetic kid practically jumping out of my chair as I spoke, and he, the busy lab director with more pressing things to do, taking drags on a Parliament cigarette until I was done.

I spun stories of our Lakeside Programming Group and all that I had done since first learning to program at age thirteen. I told him I skipped part of my senior year to work at TRW on the power grid serving millions of customers. I talked about Traf-O-Data and the customers we would surely attract as we exploited the power of the microprocessor—which, I said, was going to change everything! The hulking machines we were used to would be the size of matchbooks—and their cost would shrink with it!

I was used to wowing adults with my grasp of what was still an arcane world. Even the veteran programmers at C-Cubed and TRW were amused by my sheer enthusiasm for the topic and drive to learn more. Professor Cheatham, however, seemed uninterested. I felt intimidated. He was the director of the lab, after all.

I later learned that administrative tasks—signing students' study cards and managing the day-to-day of the lab—were his least favorite parts of his job. Cheatham was a programmer at heart. Behind his swivel chair was a terminal connected to the Harv-10 computer. It was there he worked on designing new languages, when he wasn't off meeting with Defense Department brass and securing more funding for the lab.

After thirty minutes of my enthusiastic spiel, he stubbed out his cigarette and signed my form. I would later learn that Cheatham had a reputation for giving his students autonomy and letting them experiment. He was open to new ideas. What I took as lack of interest was probably a combination of that openness and a desire to get an annoying kid out of his office so he could swivel back to the software he was writing. Whatever the reason, by the end of the day I had a key to the lab and my own account, number 4114, as well as a slightly bruised sense of my own exceptionality.

As an entering freshman, I won an academic award that allowed me to choose the type of roommates I wanted to live with. I liked the idea of being thrown together with different kinds of people. In D.C. I'd found it fun hearing the stories of other pages, all from a wide range of backgrounds. I figured Harvard would offer the same opportunity, so I asked to room with a foreign student and a person of color.

Walking into room A-11 Wigglesworth Hall—Wigg A for short—I met Sam Znaimer, from Montreal, which, I guess, technically made him a foreign student, and Jim Jenkins, a Black engineering major from Tennessee. I immediately got a lesson in my own privileged upbringing. Sam had shown up a week or two earlier than the rest of us for his student job as a janitor, cleaning showers and toilets before the excited hordes moved into the dorms. He had to work for his tuition. In time he would tell me about his background as the son of two Holocaust survivors who met as refugees growing up in an insular Jewish community. His father ran a one-man kids' shoe store, and his mom was a waitress. He was kind of goofy like me, and I liked him immediately. Jim was a self-declared military brat who had moved around as a kid but was proudly Southern, proud of his taste in certain Southern comic books and potato chips that I had never heard of. He too worked, disappearing on weekends for a job at a nearby Air Force base.

The three of us went to register for classes. To satisfy the humanities requirement, I chose Greek classics—Ulysses, Antigone, and all that—partly because I had taken the Lakeside version of the class, and partly because the Harvard professor who taught the class was legendary. I thought it would be fun and easy and leave me time for hard classes. Flipping through the course catalog over the summer, I had found an engineering class that offered independent study around design and research—any project in any field of your interest, including, the listing said, electronic circuits, heat power engineering, and, crucially, computer applications. I figured the class was so open-ended I could work on anything I wanted to explore. I signed up.

In the math section I saw the course numbers started at 1a—Analytic Geometry and Introduction to Calculus—and moved upward from there. Near the bottom of the course list, just before the independent study options, I found the highest number offered to freshmen: Math 55A and 55B, a two-course sequence in Advanced

Calculus. I liked the prominent warning in the description: "Students whose interest in mathematics is casual should not elect them nor should they be chosen on the basis of a vague desire for 'theoretical' mathematics." Students had to pass a qualifying exam just to get into the class.

I could tell that warning was meant to divide prospective math majors into the two wings of mathematics. One, pure math, was the prestigious one, the highest form of intellectual work, where the only equipment you need is your brain, pencil and paper, chalk and a blackboard. Pure mathematicians are the beautiful minds on the cutting edge; they describe their achievements as "discoveries." Anything in the "applied" wing of mathematics was seen as the suburbs of academia, where people merely used the tools that the pioneers had invented decades or even centuries earlier to perform work that was useful, sure, but not "pure."

At Lakeside, I had finished the most challenging math classes that the school offered. I had scored a perfect 800 on the math half of the SAT and received the top score on the Calculus Advanced Placement exam. Math 55 looked like a door to the pure math world. Only a tiny fraction of people could unlock it. I signed up, took the entrance test later that week, and passed it.

At 11 a.m. on the first Monday of classes, I walked into the Math 55A classroom in Sever Hall to find about eighty other students—more than I had expected. Nearly all of them were male.

Standing at the blackboard was a young professor with frizzy red hair and an equally red beard so bushy it smudged the words he was chalking onto the blackboard: "Finite dimensional vector spaces," the title of chapter 1 in the Xeroxed class notes he would hand out every week. The chalk squeaked out a list of some of the topics we'd cover in upcoming classes: axioms, fields, tuples, complex and imaginary numbers, vector spaces, isomorphisms, and a handful of others, all the way through differential equations. I had only a vague acquaintance with some of these—what the heck was a Banach space? But I recognized enough of them to know that math majors who did not take Math 55 would spend six semesters or more studying what we would cover in two. This was going to be intense. On one side of the blackboard, the redheaded teacher had written his name: John Mather.

My classmates were soon buzzing about Mather. He had made full professor in record time, at age twenty-eight. At six years old, when his peers were learning to read, Mather was already learning logarithms. He would sit at his family's dining room table, legs dangling from the chair, talking math with his father, a professor of electrical engineering at Princeton. By age eleven, Mather was absorbing calculus from his father's engineering textbooks. While in high school, he spent almost all his free time buried in books on topology, abstract algebra, and, yes, finite dimensional vector spaces. He was the first high school student allowed to take math classes at Princeton University. As an undergraduate at Harvard, he placed in the top ten in the nation in the Putnam Competition, an annual math Olympics for college students. A year later, he did it again. He was only twenty-four when he finished his PhD at Princeton, with a dissertation that laid out a major discovery, now known as the Malgrange-Mather Preparation Theorem, and had published a flurry of papers cracking a vexing problem in singularity theory so thoroughly that a colleague would later write that he "completely answered the question and in some sense killed the subject because there was nothing more to say."

Mather's career would bring further breakthroughs and countless awards. But based on what I knew of him even then, as our thirty-one-year-old professor, it was clear that preternatural talent and an early start were indispensable to becoming a world-class mathematician.

By the second Monday of Math 55, about half of us remained,

and by the end of the first month we were down to twenty-five. To survive, we realized we'd have to team up. Maybe as a herd we'd avoid being culled.

That's how I got to know Andy and Jim, who would become two of my closest friends at Harvard. They were both typical of the remaining Math 55ers. In sixth grade, Andy Braiterman taught himself algebra in three weeks while laid up in bed with pneumonia; in high school he skipped ahead and finished calculus—two years before I did. He was one of the youngest in our class, having entered Harvard at just sixteen. Jim Sethna was the son of a chemist mother and a father who had studied at MIT and was head of the aerospace engineering department at the University of Minnesota.

Andy and Jim lived in a quad on the third floor of Wigg A, directly above my room. A group of us from Math 55 started meeting in their suite's lounge to work through the weekly problem sets. Mather had created all the problems himself—there was no textbook designed for a course like this. The Xeroxed notes Mather handed out every week were of surprisingly little help.

"There are no numbers!" someone shrieked. Mather didn't break problems down into steps or explain how the concepts might be used in the real world. The handouts just signposted what we were supposed to have learned . . . somehow. It was up to us to go find books and solve problems that would unpack these concepts.

I hadn't seen anything like it. And though I had survived the culling, it was unclear where in the herd that left me.

The heart of the Aiken Lab was the Harv-10, the donated computer. It took up a big chunk of the room, five or six hulking boxes along one wall that were connected to a dozen or so terminals. Most of the users of the center were there because of the PDP-10. It was the tool for graduate students under Cheatham working on compilers, assemblers, and creating an experimental programming language called ECL.

Some chemistry post-docs working with Professor E. J. Corey were using AI software known as LHASA that they had developed to help synthesize new molecules for medicine, plastics, and other industrial applications. (Corey's advances in that area eventually earned him a Nobel Prize and a National Medal of Science.) I was amazed by the computer graphics. The program could actually draw the shapes of the molecules as they were built, atom by atom.

My first day in the lab, I noticed another computer sitting idle in the far corner. It looked like a command center for a space launch. Most computers back then didn't have their own screens, but this one had four round CRT displays arranged along an L-shaped desk. On the desk was a RAND tablet and stylus, one of the first tools for converting handwriting and hand-drawn shapes into images on a computer screen. It was an $18,000 ancestor of the pen tablets that decades later became ubiquitous tools for digital artists.

The centerpiece of this display desk was a DEC PDP-1. I knew about the PDP-1; it was the first computer model DEC sold. But I had never used one. It was one of the earliest "interactive" computers, which meant that a user could work directly with the machine, an option not available on mainframes locked in rooms or housed miles away. DEC priced it at $120,000, a fraction of the $2 million a mainframe computer might cost back then. DEC made the PDP-1 for only a decade, selling just over fifty of them. If the PDP-10 at the time was the equivalent to a late-1960s muscle car—known for raw power—the PDP-1 was a '57 Chevy—old, not so fast, but with lots of style.

Arriving in labs in the early 1960s, the PDP-1 was an instant hit with hackers who wanted nothing more than the freedom to tinker directly with a computer. A PDP-1 that DEC gave MIT was legendary for helping spawn a generation of influential hackers who learned by creating programs that were frivolous but cool for their time, playing tunes like a carnival organ and displaying an endless stream of snowflake patterns. I knew of the PDP-1 mostly due to *Spacewar!*. Steve Russell, one of the computer legends we met at C-Cubed, had told Paul and me the story of how he used the MIT PDP-1 to coax that groundbreaking video game into being.

Although the Aiken PDP-1 was outdated by then, its displays and input devices still made it a great tool for displaying and interacting with computer graphics. On one of my first visits to the lab, Eric Roberts, a graduate student in applied math, had walked me through its recent history. See those loose wires hanging from the back of the computer rack? That's where Ivan Sutherland connected his head-mounted virtual reality device, the great grandfather of the more refined VR headsets that would arrive decades later. By then, Sutherland was already famous for creating Sketchpad, software that was a precursor to the graphical user interface that would become standard on all computers. Fifteen years later Sutherland would win a Turing Award (the computer science equivalent of a Nobel Prize) for Sketchpad and be recognized as one of the fathers of computer graphics.

Eric pointed to a joystick on the desk in front of the PDP-1. That device, along with several switches and buttons, he said, were the controllers to an innovative flight simulator built in 1967 by Danny Cohen, one of Sutherland's students. It was the first known proof that a sophisticated simulation could run on a limited general-purpose computer.

He explained that a few years later, Cohen, by then a Harvard professor, worked with two graduate students to soup up the flight simulator. Their idea was radical at the time: harness the powers of three different computers connected over ARPANET. The PDP-1 did a great job displaying graphics and had all those nifty displays, and the joystick. But it was slow and not capable of producing a realistic flying experience. Eric told me that a graduate student named

Ed Taft devised software for the old computer to offload its heavy processing to the more powerful Harvard PDP-10 and another computer miles away at MIT. The experiment was a breakthrough, proving that 3D graphics and programs could work between computers over ARPANET—the proto-internet.

Cohen had recently left Harvard for the University of Southern California, and the two graduate students, Taft and Bob Metcalfe, had started jobs at Xerox PARC, the copier maker's innovative research arm. (In time, Cohen and his colleagues would become known for major contributions to software and networking: Taft joined Adobe, where he helped birth PostScript and PDF; Metcalfe co-invented the Ethernet networking technology and started the company 3Com.)

Hearing about these experiments gave me an idea for my independent study. I liked the idea of connecting the graphics-capable PDP-1 with the more powerful machine across the room. Instead of the view from a plane cockpit, I pictured a 3D baseball park, with the computer's displays each offering a different real-time camera angle of the game. A player would use the joystick and other PDP-1 controls to pitch, hit, and catch, with the computer sending data over ARPANET for the PDP-10 to calculate the complex physics of ball speed, trajectory, and a runner rounding the bases. It would be a tough program to write, requiring a lot of work to simulate the complexity of a real game. How do you train a computer to animate a player scooping up a ground ball, or stretching for a pop fly? What does the shortstop do when there's a single to left field with runners on first and third?

I wrote a proposal for a "three-dimensional, three-camera interactive graphics system" (aka a computer baseball game) and brought it to Tom Cheatham. I asked if he would be my faculty sponsor on the project. He seemed excited by the idea and signed on.

A baseball simulation was a deliberately ambitious plan. I had sold my programming skills to Cheatham. A part of me wanted to prove to him that I could live up to my own hype. Graphics and networking were two of the hottest areas in computing at the time. Both fields were in their infancy. That left lots of room for innovation and chances for a person to make a mark. Maybe I could follow in the footsteps of these other graphics pioneers. At the very least I figured I could make a cool game that my friends and I could play.

The Aiken Lab was supposed to have a faculty overseer—an associate director under Cheatham—but that job had been vacant for some time. Instead, like a lot of university computer labs back then, Aiken was run by the community of its users, a sort of self-governing cooperative of about two dozen grad students, researchers, and random hackers. These were the people who knew the quirks of the lab's computers and how to fix them when they broke. One person might know how to restore files while another could coax the system back up when it crashed. All were more than willing to help if anyone had a question. If there was a de facto leader in this group, it was Eric Roberts. Eric had a programming addiction completely familiar to me. Thanksgiving break for Eric meant arriving at Aiken Wednesday night, coding until he fell asleep at the terminal, skipping the next day's turkey, and staying through Sunday night, subsisting on candy from the machine and a couple of greasy burgers from the cafeteria. When he wasn't working on his own projects, Eric was writing user manuals, fixing the DECtape unit, or playing doctor on call for the PDP-1. When the aging machine broke down, Eric showed up with an oscilloscope and breathed it back to life using transplanted parts from a donor machine nearby.

I very quickly fell into the easygoing, democratic culture of the place. No rules other than the commonsense understanding that you stay out of the way of anyone deep in research or closing in on their thesis project. Other than that, you had free use, twenty-four hours a day. That is why in the fall of my freshman year, I quickly acquired a reputation for leaving my friends for Aiken, where I stayed long into the night trying to get my virtual baseball players onto the field.

Jim and Andy's third-floor suite became our clubhouse, and while the rest of the dorm was partying over garbage cans of ZaRex fruit punch and vodka, we puzzled through math problems, hung out, and drew one another into debates or questions that tested our thinking skills or trivia knowledge: What's larger, Bulgaria or Czechoslovakia? How many gas stations are there in the United States? One added benefit of the suite was that Jim and Andy's roommate had one of the only stereos around. I bought two LPs: Hendrix's *Are You Experienced,* because Paul had instilled in me that it was cool and so having it made me cool; the other one, the one I mostly played, was *Donovan's Greatest Hits.* The smooth Scottish singer and his tune "Mellow Yellow" relaxed me. It was good music to sit and think to. (My Donovan obsession was such that more than twenty years later Andy gave me a copy of the CD as a gag wedding gift.)

There was a certain purity to friendships back then that I appreciate more now than I did at the time. The mundane things friends do at that age, hardly notable in the moment, teach you about one another in small doses, and bond you over time. We'd travel as a pack—Sam Znaimer, Jim Jenkins, Jim Sethna, Andy Braiterman, and I—to the cafeteria to eat, or to the Wigg A basement to burn up hours playing pinball, or to the Freshman Union to watch the news.

It was the year that *Roe v. Wade* guaranteed the right to abortion and the year of Nixon's "I'm not a crook" declaration. America's slow exit from Vietnam began and the draft was suspended. These headlines were the backdrop of life in 1973, but my friends and I were mostly focused on a narrower set of concerns. We talked math, physics, history, food, and occasionally girls, though none of us had much interaction with them aside from the few classmates in Math 55.

Harvard back then held mixers that brought coeds together for drinks and dancing, often at nearby women's colleges like Pine Manor. For these rare occasions, I bought myself an expensive brown leather jacket that I paired with blue velvet bell-bottoms, which in my mind put me at the peak of 1970s fashion. My Wigg A posse and I never had any luck meeting women at these parties, though guys in our wider circle would come back claiming they had. Almost in unison the rest of us would stammer, "How do you do that?"

Math 55 problem sets were due every Monday morning. Every Sunday night, a group of us would gather in Andy and Jim's suite. Together we'd try to take the abstract problems Mather posed, give them shape and mold concrete, correct answers. They never came easily. A typical problem would give some definitions or axioms, state a theorem derived from those facts (without showing how), and then command: prove that this theorem is true. Every proof had multiple steps, and if your first step was in the wrong direction, you'd never bushwhack your way to a solution. So each problem forced you to think hard about the right approach. Once you found that, the rest typically fell into place. But getting there . . . We would do a kind of five-person brain meld to figure out what Mather was asking. Then we'd work separately, each of us trying to be the first to hit on an approach that would work. Eventually, someone would shout, "I see how to do it!" and explain their idea if the rest of us were stuck.

As the night wound on, members of the group would peel off to their own rooms to sleep. Usually Jim, Andy, and I stayed working until after midnight. That was when we'd head for Pinocchio's, a pizza place in Harvard Square. If we were lucky, we'd arrive right when they were closing and get leftover pizzas on the cheap, the cheese already congealing. We'd push on until two or three, sometimes four in the morning, then grab a few hours' sleep before rushing to class at eleven to hand in our answers.

Those first months of college, I was like a kid in a candy shop, dazzled by the seemingly limitless access to experts and intellectual stimulation. In my freshman humanities class, The Rise of the Greek

Classic, the professor, John Finley, cinematically wove Homer, Herodotus, and Aristophanes into modern life and literature. I loved the freedom my independent study gave me to push the limits of my programming, and I was energized by the camaraderie I found in Math 55 as we struggled through Mather's notes and pushed one another to improve.

And yet, late into that first semester, I felt at loose ends. I had come to Harvard from a small school, not even ninety people in my graduating class. At Lakeside, once I found my footing, it had been easy to excel and be recognized. Helping too was a tight community of teachers, administrators, and parents who supported me. They knew I was an outlier, a bright, awkward kid who needed an occasional nudge (Sign up for drama, Bill!) or door opened (Sure, take a trimester off to work). At Harvard I was on my own, swimming in a much bigger pool. Everyone had been the top of their high school class, everyone knew how to excel, and everyone was striving to be the best.

I had felt this acutely when I walked into my organic chemistry class and found myself surrounded by hundreds of students, mostly premeds determined to excel in the class, an essential hurdle in the long road to becoming a doctor. I had signed up for the simple reason that I loved high school chemistry with Dr. Morris. Organic seemed like the next logical step, even if I had no plans for medical school. Focused intently on the professor at the front of the huge lecture hall, my classmates sat with the monstrous textbook balanced on their knees as they agilely snapped together molecules from kits of colored balls and sticks. It was intimidating.

A few weeks into the semester, I stopped going to class. I rationalized that since our whole grade was based on the final exam, all I had to do was learn everything by the end of the term. And since the organic chemistry lectures were videotaped and available in the science center, I could just watch those instead of attending the lectures live. Harvard had a wonderful thing called the reading period, which gave you nearly twenty days to study for final exams. I gambled that if I got my act together during reading period, I could study the book, watch the videos, and an ace crammer like me would do fine. If there was one thing I knew, it was how to turn on a maniacal focus and learn on my own.

I threw myself into a daily rhythm that worked for me even if it seemed extreme to my friends. Between studying and programming, I could be awake for thirty-six hours at a stretch. Whenever exhaustion took over, I'd head back to Wigg A-11, crash for twelve or more hours, often fully clothed, sometimes with my shoes still on, always with my yellow electric blanket over my head to block the daylight. When I woke up, I'd gobble something quick with Jim Jenkins or Sam, maybe stop by the suite to see Andy and Jim, and then head to class, the library, or back to Aiken. I repeated some variation of that routine for months.

At the start of school I had signed up for a weekly linen service. It was a luxury for kids who could afford it. Once a week you were supposed to trade in your dirty sheets for a set of clean ones. I got my first set of sheets, but I was so preoccupied I didn't drop them off that first week. Then week two passed, then week three and four . . . at around the sixth week I was disgusted with myself. The sheets were dingy, streaked with ink and boot mud.

The man at the laundry room checked my name on a list and saw it had been at least a month and half. "Man, you broke the record!" he said with a laugh as I handed him my grimy sheets. Walking away I thought to myself, *Hey, that's an accomplishment. At least I'm Harvard's best at one thing!*

Toward the end of the semester, I walked into the video room stunned to find it full of my organic chemistry classmates rewatching the lectures they had dutifully attended all semester, textbooks open and molecule models in hand. The videos were hard to follow. Sometimes the audio cut out; other times the screen went blank, leaving the professor's words meaningless without the visual. At certain moments while watching the videos, my classmates in unison snapped together the white hydrogen atoms with black carbon ones and discussed whether the thing was isometrically symmetric, or was it symmetrically isometric? *Oh shit,* I thought. *I'm screwed.*

I got a C in that class, the lowest grade I would receive in college. I didn't take the second half of organic chem in the spring.

As a freshman, I was paired with an academic advisor to help navigate my path toward deciding a major, which students were required to declare as sophomores. I didn't get around to meeting my advisor in the fall. At the start of the spring semester, I got a call from his office to set up a time to talk.

He had gotten word that I had insisted I jump ahead to graduate classes related to computer science. I had talked my way into auditing one of those classes in my first semester—AMATH 251a, Operating Systems Architecture—and wanted permission to continue the class in the spring for credit. My other classes, meanwhile, didn't indicate a clear path toward a major. I had re-upped for the second half of Math 55, and had registered for a physiological psychology class, focused on "the behavior of organisms viewed as biological machines."

My freshman advisor—a professor in the chemistry department—and I would go on to have a great relationship; he was extremely supportive and guided me as I sorted through potential majors. But that first meeting took me aback. I don't remember exactly what I said, but I recall diving into that hyperkinetic stream of thought typical of me at the time, enthusing about how computers of tomorrow would be vastly different from the dusty old things we know today and explaining that I signed up for the psychology class because someday computers would match the power of the human brain. Absorbing this swirl of words, my advisor said, "You are very precocious!"

Up until that moment, I had never heard anyone call me that word except my mother, and the way she used it wasn't complimentary. "You're being a precocious brat," she'd say when I was talking back, challenging her on something. Having heard the word only in that context, I took it as an insult, a sharp verbal slap. I walked out of that meeting dejected, stunned that the advisor saw me in a negative light.

He was on to me: I was a misbehaving fifth-grader all over again.

"Can you believe it? The guy called me 'precocious'!" I told my friends back at the dorm, seeking confirmation that my advisor had crossed some line of propriety. No one reacted. "Precocious. That's so rude."

"But, Bill, you *are* precocious," Andy said. Now I was doubly dejected. Even my friends thought I was a brat. Andy told me I didn't know the meaning of the word. Go look it up, someone said. I did. *Exceptionally early development . . . exhibiting mature qualities at an unusually early age.*

I was the kid who was more comfortable speaking with adults than with my peers, conversant in what I thought of as adult knowledge. It was a role I played: Trey Gates the fast reader, the math whiz, the brainy kid able to converse about stocks and patents, the advent of the minicomputer or the invention of nylon. Wrapped up in that was my confidence that I was intellectually fearless, curious about everything, and ready to learn if you could teach me.

What was the age limit on precocity? At some point you became an adult and were measured as an adult. No longer just a curious kid.

For most of my school life I had viewed math as the purest area of intellect. In the bigger pool of Harvard, as obvious as it sounds now, I realized that despite my innate talent, there were people better than me. And two of them were my best friends.

In our Math 55 study sessions, even as we were helping each other, we were also subtly keeping score. That was true in our broader circle of math nerds as well. Everyone knew how everyone else was doing, for instance, that Lloyd in Wigg B aced a Math 21a test or that Peter—or was it someone else?—found an error in Mather's notes. We all grasped who among us was quicker that day, sharper, the person who "got it" first and then could lead the rest of us to the answer. Every day you strived to be on top. By the end of first semester, I realized that my ranking in the hierarchy wasn't what I had hoped. The top two spots in Math 55 belonged to Andy and Jim.

By most measures I was doing well. I earned a B+ in the first semester, which was an achievement in that class. In my stark view, however, it was less of a measure of what I knew than how much I didn't. The gap between B+ and A was the difference between being the top person in the class and being a fake. My severe take was that everyone in that class was the best person they knew in math—*up to that point.* All of us had 800s on our math SAT. All of us entered college thinking we would be the best. And when we weren't, well, we'd been victims of self-deception, we were frauds in my book.

My inability to do better in that class forced me to reconsider how I thought of myself. I so deeply identified with being the smartest, the best. That status was a shield behind which I hid my insecurities. Up until then, I had experienced only a few situations in which I felt someone was hands-down better than I was in some intellectual endeavor that mattered to me, and in those cases I soaked up what they could teach me. This time was different. I was recognizing that while I had an excellent math brain, I didn't have the gift of insight that sets apart the best mathematicians. I had talent but not the ability to make fundamental discoveries. I saw a vision of myself in ten years: teaching in a university but not good enough to do groundbreaking work. I wasn't going to be a John Mather, operating in the zone where math touches the deep secrets of the universe.

I wasn't alone. Hanging out in their suite that winter, Andy and Jim confided that they were also at a loss, also in some crisis of spirit. Both saw in Mather a model for what they'd become if they stuck with pure math. He was brilliant but seemed to live in his own world, removed from anything concrete. Though we didn't know it then, within a year Andy would burn out on pure math and need to take a semester off junior year before graduating as an applied math major (he later got a law degree and became a Wall Street tax expert). Jim would graduate with a degree in physics (and go on to be a highly successful physics professor at Cornell). Another one of our Math 55 study mates, Peter Galison, had a similar epiphany. To him pure math was like the finest art. He could appreciate the genius of Michelangelo's *David,* but he could never come close to creating something so perfect. To be a pure mathematician meant you had to believe you could become Michelangelo. (Peter would go on to be an influential professor of the history of science—at Harvard no less.)

What would I do? There were implicit expectations from my parents. In a letter I wrote that February to Ric, I said that "I was down in New York with my parents last week—seeing plays, going to fancy restaurants, etc. They are more in favor of my taking up business or law—even though they don't say so." I don't know what happened in New York, but I must have picked up the vibe that they preferred those options. "I haven't made up my mind at all."

In fact, I was already subconsciously circling the answer. Many of my Harvard friends thought my fixation on math was strange. I distinctly remember one, Lloyd Trefethen—who, as it happens, became a mathematician—prodding me to the obvious conclusion: "You're really good at the computer stuff. Why don't you do that?" Others had suggested that path, but Lloyd kept returning to the idea.

Paul and I were on the phone all the time, our conversations pointing me in the same direction. He was in his junior year at WSU and was languishing. His classes weren't challenging. He said he felt stuck in school when he'd much rather be out working, building something cool. In the back of my head, I heard the encouraging voices of the TRW engineers; maybe I could get a job at DEC. That winter we decided to write up our first résumés, ones we typed, unlike the ones we scrawled by hand years before at ISI. On mine I listed every computer I had worked on, and every major program I had written. I also noted that I was building a business in traffic flow analysis "in partnership with Paul G. Allen." I wasn't that serious about finding a job, but maybe something interesting would happen if I tried. I found a recruiter who specialized in the computer industry and sent out a bunch of résumés. I did not tell my parents.

As I came around to the idea of computers as my vocation, I was convinced that Paul and I should work together. Our conversations kept alive our mutual feeling that Intel chips and other microprocessors would upend the computer industry, even as it seemed like no one else we spoke to seemed to agree or care. Paul had some ideas for companies we could start. I thought it would be easier to discuss them if we lived close to each other.

"Why don't you take a leave of absence and move here so we can brainstorm on what to do?" I said one day that spring. I had floated the idea by him a few times before: we could both work in Boston as programmers or systems administrators, jobs that would give us access to computers, income, and time to work on a side project. But leaving college and hurling yourself into the job market was a dicey prospect. Paul didn't have the means to support himself without a job. He needed a sure bet.

In the meantime, my baseball project turned out to be far more complicated than I had anticipated. For months I had thrown myself into my program and hadn't yet fielded a game. I was able to get some critical pieces working, and Tom Cheatham was nice enough to give me an A on the project. (I am sure that Eric Roberts put in a good word for me.) Still, it ate at me that I had hyped my abilities to Cheatham and not fully delivered.

For the spring semester, I got permission to take the second half of the operating systems graduate class for credit. It was taught by two professors who served both as Harvard instructors and as engineers in the computer division of the big conglomerate Honeywell. The fact that they worked in the industry added to their credibility in my book. The younger of the two, Jeffrey Buzen, had already made a name for himself in the area of optimization. That was also the focus of our course.

The second day of the class Professor Buzen introduced us to a concept called queuing theory. To illustrate, he compared two algorithms, explaining why one was more efficient than the other. Listening to his explanation I thought, *Wow, the guy is totally off base.* Sure, he was one of the world's foremost experts on the topic, but I thought I knew better.

"You are wrong," I blurted out, dismissing his approach for what I saw was an obvious flaw. He looked flustered and attempted to explain. I wasn't having it. I shot back that his metric of efficiency was dumb and blah, blah, blah.

He started to explain again. "No, you're completely wrong," I repeated. I shot up out of my seat and stalked out of the room. What the rest of the class, all graduate students, thought about this freshman storming out of class I can only guess. I'm sure nothing good.

I paced around outside, replaying the incident in my head. After about fifteen minutes, my certainty gave way to dread. I realized, in fact, that I was the one who was wrong, completely and totally wrong. *What did I just do? What a fool I am.* It made it worse that he was one of the most congenial professors I had met. Plus he'd been kind enough to give me—an undergraduate—entry into his class.

I went back after the class let out and apologized. He couldn't have been nicer about the whole thing. Ultimately, we formed a good relationship. Professor Buzen took the effort to teach me the ins and outs of the Honeywell operating system he was working on, and my comeuppance brought new awareness that I needed to listen and learn. Even today I cringe when I think about my rudeness. My mom surely would have called me out for being a precocious brat.

At some point that spring I got a call back on one of my job applications. DEC engineers I had met at Bonneville the previous summer had helped connect me with DEC headquarters near Boston, and I'd landed an interview.

In the five years that I had been using DEC's computers, the company had grown into one of the largest employers in the state of Massachusetts. By the spring of 1974, DEC was buying up all the buildings around its headquarters and building new ones throughout the area. DEC operations now dotted Eastern Massachusetts. As the company grew, its founder, Ken Olsen, assembled a fleet of helicopters so that DEC engineers could zip between the company's facilities.

And I guess job applicants too. I was surprised when the company told me to take the subway to Logan airport, from which a DEC helicopter would whisk me to the headquarters, the fabled old mill where the company had built a world-changing computer business on the same floors where looms once wove Civil War blankets. I had never ridden in a helicopter before. Even if I didn't get the job, just that was cool enough.

Walking through the Mill and meeting these engineers was the closest thing for me at that age to visiting Mecca. It was DEC that demonstrated so clearly how rapid change in technology created openings for new ideas, new companies, and entirely new uses of computers. And it was studying DEC—Kent with his *Fortune* subscription and Paul with his computer magazines—that gave us confidence that with the right idea, we too could start our own company. Even as I clung to my solo-genius worldview, the idea that Paul and I should collaborate, build a company, grew stronger. I felt confident that if and when we decided to start our own thing, it would fall into place.

At DEC I interviewed with the makers of the TOPS-10 operating system. TOPS was the same software I had banged on at C-Cubed and that Paul, Ric, and I helped customize at Bonneville. I knew it cold. At DEC I was awed by everyone I met and basked in the feeling that I was valued for skills I had been honing for so long. They offered me the position.

It was incredibly flattering. The DEC people were kind to even consider me. And yet, I didn't take the job. I felt bad. I think at that moment I just needed a confidence boost. For an afternoon I was back in a world that I fully understood, with people who spoke my language and who affirmed that I had something to contribute. I received a few other offers that spring, including one to be a programmer at General Electric's appliance facility in Kentucky. I declined them all.

It had been a test of sorts. Could I get offers? I didn't need the actual job. The offers gave me a story to tell my friends. As if I had proof of my value to the world even without the high-class education we were all striving for.

I never mentioned the interviews and job offers to my parents. They wouldn't have understood. In fact, they probably would've been horrified to think that I might veer off the Harvard track.

In the late spring I got severe stomach pains, bad enough to send me to the ER, where they diagnosed me with ulcerative colitis. Two weeks in the hospital with a fever that spiked at 106 degrees marked the close of my first year of college. Part of me doubts the diagnosis. I've never had the problem again. I also can't help but wonder if stress, fatigue, a poor diet, and my general angst about what I was doing with my life played a role in whatever hit me that spring.

At the start of summer, I heard from Honeywell. I had applied for a job at the division's headquarters in Waltham, just a few miles from Harvard. At the interview I emphasized the "in partnership with

Paul G. Allen" part of my work history, making clear that Paul and I hoped to work together. I asked that they consider us both, and they followed up by interviewing Paul by phone. By the time they made us offers, I knew I was going back to school. Paul accepted.

In August Paul borrowed his father's Plymouth and with his girl-friend, Rita, drove across the country to start a new life in Boston.

CHAPTER ELEVEN

Wild Card

I have a recurring dream that even now can jolt me out of bed. The dream gets right to the point: panic. I'm at Harvard, it's late in the semester, and I still haven't figured out where my class is meeting. I haven't figured out the textbook I need. I'm wandering around looking for the lecture hall or the final exam room. And I feel dread: I've run out of time, and I'll never get my act together. I put off studying too long. I will fail.

I can trace the source of that anxiety to my general approach to classes from my sophomore year. Though my organic chemistry gambit of leaving everything to the last minute didn't play out as planned and caused me a lot of stress, I structured the next school year around that same approach for all my classes. I would skip the lectures and hope I could pull off a semester of learning in a few weeks of monomaniacal cramming. Then, during the time I was

209

supposed to be in those classes, I sat in on other classes that interested me. I was determined to explore as much as Harvard had to offer. Double the classes, I figured, meant double the learning.

I declared applied math as my major. In our conversations the previous year, my freshman advisor explained that since math applied to everything under the sun and virtually everything in the Harvard course catalog, it gave me license to explore. He helped me see that applied math was a wild card, a major that would allow me to study an array of classes based purely on what I thought was interesting. In my time at Harvard, I would repeatedly play this wild card to justify classes in linguistics, criminal justice, economics, and even British history. It was the perfect major for an information omnivore.

I was deliberately public about my perilous approach to my academic career. I skipped my combinatorial math class to sit in on a fascinating psychology class for the whole semester. When the time came for the finals in the two classes, which happened to be held in the same auditorium, the friends I had made in psychology saw me sitting among the math nerds and assumed I was making a grave mistake. *You're in the wrong section!*

Admittedly, it was an act: part of my long-held need to define myself in others' eyes as clever and a bit different. It was the same instinct that had led me to buy two sets of books at Lakeside so as not to appear that I was really trying—though all the while behind the scenes I was *really* trying. I reverted to shielding my insecurities with nonchalance.

Despite the confidence I had in my ability to cram, it made the end of a semester stressful. Ahead of finals, I had to disappear into Widener Library and all but live there until I was done. I enjoyed the intensity and made it work, but it led to a lifetime of disturbing dreams searching for that classroom.

—

In advance of sophomore year, my core group of friends—Sam, Andy, and the two Jims—put our names into the housing lottery together in the hopes of snagging suites at Currier House, an undergraduate dorm with two attractions: (1) it was a natural habitat for math-science types, and (2) it was coed. The second was a stronger draw for me, but I would end up spending all my time with the first group.

We didn't get our suite; I ended up sharing a room with Andy. We were compatible for many reasons, not the least of which was that we were both complete slobs.

I fell into a regular habit of playing poker with a group of Currier guys. Several nights a week we'd gather in a narrow room in the basement with a long boardroom table and play cards deep into the night. Some of these guys treated poker almost as a second major. Most of the regulars were math and science people who figured probabilities and game theory on the fly. And several had the means to quickly raise the stakes.

While I hadn't played much poker, I ranked myself above average within the group at the start. That didn't last. It was reminiscent of Math 55: gradually the lesser players dropped off, so even as my skill level improved, my relative skill compared to the group fell. But I stuck with it. Competing with these supersmart players drove me to get better and better. That feeling was addictive, even if I was losing so much money that at one point I asked Paul to take away my checkbook. I was eight years old again at the dining room table with Gami, losing but improving with every hand. Only this time it was for money.

The stakes went up and up, and the games migrated from Currier House to grungy student apartments off campus. My best run was a night at an off-campus game playing seven-card stud hi-lo. I kept winning and winning, stuffing bills into the pocket of my khakis each round because it felt too showy to leave them on the table. I also hoped that with my winnings safely stowed, I'd resist gambling more. That night I came away with something like $1,800, which was huge. The next night, same house, same crowd, I lost nearly all of it.

That wasn't a taste I enjoyed, and this would be one of the last times I played. I realized I was not good enough to come out ahead since only the very best players remained.

Paul and his girlfriend, Rita, had arrived in Boston in August, renting an apartment in the suburbs about a forty-minute drive from Harvard. By the fall, Paul was adjusting to life as a salaried employee at Honeywell, writing small pieces of large programs. My college friends already knew Paul as a larger-than-life character from my stories. Now Paul kept the mystique alive in person. It was unusual in those days for a college student to take a leave of absence, move across country to work as a programmer. With his beard and his girlfriend, his guitar and his broad knowledge, Paul fit the role of cool older brother. And as always, he was my goad—and a bit of a corrupter.

One weekend in October, I drove with a few friends to visit Paul and celebrate Rita's birthday. Paul had some LSD that we all dropped while watching *Kung Fu*. Patient Rita stayed sober, our chaperone on the chance things got weird. At night we checked out the woods around the house, stopping a long time at every tree to look at the fall colors. I watched a friend trace his finger in the dewdrops on the trunk of Paul's car, writing ∃, the symbol in logic problems meaning "there exists." He wrote another one next to the first: ∃ ∃. The two backwards Es together, side by side, to him, to us, held some profound meaning. "Bill, see this. Existence exists," he said as we stared at the dewy car trunk. It was one of those moments that seem perfectly cosmic at the time and purely silly once the acid wears off.

At the height of the evening, a curious train of logic passed through my mind. On a computer you can delete a file and even wipe out all of your stored data. Since the brain is just a sophisticated computer, I thought, *Hey, maybe I can command my brain to zero out all my memories?* But then I got worried that testing that notion might actually set it irrevocably into motion. *Better not even think about it!* Taking a shower the next day, I ran through an inventory of my cherished memories, relieved to find that everything was intact. That would be one of the last times I would do LSD.

When he wasn't working, Paul lived in his magazines, his apartment littered with back issues of *Popular Electronics, Datamation, Radio-Electronics,* and spec sheets for all sorts of computers and their components. He could easily spend an hour foraging through Out of Town News, the landmark newspaper and magazine kiosk in the center of Harvard Square. From his growing pile of paper and publications sprang many ideas for any number of ventures Paul pitched me that fall.

Most of them centered on the microprocessor. For a while, Paul was set on the idea of building a computer company in the model of DEC. DEC had exploited new technologies to lower the price of computers and greatly expand their use. Could we do the same with inexpensive microprocessors, maybe string together multiple chips to make a superpowerful computer really cheaply? What about setting up a timesharing service aimed at consumers? People could dial into our computer to access news and other useful information, like, I don't know, recipes?

We'd sift through these ideas over pizza or at Aku Aku, a Trader Vic's–style Polynesian place, talking for hours as I sipped Shirley Temples (at nineteen years old I was over the drinking age but preferred the kid's mocktail to alcohol). Because of Paul's love of computer hardware, his ideas often centered on building some kind of innovative computer. One great idea he came up with was a technique for wiring together cheaper, less-capable chips into a single powerful processor called a bit-slice computer. His question: Could we use this bit-slice technique to undercut IBM just as DEC had done a decade earlier? At the time, an industry-leading IBM System/360 mainframe computer could cost several hundred thousand dollars or even far more. I spent some time on my own studying the details of the IBM machine and Paul's bit-slice idea. On our next night out, I told him I thought it could work. We could probably make a computer for $20,000 that would be equivalent to the 360.

Still, he knew that I was increasingly cooling to the idea of building hardware. The business of manufacturing computers seemed too risky to me. We'd have to buy parts, hire people to assemble the machines, and find lots of space to pull it off. And how would we ever realistically compete with big companies like IBM or fast-rising Japanese electronics makers?

My view was influenced by Traf-O-Data's hardware challenges. For eighteen months our partner back in Seattle, Paul Gilbert, had been struggling to get our computer to work. The machine required the delicate coordination of electronic pulses that had to reach each of the machine's memory chips at exactly the same moment. A delay of a microsecond and everything froze. One wire a hair longer than it should be, or a trace amount of radiation it produced, could throw off the pulses. And did, over and over. These endless glitches fed my worries that we were courting a life of tedious problem-solving that seemed hit-or-miss, not fully in our control.

Gilbert was a self-declared perfectionist, a math-obsessed engineer who doggedly stuck with a problem until he solved it. "I don't like to be defeated. I'll get it fixed regardless of what it takes," he would say. (His girlfriend dropped him that year because he spent too much time on Traf-O-Data.)

I wrote memory test software and then the two Pauls dove in. They'd stare at the oscilloscope patiently making the diagnosis: "a glitch in the data to the line on chip seven." Kind of like those organic chemistry modules, there was a level of disorder to the hardware problems that frustrated me. I'm sure my nervous energy added to the stress. I was always pushing to see if there was something we could change or add to speed things up.

Gilbert eventually got the hardware working in the spring of my first year of college. That summer I arranged a meeting at my parents' house with potential customers from Seattle's King County. I had everything set perfectly that morning, but when the time came for my demo, the unit's tape reader broke. I pleaded with my mom to tell them that it really, truly had worked flawlessly the night before. Our guests politely finished their coffee and left. After that, we laid out more money for what we considered to be the Rolls-Royce of tape readers. All this effort and expense for a simple computer, with a single job of translating holes in a paper tape into graphs.

Again and again, my dinner conversations with Paul led back to software. Software was different. No wires, no factories. Writing software was just brainpower and time. And it's what we knew how to do, what made us unique. It was where we had an advantage. We could even lead the way.

First we needed a computer. A few companies had marketed small computers around Intel's innovation. In France a suitcase-sized computer called the Micral had used Intel's 8008—the same chip in our traffic machine—for single-purpose applications such as automating tollbooths. Another, called the Mark-8, was just a DIY project. You paid a few dollars for assembly instructions and then had to buy various parts from different suppliers and hope your computer worked once you soldered everything together. I knew that the newest Intel chip, announced earlier that year, was advanced enough to power a functional general-purpose computer. That was the 8080. As our sentinel on all things hardware, Paul would keep track of what was happening with that chip.

"Let me know when someone comes out with an 8080 computer," I told him.

Meanwhile, I agreed to see if we could get help from Harvard. In the course catalog I looked for classes that focused on computer architecture and found Introduction to Digital Computers. I didn't know the professor, but I figured he might have connections in the industry. I made an appointment and pitched my idea. I said I was really interested in the advances in microprocessors and wanted to experiment with writing software for them. Could he help me contact Intel and other companies to see if they would donate chips for research? He asked if what I wanted to do was for a specific class. I said no, it was just an area I was excited about. He replied that he probably couldn't help.

A few days later I tried again. I returned to his office to drop off a detailed proposal of my plan for the hardware and a sample letter asking for donations that, with his signature, I hoped we could send to hardware makers. Later I'd learn that he never looked at the plan. He told my senior tutor that he had neither the "time nor inclination to assist since it wasn't course-related."

Most of the people I spoke to back then about this magical chip responded skeptically. Today, if I try to put myself in their shoes, I can understand. Microcomputers were a weak distant cousin to the mainframes and minicomputers that occupied the minds of computer science academics—and most of the computer industry. Microcomputers were toys. The Department of Defense wasn't paying Harvard to research toys. No microcomputer in 1974 was going to guide a missile or pilot a submarine. At the time I was less charitable in my assessment: these people lacked imagination for what the future could hold.

By late November, Paul's girlfriend, Rita, had moved back to Seattle. Paul by then had moved into subsidized housing in Cambridge, a short train ride from me. The development was called Rindge Towers, which Paul dubbed "the Grindge," a word that seemed to capture the depressing state of the apartment, with its heavy steel doors and hyperactive cockroaches. It also kind of fit Paul's mood at the time. The love of his life had moved across the country. He was lonely. He was tired of his job. Several nights a week and most weekends he'd either come by Currier House or I'd go to the Grindge to hang out and talk about our plans.

That was the state of things one snowy afternoon in early December 1974 as I sat reading in my dorm room. The next few weeks were set. I would take the Putnam Competition exam and then finish classes for the year before flying home to Seattle for break. I was sure my mom would overschedule me with holiday parties, dinners, and gift exchanges with friends and extended family, as she had done my freshman year. She had already asked what I wanted for Christmas: *The Beatles 1967–1970,* Santana's *Welcome,* and a sci-fi book Paul recommended. After the holidays I planned to be back at school for the start of the reading period on January 6 and study like mad for finals.

Then Paul burst into my room. He'd run all the way from Out of Town News and was panting. There was slush on his boots.

"Remember what you told me?" he said.

"What?"

"You said, 'Let me know when someone comes out with a machine built around the 8080.' Well, here it is—check it out," he said, shoving a magazine into my hands. It was the January 1975 issue of *Popular Electronics.* On the cover: "PROJECT BREAK-THROUGH! World's First Minicomputer Kit to Rival Commercial Models."

I sat back in my chair and flipped to the article. The headline read, "The most powerful minicomputer project ever presented—can be built for under $400." Below that, a box listed some impressive specs: an 8-bit Intel 8080 processor, up to 64K of memory, and 78 machine instructions—almost twice as many as the 8008 chip that we had used in the Traf-O-Data system.

Paul stood there, silently watching as I pored over the six-page article and its circuit diagrams. I could feel myself rocking.

This thing was small, hardly bigger than the typewriter in front of me. It looked like a stereo receiver with toggle switches and lights.

It had no keyboard, no screen, not even a connection for a tele-type. The article said it was expandable, meaning all those things could be plugged into it, making it a fully functional computer. The first paragraph summed it up: "The era of the computer in every home—a favorite topic among science-fiction writers—has arrived! It's made possible by the POPULAR ELECTRONICS/MITS Altair 8800, a full-blown computer that can hold its own against sophisti-cated minicomputers now on the market. And it doesn't cost several thousand dollars."

The authors noted that the under-$400 price was about what you would pay for a color television.

For three years Paul and I had been talking about how new com-puters that exploited the exponential improvement of chips could change everything. I looked up at Paul. "It's happening without us," he said.

The era of the computer in every home? Was it really?

The $397 price for the Altair 8800 got you the unassembled ver-sion, a kit that arrived in hundreds of pieces. After you were done soldering and screwing everything together, you hoped it worked. At their core, computers rely on performing calculations using binary math—ones and zeros. That remains true of the extraordinarily powerful processors inside today's machines, from a smartphone to a supercomputer. But many layers of sophisticated software shield you from the fundamentally binary nature of computing. You don't need to think in ones and zeros to write software, let alone run it.

The Altair's binary aspect was on full display. Without connect-ing it to a teletype or some way to feed it programs, everything had to be entered using sixteen (of twenty-five total) toggle switches on the computer's front. Each of the sixteen switches had two positions: up represented a 1 and down was a 0. Each 1 or 0 represented a bit.

As an 8-bit processor, the 8080 chip strung eight of these bits into one byte of information.

To enter a single byte into the Altair, you had to flip at least nine switches. Inputting even the simplest of programs—say, one to add 2 + 2—required dozens of flips. Any program that performed a useful task of any complexity involved, at minimum, hundreds of flips. The computer also used binary to communicate the results of its work back to you, on rows of little red LED lights.

Even after assembly, the Altair 8800 was hardly a computer for every home.

And yet, I was sure that plenty of people besides Paul and me wanted one. For around the price of the Intel 8080 processor alone, MITS was selling an entire computer kit. For the avid community of computer hobbyists, this would be the holy grail. More significantly, Paul and I felt there would be serious business and engineering applications, because even with the add-ons, it was so cheap.

The *Popular Electronics* story hardly mentioned software. In order for people to easily write software programs on an Altair without flicking all those switches, they would need a teletype terminal and want a programming language like BASIC or FORTRAN tailored to the 8080 chip. But the authors said nothing about whether a language was available.

Our bet was that they didn't have one.

There was a big hitch, though. We didn't have an Altair 8800 or even an Intel 8080, the microprocessor that was the brain of the new machine. How would we test our code?

Paul had thought about that, and over Christmas break he called me with great news. In the prior year he had figured out a way for us to write programs for our Traf-O-Data machine by using a PDP-10 to simulate the Intel 8008 chip—effectively making the $500,000 mainframe pretend it was a $360 microprocessor. Now, poring over a manual for the PDP-10, he'd devised a way to do the same for the much more powerful Intel 8080 chip. That simulator would let us use Harvard's PDP-10 as if it were an Altair.

With that breakthrough, we made a plan. We would get Intel's reference manual for the 8080 and learn its instruction set. I would design and write the BASIC in assembly language using those 8080 instructions. As a language conceived from the start to make programming approachable to beginners, it would have wider appeal to the Altair's hobbyist market than a more advanced language such as FORTRAN. I was confident I could quickly get it up and running—maybe not the ultimate BASIC, but one that did enough to be viable and useful. And even though I hadn't finished the BASIC I'd started at Lakeside (for the PDP-8), that project gave me a head start on this one. Meanwhile, Paul would build a simulator program that could make the PDP-10 behave like an 8080 and run my code. He would also tweak software tools we could run on the PDP to monitor the 8080 code as it ran and to debug it when it didn't work.

We had never heard of the Altair's maker, a manufacturer of model rocketry electronics and calculators called MITS Inc. The *Popular Electronics* story listed an address in Albuquerque, New Mexico, and a phone number. In early January, Paul wrote a short letter to MITS claiming that we had a version of BASIC for the Intel 8080 chip. In the note, he said that we would charge $50 per copy, which he suggested MITS could resell to hobbyists for between $75 and $100. He typed the note on Traf-O-Data letterhead and signed it Paul G. Allen, President.

As the weeks went by without a response, we decided to call.

We worried that anyone who knew we were just a college kid and a low-level programmer at Honeywell would never take us seriously. That was why Paul was so definitive in his letter—that we had a version of BASIC ready to go—and that's why I wanted Paul to do the talking. He was older and had a deeper voice, and for those reasons was probably the best public face of whatever company we started. Plus, he had signed the January letter. But Paul thought I should call. I was quicker on my feet and had more experience talking business.

We compromised. From my dorm room early one night in February I dialed the telephone number listed in the *Popular Electronics* article.

When the woman who answered the phone connected me to Ed Roberts, the MITS president, I thought: *How big can this company be if I can get the president on the phone?*

I identified myself as Paul Allen calling from Traf-O-Data in Boston. I explained that we were almost finished writing a version of BASIC for the Altair and would like to show it to them.

Roberts told me that he had already gotten calls from people claiming to have the same software. He said that the first person who could produce a working version would get the deal. He added that the Altair wasn't ready yet. He said it would take another month or so before it could run any version of BASIC we had. Within a few months we would learn that despite the proclamations in that first magazine story, the Altair at that point was just a clunky prototype, a single machine that wasn't even finished.

Such was the dawn of the personal computer revolution. We all were just faking our way along.

Like most versions of BASIC, the one we wrote for the Altair was a particular kind of programming language called an interpreter. In the same way the interpreters who stand next to American and Chinese presidents translate one idea at a time, a BASIC interpreter converts one line of code at a time into instructions the computer can easily understand. One of the advantages of an interpreter is that it can work using less memory than other types of programs. Computer memory back then was precious because it was pricey.

Although Altair owners could stuff the case full of extra memory cards to add RAM, up to a maximum of 64K, the cards were really expensive: $338 for each 4K expansion card.

So I knew the biggest challenge was going to be figuring out ways to squish BASIC into the smallest possible amount of memory. Otherwise there wouldn't be any left for the BASIC programs that users would write and the data those programs would use.

The first thing I did was think back to that hike three and a half years earlier, slogging through the snowy Olympic Mountains while writing computer code in my head. That I was able to make it so small and efficient was to me proof that we could fit an entire BASIC programming language in less than 4K of memory, with some to spare. The part I crafted on that hike—the formula evaluator—was key. I just had to download it from my head now. I started with that, writing it out on a yellow legal pad. It was small and tight. *Now if I can just write the rest of the program like that, we can pull this off.*

Our big worry was time. We figured we had only weeks to finish the program and get it to MITS before someone else beat us to it. There was too much work for two people, one with a full-time job and the other a full class load. We worried particularly about a section of the program called floating-point math for handling very large numbers—"to the power of"—and very small numbers—decimal fractions—and quantities like pi (3.14159). It wasn't a hard job to write that code, but it would require lots of tedious work. We could leave that part out to make our self-imposed deadline, but our BASIC would be severely limited. You can't build a decent lunar lander game without floating-point math.

Paul and I were discussing our floating-point conundrum one night in early February while eating in the Currier House dining hall. From across the table, a student interrupted: "I've done that." Apparently, he'd been listening in on the whole conversation. He was a freshman math major named Monte Davidoff. I asked him a few questions to test if he really knew what he was talking about. He did, and he came across as very confident. I asked him if he could come by my room later to continue the conversation. We ended up speaking for several hours that night. Monte told me that he had caught the computer bug as a high school student in Wisconsin. He'd already gained a lot of experience with multiple programming languages and different computers and had even been paid to write programs for a large automotive battery maker. He also had good ideas about the floating-point algorithms we needed, so I walked him through our project to write the BASIC interpreter. He was game to work on it.

Starting the second week of February, I alternated between slouching in my red chair hand-writing code on yellow legal pads and planting myself at Aiken trying to get the code to work. I slept during the day, skipped classes, and then met Monte in my room in the early evening, and we'd head to Aiken. Paul would come straight from work to the lab. Monte and Paul would use my account number, 4114, and we'd each grab a terminal and code all night.

I worked on the main part of the program while Monte started on the code to handle math functions like addition, subtraction, multiplication, division, and exponentiation. Paul fine-tuned the 8080 simulator he had developed (the code that let us use the PDP-10 tools as if we were using an 8080-based computer). As the simulator got better, so did the speed at which we could program. I could type my handwritten code into the PDP-10 and the mainframe would emulate exactly what the Altair would do. When my Altair program crashed, I could use the PDP-10's powerful debugging tools to quickly figure out where I had made a mistake. We were sure that no one else had tricked the PDP-10 in this way. And we were sure that gave us an advantage over anyone else who might be trying to write software for the Altair.

In the pecking order of the Aiken Lab, Professor Cheatham's PhD students and the people doing serious research had priority use of the terminals. I didn't want to get in anyone's way, so we did the bulk of our work at night, when the PDP-10 was mostly idle, no one was in the lab, and we could get big blocks of time on the computer. Aside from stops at the cafeteria and a couple of movie breaks, most of my waking hours were spent at Aiken. The room temperature was kept in the low fifties—perfect for cooling the PDP-10 but cold if you're sitting there for hours on end. In my winter jacket I'd code until I'd get tired and either sleep at the terminal or curl up on the floor near where the computer threw off heat.

With Paul's simulator and his development tools, the job went fast. I could write code, pull it up on the PDP-10, and stop the program right where it found the problem. Then try to fix it and move on. I had spent a huge chunk of my life in that weird, almost magical feedback loop: *write, run, fix*—a zone in which time seems to stop. I'd sit down at the terminal after dinner and then look up surprised to find it was two in the morning.

In the midst of all of this, I realized we didn't have enough information to write the code needed to connect a teletype machine to the Altair, which would be a necessary setup for anyone who wanted to program it in BASIC. I called MITS again and spoke to the engineer who had designed the Altair. I guess my question, about how the computer inputs and outputs characters, was detailed enough to impress him. He said something like, "You're actually the first guys to ask that." Beyond the information he provided, the conversation suggested to me that we must be ahead of anyone else writing a BASIC interpreter for the MITS computer.

In March, after about six weeks of this frenzied code-writing, our BASIC was up, running, and, we thought, good enough to show MITS. We had a long list of features to add and sections to improve, but all that could wait.

Paul called MITS, talked to Ed Roberts (who didn't question that his voice was lower than the first time he called), and set up a meeting. I bought Paul a plane ticket.

The night before his trip, it occurred to me that a tiny mistake in our reading of the 8080 manual could sabotage everything. We had only run the program on the PDP-10 via Paul's simulator. Our program had never run on an Altair itself, just a computer pretending to be one. If one thing was off in Paul's simulator, our demo would be a bust. While Paul slept, I stayed up all night checking every instruction in the Intel manual against the simulator, looking for errors. When I was done, I saved the program to paper tape and hustled it over to Paul. I watched him tuck the roll into his carry-on bag.

As it happens, we did forget something. On the plane, Paul realized we didn't write a small bit of code—called a bootstrap loader—to tell the Altair to load our program in memory and launch it. Paul pulled out a notepad and madly wrote out the missing lines of code.

At MITS the following day, they had readied a machine with 6K of memory and a paper tape reader. Paul entered his bootstrap code, which took a while: each byte had to be input by setting eight data switches. He then started the tape reader. Our BASIC program took about seven minutes to feed into the computer. Finally, it got to the end of the tape, started running the program, and . . . nothing happened. It didn't work.

They tried again. And there on the terminal appeared:

MEMORY SIZE?

Paul typed in a few BASIC commands to demonstrate our magnum opus.

PRINT 2+2
4
OK

With that, the first piece of software written for the first personal computer came to life.

CHAPTER TWELVE

Be So Correct

I don't know who was more surprised, me or them!" Paul said, sipping his fruit punch over a celebratory dinner at Aku Aku. When our software combined with their computer added 2 + 2, he recounted, the MITS president was flabbergasted. "Oh my God, it printed four!"

Paul was stunned that our little program worked flawlessly on its debut. At the same time, Ed and the lead MITS engineer, Bill Yates, were floored that their machine actually *did* something.

After the simple addition test, Paul had wanted to show off more and see for himself what our program could do. Yates handed him a copy of *101 BASIC Computer Games* from which Paul typed in a version of Lunar Lander, the simple text-based game we had learned to program at Lakeside. It simulated control of the retro rockets on an Apollo moon lander. The goal was to slow your free fall so that

227

you touched down softly on the moon before running out of fuel. On the Altair that day it ran the first time.

Ed Roberts was ecstatic. He asked Paul into his office to talk business.

Through Ed, Paul learned a lot about MITS, a company we hadn't heard of before the Altair article. It was small, under twenty people. Ed had started the company in the late 1960s as a maker of transmitters for model airplanes before moving into electronic calculator kits. The increasing power and decreasing cost of chips enabled MITS and a whole bunch of other companies to enter the market with programmable kit calculators. Ed bet big, taking on debt to finance his calculator business, only to lose money amid stiff competition and a flagging U.S. economy. That was the state of MITS in the spring of 1974 when Intel announced the 8080. With his company on the brink of bankruptcy, Ed saw the chip as his savior. On a gut feeling that there was a market for a cheap functional kit computer, he borrowed more money to start the Altair business.

The story was a lesson in gambling. Ed heard that *Popular Electronics* was looking for a computer to highlight in its January issue. He pitched the magazine without a prototype or even much of a plan, but assured the magazine's editors he would have a cheap computer ready for publication. They agreed. He did have one thing: an agreement from Intel that if MITS bought a certain number of chips they'd offer a deep discount, which turned out to be around $75 per chip, compared to the list price of $375. That's how MITS would be able to offer the Altair for about the same price it would cost someone to buy just its computer brain.

MITS built a prototype and shipped it to *Popular Electronics* in New York. It never arrived (and was never found). The Altair pictured in the January issue was an empty box, a mock-up that MITS had cobbled together for the photo shoot. If I remember correctly, the front panel was made of cardboard.

Now, three months later, hundreds of people were mailing $400 checks to get an Altair. The company couldn't keep up with the deluge of orders. Paul said that the MITS office had been turned into an assembly line of workers stuffing boxes with the Altair innards and casing to be shipped out. It was clear sales would far surpass the several hundred that Roberts had forecast. And it was clear Ed's gamble would pay off: his company would be viable again.

In his office, Ed told Paul that he wanted to license our BASIC interpreter right away. Our software could turn the Altair into a useful computer. Ed knew it would help drive even more demand. "He said that we can work out the terms later," Paul told me.

Over dinner we talked through what we should put into our contract and how much we should charge.

One thing we needed was a name for our partnership. Up to that point Paul and I had been calling ourselves Traf-O-Data and using the company's stationery every time we sent a business letter. But we wanted to separate the work on traffic from whatever new business we did with microcomputers. "Allen & Gates Consulting" made logical sense, but I thought people would mistake us for lawyers. It also sounded kind of small and artisanal, whereas we wanted a name with more gravitas, like our model, Digital Equipment Corp. That name carried the weight of a behemoth. With a name like that, people might take us seriously, which still seemed like an ambitious goal for two young guys figuring it out as we went along. It was Paul who had the next thought: Since we were writing software for microcomputers, how about combining those two words? I agreed. We had our name: Micro-Soft.

Around that time, I saw Eric Roberts (no relation to Ed Roberts) at the Aiken Lab. I told him about Paul's trip to MITS and how we might have a chance to sell the software we just wrote. In his typical soft-spoken way, he gave me friendly advice: stop using the Harvard PDP-10. Since it was funded by the Department of Defense's DARPA arm for research purposes, he explained, the Harvard computer shouldn't be used to make commercial products. By then I had heard the story of how the computer arrived in Army trucks under the cloak of night and understood that the government paid for it. But I didn't know of any rules concerning its use. I told him I'd stop and would move our program off the lab's computer. Eric added ominously that a new administrator of the lab knew about my heavy use of the computer. He's not happy, Eric said.

Early that year the school had filled the long-vacant position of associate director, a job designed to manage the daily operation of the Aiken Lab and account for how the DARPA money was being used. Tom Cheatham was still the lab's director—the new person reported to him—but it was clear to everyone at the lab that there was going to be tighter control and more rules. (Later Cheatham would refer to that layer of oversight as the "bean counters.")

A few days after Eric told me to stop using the Harv-10, I drove Paul's car out to First Data, a timesharing company in a Boston suburb, set up an account, and installed our program on their PDP-10. From that point on I stopped using the Aiken Lab for anything related to our project. When I next saw Eric, I asked if I should go talk to the new associate director and explain the situation. He said not to worry. He'd tell him I had stopped.

In the back-and-forth with MITS over improvements to our BASIC, Ed offered Paul a job. That was perfect for us. We thought it would be a good idea if one of us was working directly with MITS on supporting BASIC and developing new versions of it. By April Paul had quit Honeywell and was packing his bags for New Mexico. Within days he was the sole software person at MITS, with the lofty title of director of software development.

With the Altair orders flowing in, MITS started a newsletter for sharing tips and information to the small but growing universe of users. When the first issue of *Computer Notes* hit in the second week in April, Paul called me. He read the lead story, "ALTAIR BASIC—UP AND RUNNING." Up and running? Technically true, but there was no way our software was ready for broad distribution. The story included a simple nine-line program that figured the interest, monthly payments, and total amount owed on an eighteen-month loan of $650 with a 6.5 percent annual interest rate. "There are two keys to the new computer revolution," the story went on to say. "One is computers must be inexpensive and the other is computers must be understandable. With the Altair 8800 and Altair BASIC, both of these criteria have been met."

No one reading that would know that all we had was a rudimentary 4K version of our software, still in need of months of testing. We also hadn't signed a contract yet. We had only recently found a lawyer and started mapping out our agreement. Until that story, only a handful of us knew about our BASIC. Now thousands did.

"I want to see you in my office tomorrow at ten. I'm in Room 20," the associate director said when I picked up the phone in my dorm room. It was the middle of reading period, May 14 to be exact, and I was studying for finals. I instantly knew I was being summoned to Aiken to talk about my computer use.

The next morning, the associate director confronted me without any preamble. Why was I spending so much time at the center? What was I working on? Who was I bringing into the center?

I told him I wrote a version of BASIC for a microcomputer, collaborating with Paul and Monte. I told him about Paul's trip to MITS and about the contract we were negotiating. To anyone who was regularly using the center, nothing I said would be new. I was always open with everyone in the lab about what we were doing.

He seemed to already know the answers to a lot of his questions. The center had recently introduced an accounting program to track how much time each person was using the computer. He placed a piece of paper in front of me showing the results from user 4114, my account. I had racked up 711 hours in the month of February and another 674 hours in March. Given that there aren't that many hours in a month, that seemed like a lot to him. He was flabbergasted that when he did the math, 711 hours meant that Bill Gates and his "associates," as he called Monte and Paul, were using the center an average of eight and a half hours each day of the twenty-eight days in February. How was that possible? I wasn't sure he understood that it was common practice to leave the terminal unattended for several hours while the computer crunched through a job on its own. At times we were using two or three terminals simultaneously, so I was sure the hours were double or even triple the time we actually spent at the center.

Maybe that didn't matter. Beyond computer time, at issue was the fact that I brought unauthorized people—Paul and Monte—into the lab and that we worked on a commercial project. He explained that the government would be concerned that commercial work was performed under the DARPA contract.

As he looked at me across his desk, I'm sure he saw an undisciplined undergraduate, unwisely given access to his center, who sneaked his two accomplices into Harvard's secure computer room where the three worked on some mystery product late at night to avoid detection. In this scenario, if the generals at the Department of Defense ever uncovered this scheme, they would have no choice but to cut off their generous funding of Harvard's cutting-edge Aiken Computation Laboratory.

That outcome seemed far-fetched to me. I guess I showed it. My lack of contrition in the moment seems to have bothered him. In notes I recently found in my Harvard records, he wrote, "He [me] did not understand the ramifications of his activities and seemed totally unimpressed when I explained them to him." Other notes in my record have him commenting that I was "a wise ass."

Perhaps I was. My ability back then to filter my reactions wasn't very highly developed. The lab that he now oversaw previously had no rules, no strict oversight. Many of the users were working on their own side projects, including one who used the computer to write other students' essays and theses for money. Our use of the computer didn't get in the way of anyone else; the machine would have been idle if we hadn't been using it. We also hadn't been hired by MITS to build the software. It was done on spec, a bet that if we could write it, the company might buy it.

I'm not sure more contrition would have even helped. It seemed like a decision had been made.

"I want to remind you that you're speaking before a witness," he said at one point, indicating that his administrative assistant was sitting at her desk nearby. *Witness? Am I in some legal peril?* I thought. I said I would reimburse the center for the time I used the computer and added that I'd put the version of BASIC written at Harvard in the public domain where anyone could access it.

He told me to hand over my key to the Aiken center. He then deactivated my account in front of me. He said he was going to immediately inform the Administrative Board.

The Administrative Board? That meant the dean and a committee of administrators and faculty members would hear my case. Two days later I learned what was at stake. My senior tutor (an upperclassman advisor) explained that in the worst case, the board could expel me from Harvard, and if they found my actions particularly grievous, they would expunge my record, which meant all but erasing the fact I had ever attended the university. Gulp.

I didn't call my parents often back then—once every three weeks or so. I also hadn't shared very much with them about what I was doing with Paul and BASIC.

Now, in one call, they learned everything.

As always, my dad went right to the key questions: Were the rules of the lab written down and communicated to you? How does the school distinguish your use of the computer from that of professors who use university resources for their commercial work? Will you get to see the testimony of others? At some point he called the school and asked similar questions. My dad wasn't the type to ever play the bad cop, but given his temperament—measured, logical, succinct, and not prone to small talk—he could be intimidating all the same. I'm sure whoever he spoke with was left with the impression that he was watching closely. Whether explicit or not, I'm sure his message was, Whatever your verdict, your process had better be fair.

After all these years, I don't remember the details of my parents' involvement in my Aiken mess. I know my father flew to Boston to see me and assess the severity of the situation. I know that he was worried that Harvard might run roughshod over me. And I know that the prospect that I might get kicked out of Harvard deeply distressed my mom. She worried about me.

I'm sure she worried too about our reputation as a family in the community. By that time, she had achieved the kind of success that she had been working at for many years: the first woman to be director of a large Washington bank and the first woman president of King County United Way (and later chair on the national level of the charity as well). That year she was also named to the Board of Regents at the University of Washington. All this while also serving on the boards of the Children's Hospital and Seattle Foundation. Kristi was starting an accounting job, on a path to the kind of career that a generation earlier was all but closed to women like my mom. It was a proud day when Kristi got her job at Deloitte. Libby, by then ten years old, was a standout in three sports (finally my mom had a child who shared her athleticism!). And then to have a son at Harvard and performing well academically completed the picture of the successful family she had sought for twenty years, maybe longer.

For that son to drop out of college would be shocking. To be kicked out, even worse.

I felt the weight of all this as I sat at my typewriter and over the course of one long night wrote a letter to the Administrative Board.

The document—I still have a copy—was a defense of my actions, an apology, a critique of Aiken, a narrative of our project, and a snapshot of an industry on the verge of revolution. I wrote that the advent of the microprocessor by 1974 meant that suddenly computers could be "made smaller than a matchbox." I included that "Paul Allen is a firm believer that microcomputers are the wave of the future" and expressed our interest in trying to be part of that wave.

I felt terrible that Monte was dragged into this mess. The board was also considering disciplinary action against him. He was a freshman, just starting his college career. Already the project had hurt his grades. In my letter I emphasized that I was in charge of the project, I had brought Monte into the lab, and it was my mistake. I felt strongly that he should be fully cleared.

When I was done writing, I read the ten pages to my parents over the phone. My father suggested I should be more conciliatory. On his advice, I concluded my letter: "I apologize for my mistakes. I feel I showed serious misjudgment in relation to the selling of the Basic. I believe I can continue to be an asset to the Harvard Community, and I ask that you not put a blot on my record that will hamper my pursuits in the future."

On May 19 I was at my typewriter again, writing to Paul. "I've been thinking about Micro-Soft a lot tonight and thought I'd get some thoughts on paper and send them to you." I wrote out bullet points for our MITS negotiation and outlined technical details of new products. The letter is a three-page window into the mind of a new business owner, grinding through details: how we split any profits, manage our expenses, and avoid a cash squeeze given the need to pay our lawyer, rent an apartment, and cover living expenses for the two of us and an employee, a friend from Lakeside. If either Paul or I "drops off the scene in a pretty substantial way (going back to school)," I worked out how we'd split income from future contracts. "I don't think it will be a problem . . . by then we'll be hundred-thousanders anyway," I predicted.

One week later, I was in my dorm room studying for final exams when my senior tutor called. The Ad Board had just met over my case. They voted to "admonish" me for improper and unauthorized use of the lab. What does that mean? He explained: I got off easier than he thought I would. No punishment.

Of the three areas of concern—computer time, building a commercial product, and bringing unauthorized people into the lab—they found only that I violated the third. I should have sought approval before bringing Paul and Monte into Aiken. Thankfully too, they decided to "scratch" the case against Monte, which in Harvard parlance meant that he was cleared of everything.

I was lucky that the board realized the lab had been very loosely run and had virtually no set rules. Everyone interviewed for my case confirmed that fact, but I'm sure my Aiken guru Eric Roberts helped a lot. In his statement to the board, he wrote that, though he was opposed to the commercial outcome of our work, "I feel that Bill's action must be considered in light of the Center's traditional casual attitude, and that the Center must bear a share of the responsibility for not setting any standards for machine use." Eric would go on to start the first computer science department at Wellesley College and later teach thousands of students at Stanford and other universities.

I'm not sure why I don't have better recall of my parents' worries during my Aiken problems. I was very independent and also less in tune back then with other people's emotional states than I am now. I do know that I felt at the time that since I caused the problem, it was up to me to get out of it. One record from that period I have is a Christmas letter from Gami. As expected, she took a firm, principled view of my mess. Her thoughts, I'm certain, reflected those of my parents:

I'm sure you recognize you have a wonderful talent and we're all proud of your creativity and diligence in pursuing each idea. Be sure you stand on the highest ethical standard. Bend over backward to look at each facet of your endeavor from every angle. Perhaps I am concerned because I feel temptations are so great to let up a little here and a little there, forgetting our whole goal is being jeopardized. Your experience at Harvard, although you were somewhat exonerated, is still a warning to be above board in every step you take. Having seen lives destroyed because the individual thought the end justified the means, should keep us on our toes. I want you to be alert. Let your work be so correct that in no way can it be construed as improper. You're a great young man—I'm for you and I love you. See you soon, Gami

In my Harvard records, fifty years later, I found notes from an interview with Tom Cheatham conducted as part of my Administrative Board review. He was the person who opened his lab to me and who became my academic advisor sophomore year. I would have him again as a professor within a year. But I wasn't aware of his stance on my case.

I had met with Cheatham at the beginning of our BASIC project and told him that I was going to work on the tools and attempt to write an interpreter. He was enthusiastic, if busy, so we didn't get into details. It was a rare interaction between us. By that point I felt that he was tired of me filling our meetings with excited talk of all the technologies I was thinking about and projects I thought the lab should be taking on. We reached an implicit understanding that if I needed something signed, I'd drop it off with his assistant and then pick it up once he'd signed it. After I realized there might be a problem with my work on BASIC in the lab, I made an appointment to see him. He didn't show up. That was our relationship at that point.

I always felt nervous speaking with him, and we both probably felt more comfortable not meeting. It was an unusual dynamic for me. I found most professors at Harvard very approachable and built relationships with them based on long talks about math and programming; some even contributed directly to my evolving thinking about the future of the computer industry.

At the time of the Aiken controversy, I assumed that Cheatham was not in my corner. But the Harvard notes reveal that in fact he stood up for me. He told the board that it would be a "travesty of justice" if I was forced to withdraw from Harvard and that he "would be delighted to have BG computing at the Center next year." He seemed to know my general state of mind. The origin of the whole thing, he said, according to the notes, was that "BG began project out of boredom—a sophomore who already is bored with graduate courses" and got into microcomputers for something to play with. All of that was certainly true. In retrospect it's clear that he supported me, and I'm grateful. I only wish we had forged a better relationship back then. Tom Cheatham worked at Harvard into the late 1990s, and continued researching ways to help programming evolve from its artisanal roots into more of an engineering discipline. When I read my Harvard files many years later, I learned that he'd died in 2001.

The tension over my use of Aiken was rooted in the way computing had always been: a scarce, protected resource. A lot had changed since Howard Aiken built his huge Mark I mechanical calculator in the 1940s, when you could count the number of computers in the world on your fingers. By the time DEC sold its first PDP-10 in 1966, there were thousands of computers in the world. By 1975, when the Altair arrived, there were even more. But computers were still expensive and access to one required some special connection or accreditation, a key to a room, or if you were lucky, enlightened teachers at your high school.

Though no one could fully grasp it at the time, that scarcity was about to give way to plenty, and computers would very quickly be available to millions of people. The BASIC program we wrote that caused such a stir would play a central role, as would the work of thousands of other people. Suddenly the notion that a teenager could create something of value on a computer would go from far-fetched to commonplace. And the cost of computing would fall so fast that it would soon be nearly free.

CHAPTER THIRTEEN

Micro-Soft

W hen I arrived in Albuquerque in the summer of 1975, the former sandwich shop that MITS called its head-quarters had been transformed into a makeshift com-puter factory of long tables thrown together with two-by-fours and plywood. On any given day you'd see a dozen or so people stuff-ing electronic parts into boxes that got shipped out as fast as pos-sible, but not as fast as many customers wanted their new $400 kit computer. The real die-hard fans drove hundreds or even thousands of miles to MITS to pick up their Altair. Coming to work in the morning, it wasn't unusual to find RVs camped out on the corner of Linn Avenue and California Street waiting for their Altair like it was a takeout pizza. That office, in an aging strip mall surrounded by a check-cashing place, a laundromat, and a massage parlor, was ground zero for what would come to be called the personal com-puter revolution.

The father of it all, Ed Roberts, had the right idea, but vastly underestimated its popularity. He had forecast MITS might find about eight hundred customers a year willing to shell out the money for the novelty of having their own computer. Instead, in those first few months, orders came in from thousands. Altair buyers didn't seem to care that you couldn't do much more with it, once assembled, than flick switches and make lights blink. They were mostly engineers, doctors, small business owners, students, and other hobbyists who had the means to splurge on electronic gadgets and the free time to tinker with them.

In Menlo Park, California, a group of thirty-two hobbyists had gathered in March in a garage to swap information on the Altair. Ahead of that meeting, one member had driven from California to Albuquerque just to see if the company behind the mail-order computer was real. He had met Ed Roberts and learned that MITS had taken orders for far more computers than it was prepared to deliver. By the club's next meeting, members got their first glimpse of an Altair. With no software, keyboard, or display, the computer's new owner, a carpenter named Steve Dompier, toggled in a simple program. When he flicked the final switch, the Altair played a staccato rendition of the Beatles' "Fool on the Hill" through— surprisingly—an AM radio. (He followed with "Daisy, Daisy," which, as everyone listening probably knew, was the first song ever played on a computer—in 1957—and the tune the HAL 9000 computer sang as it slowly "died" in *2001: A Space Odyssey*.)

In time the group would call itself the Homebrew Computer Club. Within months, its membership would swell into the hundreds. Homebrew-like clubs popped up around the country. Like me, all these early personal computer fans had grown up with the understanding that computers cost hundreds of thousands of dollars. Now for under $1,000, anyone could own one, even if it couldn't do very much.

To stoke this small but enthusiastic market, Ed Roberts loaded his blue Dodge camper van with a few Altair computers and hired a college student to make a whistle-stop tour of U.S. cities. The Blue Goose, as the van became known, met hobbyists at the local Holiday Inn, where MITS employees showed off the Altair running our BASIC, before rolling into the next city.

In June I flew to San Francisco to join a group of MITS employees and the Blue Goose for a few days, to visit the Homebrew Club and other hobbyists. This was my first time in Silicon Valley, a name that had been adopted only a few years earlier thanks to the prevalence of semiconductor firms like Fairchild and Intel. The trip was an education for me. Many of the hobbyists I met viewed the Altair and the whole concept of the personal computer through a counterculture lens. Cheap or free computers fit into the hippie zeitgeist of the 1960s and early '70s. They represented a triumph of the masses against the monolithic corporations and establishment forces that controlled access to computing. Even if some of the engineers worked at defense contractors like Lockheed or large electronics companies like Hewlett-Packard, their passions in technology were very much rooted in the ideology of social change and the free flow of ideas. Among the groups I met was the People's Computer Company, which was no more a company than was the band that inspired its name—Janis Joplin's Big Brother and the Holding Company. PCC was more like a club that offered cheap computer access and free computer classes, mostly to schoolkids. The inaugural issue of the PCC newsletter set forth their mission:

Computers Are Mostly
Used Against People Instead Of For People
Used To Control People Instead Of To
Free Them
Time To Change All That . . .

The one stop on our trip that would be remembered by many was a demonstration at Rickey's Hyatt House, a hotel in Palo Alto. This was just months after Paul, Monte, and I had written our version of BASIC on Harvard's computer. That program, 4K BASIC, was rudimentary, a rough working prototype we planned to hone that summer. But it was the only programming language MITS offered for the Altair, and so in those early demonstrations it was the star of the show. With it, Altair fans got to actually *do* something with the $400 box.

Twenty-five years later, one journalist would call that evening at the Hyatt "the day someone stole Bill Gates's software." The hotel conference room was packed with a couple of hundred people, including many members of the Homebrew Club. While a MITS employee demonstrated the Altair, someone reached into a cardboard box and grabbed a spare paper tape of the 4K BASIC. I hardly have a memory of that evening, let alone whether I noticed the missing code—that would come a few months later. Eventually the tape found its way to a Homebrew member who churned out seventy more tape copies of software, handed them out at a Homebrew meeting, and encouraged everyone to make more copies. Within weeks, dozens, maybe hundreds, of copies of 4K BASIC were floating around—weeks before we were done with a version we had planned to sell.

In line with the hippie ethos of the nascent personal computer world, it was generally accepted that software should be free. Software was something to be copied from a friend, openly shared, or even stolen. In many ways it was like music back then. For all the Bruce Springsteen fans who would buy *Born to Run* that summer, many others borrowed the album from a friend and recorded it on a cassette for free.

Hardware was a different story. It was tangible. It sat on your desk. You could hear the whir of its cooling fan. Put your hand on the case, you'd feel the heat of the power supply. Pull the top off, you'd see all the tiny parts neatly soldered in place with the microprocessor brain, a magical device so sensitive it was fabricated in a dust-free factory. By contrast, software was virtual, bits of information invisibly stored on a magnetic tape or as indecipherable markings on a roll of paper. It took a leap of imagination to see that someone had spent thousands of hours designing, writing, debugging, and doing their best to get it to run. And since it had always been free, why shouldn't you give it away?

But Paul and I wanted to build a business. Our conviction, arrived at over many late-night talks, was that as personal computers got cheaper and cheaper, and spread into businesses and homes, there would be a nearly unlimited corresponding demand for high-quality software. Even as we worked on that first version of BASIC for MITS, Paul and I were talking about what other kinds of software people would need for their personal computers. We could make programming tools such as code editors and versions of other popular languages like FORTRAN and COBOL. After studying the operating system running DEC's PDP-8 minicomputer, which like the Altair had very little memory, I was pretty sure we could also create a whole operating system for a personal computer. One day, if things went as we hoped, Micro-Soft would be what we called a "software factory." We'd provide a broad range of products that would be regarded as the best in the business. And if things went really well, I thought that maybe we could have a big team of skilled programmers working for us.

At the time, if anyone asked what our goal was, I'd describe the software factory vision, or just say that we wanted to get our software on every personal computer in the world. The response would be an eyeroll or a look of bemusement.

A crowd of chip makers had quickly followed Intel. Motorola, Fairchild, General Instrument, Signetics, Intersil, RCA, Rockwell, Western Digital, National Semiconductor, MOS Technology, Texas Instruments, and others were making 8-bit microprocessors similar to the Intel 8080. Any of those chips could potentially be the brains of a personal computer. Each time a new chip was released, Paul would find a technical article with its specs and then we'd hash out whether it would be worth the time to write the software.

Everywhere we looked, the seeds of an industry were sprouting. In April, a Homebrew Club member and his friend started Processor Technology in Berkeley, California, initially to sell add-in memory cards for the Altair; within a year they would market their own computer, the Sol-20. A Stanford professor named Roger Melen was visiting *Popular Electronics'* New York office in late 1974 when he happened to see the mock Altair before it was announced. He was so impressed that he changed his flight home, stopping in Albuquerque to see Ed Roberts. Soon Melen and a friend from Stanford developed Altair add-ons, including a digital camera and a joystick, and in time they would roll out a microcomputer, the Z-1. (Their company name, Cromemco, was a derivation of a dorm at Stanford, Crothers Memorial.)

Inspired by the Altair and its Intel 8080 brain, an engineer at Hewlett-Packard named Steve Wozniak bought a MOS Technology 6502, the cheapest microprocessor he could find, and quickly built a prototype of his own computer. Like a lot of Homebrew members, Wozniak was motivated by the thrill of engineering and the pride of building something that he could share with the club. That is, until his friend Steve Jobs saw the prototype. Jobs had recently returned from a seven-month sojourn in India, where he'd gone, he later said, to find himself. Within a year, he'd shed his saffron robes, grown out his hair, and convinced Wozniak that his computer hobby was a business. Before long they'd christen their company Apple and begin selling their first computer, the Apple I.

My parents had expected me to spend the summer in Seattle taking a class or two at the University of Washington, as I had the summer before. Instead, I was in New Mexico. And soon I would tell them that I was going to take a semester off from Harvard and stay in Albuquerque. They were concerned but, as far as I can remember, they didn't push back. Maybe after the Administrative Board's admonishment they thought a break would be good for me; by winter, they probably figured, this foray into software would either end or morph into a side job I'd maintain when I returned to school to finish my degree.

My father would use the word "organized" in a way that meant a person had things under control. If you were organized, you had a plan, you were deliberate, you had set a goal, and you had worked out the steps to achieve it. I wanted to show him and my mom that I was organized, that I knew what I was doing with this Micro-Soft venture, even if I knew it might fail.

I kept a mental list of the number of times I had to ask my father for help. The first was the clash Kent and I had with ISI over our payroll program and the second the dispute with Harvard's Administrative Board. As I set out to build Micro-Soft, I hoped I wouldn't have to go back to him again, particularly as I told my parents I could manage both the company and college.

Software companies didn't exist—or at least the kind of software company Paul and I wanted to build didn't exist. And our product was something our potential customers thought should be free. But we had our one customer and faith that we could build from there.

Our first home in Albuquerque was a shared room a couple of blocks from MITS at the Sundowner Motor Hotel, before Paul and I rented a two-bedroom apartment, number 114, in a complex called Portals, a short drive from the office. Portals was cheap and had a pool, though I don't think either of us ever had the time to swim in it. Paul and I each took a room, and when Monte Davidoff showed up to help write code for the summer, he arranged a bed of couch pillows on the shag rug. Chris Larson, my friend from Lakeside who was helping manage our Traf-O-Data business, came down for the month of August. He and Monte shared the living room–cum–bedroom, an arrangement that seemed to work, since Monte liked to code alone all night, crashing on the couch pillows just as Chris got up in the morning to head to work.

Our headquarters, to the extent you could call it that, was part of MITS, in an area off to the side of the building. We had a few terminals that we used to dial into a PDP-10 across town at the Albuquerque School District. Paul had cut a deal to lease time on the computer, but it meant we usually worked at night when it wasn't burdened by the district's use. We didn't have a printer, so at the end of each day one of us would drive a few miles to the district and retrieve reams of perforated computer paper containing our secret code.

As MITS's director of software, Paul spent much of his day porting our software to the Altair and fielding calls from confused customers trying to navigate their new purchase. For Micro-Soft, Paul helped set our technology direction and was the keeper of our development tools. The work that he had done to create the simulator for the PDP-10 and related tools would pay dividends for years. Not only did they enable us to create our first BASIC without an Altair (or Intel 8080), over time Paul would adapt the tools so we could write versions of the language and other software for different processors. His work had helped put us in the lead on BASIC and would give us a big edge for a long time.

Meanwhile, I dove back into BASIC. On top of fixing bugs in the 4K version, we planned another two versions: one 8K and a 12K, which we called Extended BASIC. If we were novelists, 4K BASIC would have been our outline, a mere sketch of the story. The 8K version layered in more exciting action, fuller characters; the Extended version was a complete draft of the novel, which in the computer realm meant it had things like ELSE statements, and double precision 64-bit variables, features needed to write better programs.

We had signed our contract with MITS in late July, bending to

Ed's insistence that we grant MITS exclusive global rights to all of our BASIC versions for the 8080 chip. The deal paid us $3,000 up front, and we'd get a royalty for every copy of 8080 BASIC that sold with an Altair, between $10 and $60, depending on whether it was 4K, 8K, or Extended. The royalties from those sales were capped at $180,000. The deal also gave MITS the exclusive right to sublicense the software; any company that wanted to use 8080 BASIC in their products would have to get the source code—the recipe to BASIC—through MITS, not Micro-Soft. MITS agreed to split any proceeds from those sublicenses with us. If lots of companies used the Intel 8080 in their products, it could translate into a significant business. But in July 1975, that was a big unknown.

Following the success of the Altair, Ed planned to offer a cheaper version called the Altair 680, using Motorola's 6800 processor. He would need a version of BASIC that worked with the Motorola chip. We said we'd write it. Also at the time, floppy disks were becoming a viable replacement for paper tape storage, and Ed wanted to sell drives for the Altair. Which meant yet another version of BASIC. We agreed to write that one too.

With so much work, I called Ric at his parents' house in Seattle to see if he'd be willing to delay his last semester at Stanford. I told him we needed to write BASIC for the Motorola 6800 chip. How about living in Albuquerque for the fall and making some money? By late September, Ric had moved into 114 Portals with Paul and me, taking over the couch as Chris Larson headed back to Lakeside and Monte to his sophomore year at Harvard.

Of the three of us, Ric was the least settled, seemingly constantly ruminating not only over decisions like whether he should go to law school or business school but over deeper questions about his identity. Two years earlier, when we all spent that summer together coding at TRW, Paul, Ric, and I had shared an apartment in Southern Washington. At different times during that summer, Ric had taken Paul and me aside individually and confided that he was gay.

He was relieved when we each told him it made no difference to us—we were friends. We joked that we already kind of knew: Ric, after all, was the only one of us who had *Playgirl* magazine in the apartment.

At the time I probably didn't fully appreciate how much courage it took Ric to come out. In the early 1970s, homosexuality was still widely stigmatized, and the gay rights movement was just starting; there wasn't a lot of support available. And it's not like our group spent time baring our emotional selves to each other. We were close friends, partners in our little ventures. We goofed around, spent time talking technology, eating out, and seeing movies. But we didn't often, if ever, reveal our deepest feelings and vulnerabilities. In some ways we were still the same adolescents who first met in the Lakeside computer room.

Our team dynamic was also unchanged. Paul continued to soak up all the latest technology news and data, processing it into ideas that might help advance Micro-Soft. Ric's strength was to bear down on a job and methodically tackle every step until it was complete, which for coding was exactly what we needed. I was the one mapping out our strategy and vision, always worried that we weren't moving fast enough or working hard enough. This had been the case ever since we all worked on the payroll job in high school. At Lakeside that arrangement gave Paul the space to do the work he liked—and was best at—and leave the rest to me. Now, as we were getting Micro-Soft off the ground, we naturally assumed those roles: Paul focusing on technology innovations such as his simulator and tools, and me writing new software and handling most of the business side. Recently I had overseen the contract negotiations with Ed Roberts. While I was in Boston, Paul had attempted to get Ed to sign the contract, but he hadn't been able to pull it off; those kinds of face-to-face negotiations were probably Paul's least favorite part of our new venture.

We had landed MITS from two thousand miles away with a

couple of long-distance phone calls and a $240 flight to Albuquerque. But to find the next customer and the one after that, we needed to sell ourselves and our products by writing letters, attending trade shows, visiting companies. We had a lot to figure out: How much should we charge? How do we market? How do we hire employees? Figure out all the payroll and taxes? To Paul those were mundane jobs. If everything went as we hoped, they would only grow in number and complexity.

A few days after signing our deal with MITS, I typed out my feelings in a note to Paul:

"Micro-soft can do well because it is able to design and write good software and because it is able to take people, like Monte . . . teach them, choose a project for them, provide resources and manage them. The monetary, legal, and management decisions involved are very difficult, as I'm sure you know. I feel my contribution towards these tasks entitles me to more than %50 percent of Microsoft."

We should split ownership of the company sixty-forty, I continued firmly. I thought that was only fair. "I have great optimism for our work together. If things go well I intend to take a full year off from school," I wrote in closing. Paul agreed to the split.

As I started this journey into trying to turn our ideas about software into a viable business, I found a model in DEC's Ken Olsen. He learned as he went, and over time became a master of his business. As an engineer, I figured he had to be strong in math, and since math demanded logical thinking and sharp problem-solving, I reasoned that he—and by extension, I—could pick up whatever skills and knowledge were needed. Linear algebra, topology, and the rest of Math 55 tested my limits. By comparison, payroll, finance, even hiring, marketing, and whatever else it took to run a company would be well within my grasp. It was a simplistic view that years later I would be disabused of, but, hey, I was nineteen and that's how I saw it.

—

Life that fall was mostly a whirl of writing code for days on end and sleeping only when I had to, and often wherever I happened to be. I'd catnap at the terminal or just crawl onto the floor next to it. Paul would finish his day job at MITS, walk over to our part of the building to put in a few hours on Micro-Soft, then go home to sleep for a bit before returning at 2 a.m. to find me still at the terminal. As MITS employees arrived at work later that morning, Paul and I would head to Denny's for breakfast, then I'd go back to 114 Portals to sleep for the rest of the day. By that time we had also set up a terminal in our living room that you would connect over the phone line to the school district computer. Most days, Ric rolled off the couch and planted himself at that terminal, hammering out the 6800 BASIC code. On the floor would be strewn pages of our 8080 BASIC code he used as a guide.

We never cooked at home, and aside from a jar of pickled pigs' feet that Chris bought as a joke, our refrigerator was mostly empty. We ate every meal out, often at Furr's Cafeteria, one of a small local chain of restaurants, where I tried chicken-fried steak for the first time, and then by habit ate it nearly every time we went to Furr's from then on. I remember lots of Mexican food, consuming buckets of chile con queso and daring each other to eat a certain blistering green chile hot sauce.

When Paul left Boston in the spring, he had bequeathed to me his Plymouth, by then on its last legs. When I flew west two months later, I left the car where it was parked, knowing that eventually it would get towed to a junkyard. That first summer in Albuquerque, Paul dedicated a chunk of his MITS salary every month to finance his first new car, a 1975 Monza in sky blue. He used to talk about how one day he hoped to make enough money to buy a Rolls-Royce. For now, a two-door Chevy hatchback would have to do. That blue Monza was our unofficial company car, used for fetching our print-outs from the school district, taking us for more chicken-fried steak, and cruising the flat endless roads that stretched out to the west and the winding roads through the Sandia Mountains to the east. The car was light and had a V8 engine and rear-wheel drive, so it would fishtail very easily if you weren't careful. Soon after Paul got the car, Chris and I were joyriding in it when I took a turn too fast and landed the front end in a barbed-wire fence. That was probably the one time I saw Paul close to crying. I paid for the repainting, but I always felt terrible. Paul loved that car, which from then on was called the "Death Trap." Within a year, I was arrested for speeding in the Death Trap. The cop didn't appreciate my joking around and threw me in jail for the night. I called Paul, who bailed me out in the morning with the loose change and dollar bills scattered on my dresser top.

One Friday, Paul and I tagged along with MITS employees to a dive bar on Central Avenue. Since the drinking age was twenty, I wasn't allowed inside, but the bartenders turned a blind eye when MITS colleagues brought their pints to the picnic tables out front. The whole post-work happy hour culture was a new phenomenon to me. Up until that day, I had a very naïve belief that companies were all managed efficiently, and all employees were motivated, loved their jobs, and were pulling together with management in the same direction. The idea that a company was a human organization with all the attendant human foibles and failings simply never occurred to me. That first Friday, followed by others, disabused me of that simplistic view. As the beer flowed so did the complaints. MITS was at the center of a booming new industry, and yet it was a frenzy of confusing initiatives, half-baked strategies, constantly shifting plans—and ultimately, sometimes angry customers. Even some of the most senior people laid the blame on their boss, Ed Roberts. And they were frank about why: everyone was too scared to raise their concerns.

Ed was big—tall and heavy—and had a booming voice that thundered through the office when he wanted something done. People attributed his command-and-control management style to the U.S. Air Force, where Ed had worked with lasers as part of a weapons laboratory. When he spoke, he expected you to listen; he intimidated his staff, and he knew it. I'm sure that force of will is part of what made him a serial entrepreneur, the type of person who can bend the world around him into the shape he wants. Paul was deferential to Ed, which I think Ed expected. I wasn't. I approached Ed more as an equal, as I had always approached adults well before I was one. In the beginning, he seemed to get a kick out of this. He was a natural storyteller and had a command of a wide range of subjects; I'd listen, then counter with my opinion. He appeared bemused by my whole affect—the energy and intensity, my need-to-hash-it-out-now personality. We had great talks, and I learned from him. Yet at the same time, he saw Paul and me as kids for whom he was doing a favor—hence, Ed's nickname for me: "the kid." He was in his mid-thirties, had five children, had birthed a hit computer, and was the president of a hot company with a big future. I remember thinking, *We are a minor thing to Ed and MITS.* When he sat on our contract for a few months, I flew to Seattle to bide my time until he signed it. In his view, this constituted insubordination.

Once we signed the contract, I was game for anything. Paul and I traveled with the Blue Goose camper van and started writing articles on software in *Computer Notes,* the MITS newsletter, dispensing programming tips and running a monthly contest with prizes going to the Altair owners who wrote the best software. In a company that knew little about software, Paul and I were outliers brimming with energy and ideas. Paul's late-night programming to ear-splitting Hendrix solos and my excited, always-on intensity only underscored the impression that we were different. Paul liked to tell the story that Ed Roberts instructed MITS employees to avoid bringing customers back into the software area, which Paul chalked up to the fact that we were unshaven and unshowered. Ed once entered our office and nearly tripped over me sleeping on the floor.

Anytime I wasn't sleeping, coding, or writing a letter trying to drum up business, my mind was locked on the next step: people to hire, deals to cut, new customers. When I got going, everything on my mind just spilled out to anyone who would listen. At dinner with Paul and MITS people, I could talk for an hour, rocking in my chair, sipping my Shirley Temple while spinning visions of how we'd get our software into every personal computer, or why the Motorola 6800 was better than the MosTech 6502, or why a small business would buy a Sphere 1 rather than an Altair. My mind needed to make order of everything I heard, every new piece of information that I was soaking up. I'd talk and talk and then notice that everyone else was done eating. I'd leave the restaurant having not touched my food. *Maybe I'll go to Denny's in a few hours. Or not. I think you can go a whole day without eating?*

The happy hour crowd goaded me to push Ed to make changes they felt the company needed. "Hey Bill, why don't you go tell Ed that we're doing too much and we should focus more. Hey Bill, you should go tell Ed that we should scrap his idea for a new Altair." I had grown up a little bit since the Lakeside computer room days when Paul first learned how easy it was to poke me into action. But not much.

MITS had taken a booth at the New Mexico State Fair in September. It felt funny to be standing at our booth with a fifty-pound computer, waiting for someone to put down their cotton candy and get their first lesson in the BASIC programming language. But we were optimistic. A few people stopped by, but often just as we started the demonstration, the computer crashed.

The Altair shipped with very little memory—just 256 bytes of RAM—which was like driving a car with a soda-can-sized gas tank. That constraint spawned several companies devoted to selling memory boards that customers could buy separately and slot into their Altair.

Ed Roberts hated those board sellers. They were "parasites," he said, that were eating into a business that was rightfully his. Part of the problem was that MITS made very little money on the Altair itself. That put pressure on Ed to come up with peripherals and other extras that could be sold at a profit. Memory boards were the first crack at that. But MITS's boards were flawed, in part because it bought memory chips that were flawed. That's why our state fair demo crashed and why suddenly hordes of Altair customers were complaining. These boards were a big topic for the happy hour crowd. It was clear that MITS should stop selling them. You should tell Ed, they said.

I wrote software that diagnosed the problem as a combination of the design of the cards and the fact that certain memory chips leaked their electric charge too quickly. I showed the results to Ed and said he needed to stop selling the boards until we could fix the problem. He told me he couldn't. "You don't understand that the banks are breathing down our necks!" he yelled. I didn't back down. I shot back: "Stop selling the boards! We'll get this solved—just stop selling the boards until we do."

Instead, he kept shipping them and they'd boomerang back so fast that MITS customer support couldn't keep up with the complaints and demands for replacements. In *Computer Notes,* Ed apologized for the card failures. MITS, he said, was trying to train customer support people faster. "Please bear with us. We are trying!!!" he wrote.

I would come to see Ed as the consummate entrepreneur, a polymath curious about many things and willing to put aside the hard details in pursuit of a grand idea. The type of person who comes up with the Brilliant Idea isn't often the best person to turn it into a business.

In the time I knew him, Ed would find any number of new passions and pursue them with gusto. With cash flowing into MITS from Altair sales, he bought a Cessna 310 in September 1975, which is how I ended up seated behind him in the twin-engine plane two months later. We flew from Albuquerque to Kansas City, Missouri, to attend a meeting of personal computer–related companies working on a standard for how computers store data on cassette tapes.

The conference was fine. I got a chance to practice my salesmanship, meeting with other companies and explaining Micro-Soft and BASIC. And we knocked out a standard, though it eventually would be forgotten as floppy disks replaced cassette tapes.

One thing that remains from that conference, however, is my memory of the trip back to Albuquerque. We took off on Saturday afternoon after the conference ended. As we hit 7,000 feet, Ed suddenly said that the left engine was losing oil; he had to shut it off and fly on a single engine. From the back, I watched the sweat pour off his face as he fought to keep the plane from lurching to the left—I learned the word "yawl" that day—and flew back toward the airport for an emergency landing. I don't tend to get scared. I like driving fast. I love getting tossed around on a roller coaster. But seeing Ed sweating and fighting to keep the plane on course scared me. I remember thinking: *Is Ed a good pilot or not? I should have asked about that earlier.* When we landed—safely, I should add—I swore I could see a wave of relief wash through Ed's body.

We stayed another night in Kansas City, where a mechanic inspected the plane and told Ed he could find nothing wrong. The next morning, we took off and, déjà vu at 7,000 feet: the left engine lost oil again, forcing Ed to make his second emergency landing in two days. Despite my taste for risk, this was too much. I left Ed and his plane and took a commercial flight to Albuquerque.

At night I would often leave our apartment and take long walks on the flat streets around Kirtland Air Force Base. The area was quiet during those hours, the perfect place to walk and think, sometimes about coding problems but usually about some part of our

Micro-Soft plans. Walking in December 1975 before flying home to Seattle for Christmas, I reflected on the eight months since we founded Micro-Soft. We had made a lot of progress. It was amazing to think that thousands of people were using software that we had made. Still, I worried that we were dependent on royalties from MITS, and that too many people were opting for the old, copied version of BASIC and not paying us for the latest versions. For every hundred Altairs MITS sold, maybe ten included our software, thanks to the rampant spread of the pirated version. As a measure of where we stood, Micro-Soft that year would declare taxes on revenue of just $16,005, which included the $3,000 MITS gave us up front. As for future business, we had made lots of connections and generated promising leads, but no deals yet.

Within a month or so, I was due back at Harvard. As planned, I had taken off just the fall semester to get Micro-Soft going, and starting in early February of next year I would try to juggle Micro-Soft work with a full course load. Paul was balancing demands as a full-time MITS employee with his role at Micro-Soft. Ric, meanwhile, was also heading back to college for his final semester. He was ambivalent about whether he'd stick with us or even what he'd do next. That left no one thinking about the company full-time.

And yet at that point I didn't think we were going to miss out. I was incredibly optimistic, maybe overly so. I was confident about the trajectory of the personal computer business. I felt that we were close to landing some deals, and we didn't have any significant competitors as yet. A free version of the language, called Tiny BASIC, had just emerged from the People's Computer Company in Silicon Valley, but it was lacking compared to ours.

On that walk, I convinced myself that I could both run a company and be a full-time student. All that time I had put into my baseball program was time I could now dedicate to Micro-Soft. I also felt that everything I was learning at Harvard was still foundational to who I was becoming; in particular, I had started to develop a rapport with several computer science professors and thought I could learn a lot more from them—and gain knowledge that would help Micro-soft. Plus, I loved college—loved the frenetic learning pace, the late-night talks with people who knew things that I didn't. Despite my tough freshman adjustment period, I had settled into a good rhythm my second year. Looking back now with the knowledge of how the Micro-Soft story would play out, it seems obvious that I should have just quit school at that point. But I wasn't ready. And, of course, neither were my parents. I went home for Christmas and all the usual Gates traditions, including my mom's homemade card, one that veiled her worries about me with a corny rhyme: "Trey took time off this fall in old Albuquerque; His own software business—we hope not a turkey. (The profits are murky.)"

I had returned to Albuquerque after the holidays when I got a call from my parents, who told me that my father was a top pick for a federal judgeship. The chief judge of the U.S. District Court in our area had died suddenly while playing tennis, and the Ford administration had my father at the top of the list to replace him. It was amazing news. But my dad confided that after some thought, he had declined. His law firm had been through a tough period, and he felt the timing was inopportune. Leaving would have been a blow to the firm.

In my dad's world, a judgeship was the top of the heap, as prestigious a position as you could get. But he felt he owed it to his colleagues to stay. Plus, as the wife of a judge, my mom might have had to cut back her activities at a time that her career was thriving.

The call came less than a week before I was set to fly to Boston. I checked into the Four Seasons Motor Inn to finish writing out the code for the disk version of BASIC. I had been too busy and now it was down to the wire. Working sixteen hours a day, I scratched out the code on a yellow pad and lived off takeout for four days. In between coding sessions, I drafted a letter to my dad.

I rarely wrote letters to my parents back then. There was nothing that couldn't be covered in our periodic Sunday-night phone calls. Now, however, writing a letter seemed the best way to communicate how I felt about his decision. After we hung up, I thought a lot about my dad's resolve. He considered a judgeship the highest calling of his profession, and for a long time he had hoped that one day he would have the chance to serve. So close to the brass ring and then—based on deeper loyalties to his firm, and to my mom—he let it pass. I confessed that I was surprised. "It's great to decide that you're happiest with what you're doing even when a long-sought opportunity presents itself. Ever since I knew you were thinking about a judgeship, I've thought you would be a great one. It's too bad you would have had to give up so many of the things you enjoy now, but you can't have the best of both worlds," I wrote. I closed with my worry that I was a factor. "I really hope the financial burden of my education didn't affect your decision since I am quite willing and able to pay for it myself. With love, Trey."

I read that letter now and can't help but smile at the tone, as if I'm the dad conveying understanding of my son's decision. As heartfelt letters go, mine wasn't dripping with emotion. Our relationship wasn't like that. We didn't express our deeper feelings to each other often. So this was a big deal. I had never offered my opinion to my dad on his career choices. I had never felt qualified or mature enough to have an opinion. Plus, he was always so in control and so organized, he didn't ever seem to need the input.

Between the lines was the message my father surely received, which was that I was mature enough to understand that he had turned his back on prestige in lieu of something more important. But I also wanted to communicate that I was sophisticated enough to understand the nuances of his decision. I wanted to convey that I was now mature enough to look after myself. Elsewhere in the letter I recounted how hard I was working, that I was holed up writing the disk code, which "is extremely complex and requires real concentration so I isolated myself to get it done."

Days later, he replied. No, he said, paying for my education didn't play into his decision. "I really liked your letter expressing your interest in the decision about the judgeship. It was just as you say— I'm so secure and happy in what I'm doing that a big change would just be silly," he wrote. "Your mother and I were very touched at your concern about this and your willingness to pay your own way."

He closed his note: "Hope you are getting organized. Love, Dad."

In Boston, I returned to Currier House, poker games, and the puzzles of applied math. It was easy to fall back into the rhythm of school. Almost immediately, however, I felt the pull of Micro-Soft. We had found a major customer.

NCR was one of the biggest computer makers at the time, one of the "seven dwarfs" who competed with IBM. In addition to large mainframe computers, NCR made a product called the 7200 that was a combination of a keyboard, a nine-inch screen, and a cassette recorder. There was a class of devices back then called dumb terminals, including the terminal we used at Lakeside (and were using to connect to the Albuquerque School District computer), which were basically keyboards with a display or printer for accessing programs running on a large computer. With the introduction of inexpensive processors like the Intel 8080, companies such as NCR were expanding the number of tasks their terminals could execute, creating a new class of "smart" terminals.

That spring we had signed the deal to tailor 8080 BASIC to the NCR 7200 for what at the time was the staggering sum of $150,000. Since MITS had the exclusive rights to sublicense our software, we'd have to split that amount with them evenly.

The NCR negotiations came right as classes were starting, which meant we needed to find someone to manage the NCR job. I wrote a letter to Ric in which I estimated that it would take one person two and a half months of work, which would involve all rewriting and additions needed to adapt BASIC for the NCR terminal. That time, I told him, was measured in "Gates-months," a self-referential attempt to make it clear that I meant hard work, full-time, with no distractions. In his reply, Ric informed me that after graduating in the spring, he'd likely go on to a master's degree or to law school. I'd have to find someone else.

Though the MITS computer continued to sell well, only a small portion of customers were paying for BASIC. In the fall Ed Roberts had devoted his column in the MITS newsletter, *Computer Notes,* to gently chastise his customers about ponying up for the software. I didn't think he was forceful enough. In my dorm room one night that winter I had typed my feelings on a single page of paper and sent it to one of the happy hour crowd, a writer at MITS named Dave Bunnell who edited *Computer Notes.* Dave had mailed copies of my letter to a bunch of computer magazines and to the Homebrew Computer Club's newsletter, before publishing it in the February 1976 issue of *Computer Notes:*

An Open Letter to Hobbyists

To me, the most critical thing in the hobby market right now is the lack of good software courses, books and software itself. Without good software and an owner who understands programming, a hobby computer is wasted. Will quality software be written for the hobby market?

Almost a year ago, Paul Allen and myself, expecting the hobby market to expand, hired Monte Davidoff and developed Altair BASIC. Though the initial work took

only two months, the three of us have spent most of the
last year documenting, improving and adding features to
BASIC. Now we have 4K, 8K, EXTENDED, ROM and
DISK BASIC. The value of the computer time we have used
exceeds $40,000.

The feedback we have gotten from the hundreds of
people who say they are using BASIC has all been positive.
Two surprising things are apparent, however, 1) Most of
these "users" never bought BASIC (less than 10% of all
Altair owners have bought BASIC), and 2) The amount of
royalties we have received from sales to hobbyists makes the
time spent on Altair BASIC worth less than $2 an hour.

Why is this? As the majority of hobbyists must be aware,
most of you steal your software. Hardware must be paid for,
but software is something to share. Who cares if the people
who worked on it get paid?

Is this fair? One thing you don't do by stealing software
is get back at MITS for some problem you may have had.
MITS doesn't make money selling software. The royalty
paid to us, the manual, the tape and the overhead make it
a break-even operation. One thing you do do is prevent
good software from being written. Who can afford to
do professional work for nothing? What hobbyist can
put 3 man-years into programming, finding all bugs,
documenting his product and distribute for free? The fact
is, no one besides us has invested a lot of money in hobby
software. We have written 6800 BASIC, and are writing
8080 APL and 6800 APL, but there is very little incentive to
make this software available to hobbyists. Most directly, the
thing you do is theft.

What about the guys who re-sell Altair BASIC, aren't
they making money on hobby software? Yes, but those who

have been reported to us may lose in the end. They are the ones who give hobbyists a bad name, and should be kicked out of any club meeting they show up at.

I would appreciate letters from any one who wants to pay up, or has a suggestion or comment. Just write to me at 1180 Alvarado SE, #114, Albuquerque, New Mexico, 87108. Nothing would please me more than being able to hire ten programmers and deluge the hobby market with good software.

Bill Gates
General Partner, Micro-Soft

The letter was a shot heard round the world of computer clubs and hobbyists. Prior to that letter, if any Altair user knew the name Micro-Soft or had heard of Bill Gates, they would probably have had little to say. We were all but unknown. Now Micro-Soft was suddenly grist for an ideological debate over the future of software. Free? Or for a fee? A handful of readers supported me, echoing my point that without a financial incentive, few people would write the software everyone wanted. A computer technician in the psychology department at Eastern Washington State College wrote to congratulate me on "your decision to speak up. . . . I have come to truly appreciate good software and the men and women who have spent countless hours in development and debugging. Without programmers a computer is simply a large (or small) hunk of silicon or and metal."

Other people slammed me. "To the problems raised by Bill Gates in his irate letter," wrote the editor of one new computer magazine, "when software is free, or so inexpensive that it's easier to pay for than it is to duplicate it, then it won't be 'stolen.'"

Ed Roberts was outraged. Though he agreed that software should be paid for, in his eyes, I had crossed a line by insulting his customers. A week or so after the letter was published, I was back in

Albuquerque, and Ed was screaming at me. "You don't even work for our company!" he yelled. I felt really bad about putting him in a difficult position and regretful that I hadn't been more diplomatic in my letter. Since it went out on MITS stationery, my screed made it seem—to Ed and probably many others—that MITS itself was calling its customers thieves. Ed told me that I would work with a MITS employee to write another letter. In it, I would apologize. And that, he said, would be the last time I would write an open letter.

Days later, on March 27, 1976, I nervously walked onstage at the grandly named World Altair Convention, held at an airport hotel in Albuquerque. The confab was dreamed up by Dave Bunnell—the MITS writer—as a way to further spread the buzz over the Altair. Ed Roberts was stunned that over seven hundred people showed up. Thanks to the open letter, my reputation preceded me. This would be my first professional speech. I had carefully crafted my talk—an update on BASIC as the future of software—and put on my best tie and my only sport jacket to lay out an argument for why software was the most important part of the computer. It sounds obvious now, but it took some imagination to envision how these machines could evolve. My main memory of the talk is that when it ended, a scrum of people formed around me asking questions. I had never experienced that before, strangers circled around, all eyes on me. I rocked as I talked, my mental metronome kicking in as I dropped into the comfort of explaining the technical details of software and the business we were trying to build. I don't remember how much time I spent addressing my larger worry about people not paying for software, but I'm sure I had to field plenty of questions about that as well.

Before I left Albuquerque, Ed had me write my follow-up letter, which Dave Bunnell printed in the April *Computer Notes* and sent around to other publications. "A SECOND AND FINAL LETTER" was less the apology that Ed wanted and more a reasoned rationalization for commercial software. No, not all computer hob-byists are thieves, I wrote, followed by my attempt at diplomacy: "On the contrary, I find that the majority are intelligent and honest individuals who share my concern for the future of software devel-opment." At the same time, the future of the personal computer hinged on good software getting written, and that meant the people writing it needed to be paid. "Software makes the difference between a computer being a fascinating educational tool for years and being an exciting enigma for a few months and then gathering dust in the closet," I wrote.

The hope that with paying customers we could hire coders be-came a reality that spring, as money from the NCR deal and a few others—about $20,000 a month—allowed Micro-Soft to hire its first employee. In April I called Marc McDonald, a fellow Lakesider a year younger than me. He had been part of the broader computer room gang and was now in his sophomore year studying computer science at the University of Washington. The classes weren't that great, he said, so he was spending a lot of time at a job program-ming on a PDP-10 at the health science school. Marc was probably our company's easiest hire ever: I offered him $8.50 an hour, he said yes, and within days he drove to Albuquerque and took over the couch at 114 Portals. A few days later, I got a letter from Ric; he'd had a change of heart about going to graduate school and wanted to rejoin Micro-Soft. He suggested a partnership. "I'd genuinely like to concentrate my efforts on making Micro-Soft reach its full poten-tial," he wrote. He was willing to work with the company for "a long while as I can see, of course, considerable profit, both economic and otherwise, in it."

Over the next weekend, Paul, Ric, and I worked out the details on the phone. We would set up a three-way partnership that would accommodate my being in school and Paul working at MITS for at least another six months. Ric would head to Albuquerque the follow-ing week to get us set up with Micro-Soft business cards, stationery, and a PO Box, then barrage potential customers with letters offering our software and consulting. We might even spring for an answering service on the chance that orders would start flooding in.

If I stayed in college, I would work part-time and handle legal and financial management and whatever programming we needed. Ric would manage the company and serve as president while I was in school. While continuing to work at MITS, Paul would be responsible for finding Micro-Soft new technology opportunities and maintaining our relationship with existing customers, including MITS, NCR, and another smart terminal maker we had landed called Data Terminal Corporation.

I scribbled down our business plan on seven pages of copier paper. My guiding principle was not getting ahead of ourselves and drowning in costs. That meant we'd each get paid nine dollars an hour. "The $9 figure for partners is enough to live nicely on, and will not be changed dependent on success, individual effort, individual luck etc. The only basis for changing this will be if it needs to be lowered because MSoft cannot afford it."

Our two main goals, I wrote, were (1) grow in size and reputation, and (2) make money. That letter marked the next phase of a concerted effort to establish ourselves as an independent company. We all agreed to make Micro-Soft our main priority for at least the next two years.

CHAPTER FOURTEEN

Source Code

icrocomputers catch on fast."

That was the headline in an issue of *Business Week* I bought the summer of 1976, about a year after we signed our contract with MITS. I liked the story because it wasn't in the trade press or a computer hobbyist newsletter, the typical publications that followed our corner of the computer industry. I figured *Business Week* readers were investors and executives—mostly people who had yet to own a computer themselves but might be inclined to buy one if they were easier to use.

With a blue ballpoint pen, I highlighted what I saw as the key paragraph: "Already, the home computer industry is beginning to look like a miniature version of the mainframe computer business—down to the dominance of one competitor. The IBM of home computers is MITS Inc., founded seven years ago by engineer H. Edward Roberts in the garage of his Albuquerque (N.M.) home." The story

269

noted that MITS had sold eight thousand Altair computers and brought in $3.5 million of revenue the previous year. There were competitors, the story noted, but the Altair's early lead made it the industry standard.

The article brought a rush of phone calls into MITS from as far away as South Africa; people wanted to connect with the hot company in the story, either by becoming distributors, opening computer shops, or working as consultants helping introduce the Altair to business customers. MITS employees were gushing over the article and hoped it would lead to even more sophisticated applications of their machine.

As I read, I thought, *Even if MITS is the IBM of the moment, that isn't going to last.* One reason: if IBM ever decided to make a personal computer, there's a good chance it would replace MITS as the IBM of the moment. I knew that Ed Roberts was also worried that major electronics companies would push their way into the fray. In Ed's eyes, the scariest of those companies was Texas Instruments. In the early 1970s MITS had pioneered programmable kit calculators, which are used by engineers and scientists. Once that market reached a certain size, big companies, led by Texas Instruments, swooped in with assembled low-priced alternatives and nearly killed off MITS. Ed deeply feared a repeat with personal computers.

It was clear to all of us that Ed was growing tired of running MITS. Less than two years after unveiling the Altair, his work life was an endless headache of customer calls, complaints from Altair dealers, and the day-to-day hassle of a company that had swelled from a handful of people to well over two hundred employees. On any given day, a frustrated employee would harangue him because a colleague got paid a few more cents an hour. At least once, he fired someone but felt so bad about it, he soon rehired them. Ed had a soft spot that didn't always square with his often gruff exterior.

It worried me that we were still so reliant on MITS. Royalties from licenses of 8080 BASIC for the Altair were still our largest source of revenue. Licenses of our source code for that version of BASIC were picking up. Around that time, we landed General Electric, which gave us $50,000 for unlimited use of the 8080 BASIC source code. Following the NCR deal, a bunch of other smart terminal vendors had contacted us. I visited one of them, Applied Digital Data Systems, on Long Island. I flew into New York's JFK intending to drive a rental car to ADDS in Hauppauge, about an hour away. My plans were thwarted by a rental agent who informed me that he couldn't rent me a car: I was too young. Someone from ADDS collected me from the airport. It was an embarrassing start to the relationship. Still, they were interested, and so began a protracted back-and-forth as we worked out a deal.

Of course, since MITS held worldwide rights to 8080 BASIC, any time we found a customer for the source code, the contract would have to go through MITS. If we signed a deal, we then had to split the revenues with them. Gradually, that summer, we began to try to wean ourselves off MITS. We started the search for our own office and began work on products that could draw in new customers.

The job of finding those new customers mostly fell to Ric, who had taken on the role of general manager. In the months since we had agreed to a three-way partnership, Ric had experienced a change of heart. To be a partner meant he'd have to focus entirely on Micro-Soft; he wanted time to branch out and enjoy a well-rounded life. He went to church, lifted weights at the gym, took off time to visit friends in Los Angeles. Though Ric had come out to Paul and me years earlier, it was in Albuquerque that he fully embraced who he was. In a nod to that new life, he bought a Corvette with a personalized plate that read "YES I AM," in case anyone wondered. He blossomed socially and found his first love.

After Ric had opted out of the partnership, Paul and I agreed that we would continue to split ownership of Micro-Soft sixty-forty. Officially we each used the title "senior partner," though as a parody of big-company business types, we adopted grandiose titles among ourselves: I was "the President," and he was "the Veep." As general manager, Ric handled marketing and most of the day-to-day work, from dealing with MITS to depositing checks and finding our office space. He was meticulous, recording every interaction in a notebook titled "The Micro Soft Journal." Today it's an artifact of what it was like doing business in the 1970s: typed letters and phone call after phone call to company after company, hoping to reach someone who might be interested in buying our software. A sample:

Saturday, July 24:
2:45 Try Steve Jobs. Give his mom message.

Tuesday, July 27:
10:55 Try Steve Jobs. Busy.
11:15 Steve Jobs calls. Was very rude.
11:30 Try Peddle again. Must talk to him.

Peddle was Chuck Peddle, an engineer at MOS Technology, the maker of the 6502 chip that Steve Wozniak had used in the Apple I. A few years earlier, Peddle had left Motorola with several other engineers to join MOS Technology, where they created the 6502. The chip was similar to the Motorola 6800 microprocessor. We had developed a version of BASIC for the Motorola chip, so Ric had started to write a version for the 6502. But we needed a customer. All through the summer and early fall, Ric filled his journal with his attempts to reach the company by phone: *12:55 Try Peddle again; called Peddle at MOS Technology. Out on vacation. Call Peddle. Busy.* Steve Jobs, meanwhile, told Ric that Apple had a version of BASIC that his partner Wozniak designed, and that if it needed another one, Wozniak would write it, not Micro-Soft. However Steve delivered that news, I guess Ric found it off-putting.

The popularity of BASIC gave Micro-Soft its start, and we would continue to adapt the language to different microprocessors as Ric was doing with the 6502. And yet BASIC, for all its ease of use and popularity with hobbyists, wasn't the language that more serious computer buyers wanted. Scientists and academics used FORTRAN; businesses, COBOL. Meanwhile, FOCAL was a BASIC alternative popular among the many users of DEC minicomputers. In a push to expand, we got to work on versions of all three. We also started pitching Paul's development tools to customers. Early on, Paul and I had envisioned Micro-Soft would offer a broad array of software products—the software factory idea. We weren't anywhere near that yet, but building an array of languages and development tools was a step toward that future.

To support the development of new products, in late summer we started hiring our first full-time employees from outside our Lakeside circle, including Steve Wood, who had just finished his master's degree in electrical engineering at Stanford, and his wife, Marla Wood. Until that point, we were a band of friends whose futures didn't worry me. If everything blew up, I was confident that we'd head off in our various directions and be fine. But now we were hiring people we didn't know and asking them to move to New Mexico and cast their lot with us, an eighteen-month-old company with an unclear future. It was a bit daunting. To me, those early hires made Micro-Soft feel like a real company.

I was in Seattle that summer to write what I thought would be *the* product for our future, a programming language called APL, which was short for, well, A Programming Language. IBM, which had developed the original version in the early 1960s, continued to champion it in the 1970s and offered it on a variety of computers. The language was highly regarded by serious programmers, many of whom thought its popularity was poised to grow. If we could come up with our own version, I figured we could ride that wave and expand into the business market beyond the hobbyist roots of BASIC.

APL also appealed to me as a coder. It has very concise syntax, allowing you to execute in just a few statements what would take many lines of code in other languages. That made writing a version for a personal computer a tricky puzzle of compressing great complexity into a small package. I labored day and night to get it right, working off a portable terminal I had set up in my bedroom and paying my parents for the dial-up phone charges. Libby, then age twelve, would stand in my doorway wondering what her crazy brother was up to, glued to his computer terminal all day. On breaks she'd battle me in Ping-Pong. (I never did manage to crack APL, but my Ping-Pong game improved.)

That summer would turn out to be the last time I lived in my parents' house. When I think about it now, I have much greater appreciation for the role my family played during that early period of Micro-Soft. As proudly independent as I imagined myself, in truth my family supported me in ways both practical and emotional. Throughout the year I regularly retreated to Gami's place on Hood Canal for much-needed periods of reflection, and that summer was no exception. My father was always at the ready to help me work out some legal issue. Kristi, meanwhile, now twenty-two and thriving at Deloitte, was handling Micro-Soft's taxes.

To my parents, it must have seemed that I was finally getting organized in my father's sense of the word. I had my own business and, while I had taken a semester off from college, I was returning in the fall for what would be the second semester of my junior year. They were happy with my plan and understood that I found college intellectually fulfilling in a way that was distinctly different from Micro-Soft. I signed up for a course in British history during the Industrial Revolution and used my applied math wild card to talk my way into ECON 2010, a graduate-level economic theory class.

There was another undergraduate in the class, a math major named Steve Ballmer.

The previous year, a Currier House friend had suggested that I meet a guy who lived down the hall. "Steve's a lot like you," he said. By then I could instantly recognize other people—Boomer and Kent were prime examples—who emitted my kind of excess energy. Steve Ballmer had it beyond anyone I had ever known. Most of the male Currier residents were nerdy math-science types who kept to their own and whose social lives revolved around playing Pong or poker in the dorm basement. Steve didn't fit that model. He had an unusual combination of brains and physicality and was effortlessly social. He was way more active on campus than anyone I knew, overseeing advertising at *The Harvard Crimson,* serving as the president of the literary magazine, and managing the football team.

I went to one game that fall and from the stands watched Steve expend as much energy pacing and bouncing on the sidelines as any Harvard player deployed on the field. Every particle of his being was trained on that team. You could tell that he really cared about his role as manager. It was hard not to get caught up in his exuberance. Steve expanded my social circle, and through him I was nominated for membership in the Fox Club, a male-only club with black-tie parties, secret handshakes, and other archaic rules and rituals that I would normally have avoided. But since Steve was a member, I agreed to be considered, and was accepted.

As it turned out, we didn't spend much time in ECON 2010 together; given my continued approach to skipping classes until the final and Steve's packed schedule, neither of us attended the three hours of weekly lectures. We agreed we'd risk it all on the final. Late at night in the dorm, however, Steve and I had long talks about our life goals reminiscent of my conversations with Kent. We hashed out the benefits of working in government versus for a company, and which of those options would enable us to do more to improve society and have a greater impact on the world. He typically argued on the side of a big role in government. Not surprisingly, I took the side of corporate interests. It was, after all, the job that was on my mind most of the time.

As the semester progressed, I began to feel extremely conflicted about Micro-Soft. Up to that point, the company seemed manageable from afar, particularly with Ric overseeing the day-to-day. But as we were growing, so did the complexity of the business details. Often when I'd check in with Paul or Ric, I'd hear about some new issue that I thought wasn't being handled. The more I learned about the GE deal, for instance, the more I came to believe we had underbid them for the work we promised. Ric wasn't tracking the money for employee business trips, and we were way over budget on travel; we were owed $10,000 from NCR, but neither Paul nor Ric knew when it was expected. One of our biggest problems was MITS, which hadn't paid royalties it owed us related to Altairs that included extra memory. Since most of our revenue came from MITS, we needed every bit of it to keep Micro-Soft going until other sources panned out.

I made my frustration clear in early November. After a rare night of partying with Steve and my new social club friends, I went back to my dorm and typed a letter to Paul and Ric, warning them that "I went out drinking for the first time this semester tonight so I might not be too coherent, but I decided to write this tonight so I'm going to."

Reading the letter now is a reminder that even as our company was taking off, we were still working on the traffic venture and helping Lakeside with its schedule. I began with a page of technical directives related to those two projects. But the focus was Micro-Soft, and all the things that were falling through the cracks: travel expenses, employee oversight, customer follow-up, and contract negotiations. I groused that they still hadn't lined up a company credit card. Paying $800 in some kind of penalty was another beef, as was the ongoing issue of getting MITS to pay our royalites. I wrote: "Spending $14,000 since I've left and not thinking about cash flow or taking care of the memory royalty is the way to send us down the tube."

I closed the letter: "For all that talk about hard work and long hours, it's clear that you guys haven't talked about Microsoft together or even thought about it individually, at least not near enough. As far as 'putting out your last measure' the commitment just isn't being met. Your friend, Bill."

The warning about the drinking aside, my tone wasn't unusual for the time. Of the three of us, I had always been the taskmaster, the one who incessantly worried about losing our lead, and fearing that if we weren't careful, we'd be sunk. We'd watched C-Cubed go from promising start-up to having creditors drag the furniture away eighteen months later. And in just the past year, we were witnessing the growing troubles at MITS, which had the lead but seemed to lack the management rigor to maintain it. We were a young company figuring out all the functions of business: legal, human resources, tax, contracts, budgets, and finance. We knew the core job of developing software. I worried we weren't learning everything else fast enough.

A couple of weeks later I was in Albuquerque for ten days over Thanksgiving break to work through some of the issues in my tough-love letter. We had just moved into our first true headquarters: rented office space on the eighth floor of a new ten-story building, Two Park Central Tower. It was one of the tallest buildings around, offering an incredible view of the sunsets over downtown Albuquerque and rainstorms far off in the desert. The space had a reception area and four separate offices, and more that we could rent as we expanded. (Around that time we officially incorporated Microsoft in New Mexico—without the hyphen.)

My trip coincided with Paul's decision to quit MITS and dedicate himself exclusively to Microsoft. I don't remember if my concerns about our company factored into his decision; I don't know how pressured he felt by me. I do know that Paul was tired of MITS. As Ed's stress grew, so did the tension between him and Paul. At one point they had a blowup over Ed's insistence that Paul ship software that wasn't ready; Paul gave notice soon after. Whatever his reasons for leaving, it was good news for us. He would be able to spend more time guiding our new employees on the technical development of FORTRAN and other products.

I reviewed the cash flow with Paul and Ric and worked through the finances of expanding our office space as we hired more people. We were getting a lot of inquiries for our 8080 BASIC and were trying to nail down contracts from companies including Delta Data, Lexar, Intel, and ADDS, the smart terminal maker I had visited on Long Island. Increasingly, though, Ed didn't sign.

That was troubling. But we hoped to quickly find new revenue from other products. One was the 6502 BASIC that Ric was writing. In late August a company called Commodore International announced that it had bought MOS Technology. Commodore had been a leading maker of calculators that, like MITS, got trampled by Texas Instruments. But also like MITS, it had the expertise to design and build a personal computer. And now Commodore had the chip for it.

One afternoon just before Thanksgiving, Ric called Chuck Peddle, his contact at MOS Technology, now part of Commodore. After months of missed calls and messages, Peddle said that Commodore was interested in our BASIC and that our price was agreeable to them. It was great news. (Within a few weeks Paul would flag a story in the *EE Times:* Commodore planned to build a general-purpose computer based on the 6502. We needed to finish the BASIC for it as soon as possible.)

A little over an hour after Ric spoke with Peddle, we got a call from a software manager at Texas Instruments. The TI manager informed Ric that his company was working on a computer built around one of its own chips. He wanted to see documentation on our BASIC and on our company. He said they would have to convince TI's management to go with us, but TI's interest alone was a huge breakthrough. Aside from IBM or DEC, there was no other company whose entry into personal computers had been more highly anticipated. TI had a brand name, engineering prowess, and marketing skill. It was also the company that Ed Roberts had long feared. TI's deep pockets and aggressive pricing had almost sent MITS to the grave once, and it could easily do so again.

I was back at school when we heard rumors that a group of men in pin-striped suits had been spending time at MITS. MITS wasn't a natural habitat for suits. They stuck out. Eventually we learned that the men were from a company named Pertec. Pertec? I had never heard of it. I went to Widener Library (yes, this was before you could search for things like this on the internet) and found a write-up. Pertec, or Peripheral Equipment Corporation, was a publicly traded maker of disk drives and other storage devices for large computers. It was based in California, and it was big: over a thousand employees and nearly a hundred million dollars in annual revenue.

Pertec made an offer in early December to buy MITS for $6 million. If the deal went through, Ed Roberts would be rewarded for his innovative idea to build a microcomputer. And with funding from a parent company, maybe MITS could stave off Texas Instruments and any other interloper that wanted to steal the computer market from it.

Soon after Pertec began courting MITS, everything Microsoft-related stopped completely. Royalty payments stopped; licensing deals stopped. Ed had already told us that he refused to sell our BASIC to any company he thought would compete with MITS. By late 1976, his definition of competitor had widened to include the entire industry.

Over Christmas break in Seattle, I got a letter from Ric. Another change of heart: He was going to leave Microsoft. After further soul searching, he had reached the conclusion that he wanted to live in Los Angeles, where he thought he could build a vibrant social life. There was also a small but established software company in L.A. that wanted to hire him.

I felt abandoned. When we spoke next, I accused him of misleading me the prior spring when he assured me of his commitment to Microsoft. He countered that he had never promised to stay long. We went back and forth about money, and all the work we still had ahead of us. Eventually we calmed down. I asked if he could stay until March to finish the 6502 BASIC for Commodore. I said we'd pay for the work he was doing plus the salary that his new company promised until he left in March. He agreed. He then flew off to the Consumer Electronics Show in Chicago, where our new partner, Commodore, debuted the Commodore PET 2001, an all-in-one computer with a built-in monitor, a keyboard, and a cassette tape player (for storing data). It came in a molded-plastic case and looked different from any previous personal computer, more like something you'd find in a home than on a hobbyist's workbench. That was the point.

I was visiting my grandmother on Hood Canal over the holiday break and stepped out one night for a long walk. I vividly remember making my way down the two-lane Route 106, which snakes along the southern strip of the canal, thinking through the problems with MITS and the larger question of how to manage Microsoft over the coming year. MITS and its suitor Pertec were making no effort to sell our software, and they were blocking deals even as more and more companies were soliciting us. It felt like the industry was finally starting to take off and there was no way we were going to get left behind, I told myself. Wrapped up in this was my sense that it was getting harder and harder to live life as a college student with a sideline software company.

Paul and I were totally aligned on the vision to create the leading

PC software maker. That goal was like a prize we could glimpse on the other side of a river. But it was clear to me by the end of 1976 that the ambition to be the first to get there—to be the fastest to build the best bridge to the other side—was stronger in me than it was in him.

Like one of those watertight hatches on a submarine, I could shut out the rest of the world. Driven by the sense of responsibility I felt for Microsoft, I had closed the hatch door and locked the wheel. No girlfriend, no hobbies. My social life centered around Paul, Ric, and the people we worked with. It was the one way I knew to stay ahead. And I expected similar dedication from the others. We had this huge opportunity in front of us. Why wouldn't you work eighty hours a week in pursuit of it? Yes, it was exhausting, but it was also exhilarating.

Despite my self-confidence and proclivity to figure out things on my own, I was coming to the realization that I needed the kind of help that Paul wasn't prepared to give. He was a partner in some of the most important ways: we shared a vision for the company, and we worked well together when it came to questions of technology and who to hire to build software. But none of that would matter if the business foundation wasn't secure. Keeping Microsoft going was a lonely job. I needed a twenty-four-hour-a-day business partner, a peer who would hash out and argue through big decisions with me, someone who would pore over scribbled lists of which customers might or might not pay and discuss what our bank account would look like as a result. Shouldering a hundred things like that every week on my own was a burden that at that time I felt should be acknowledged by an even bigger stake in what we were building.

On that walk along Hood Canal, I decided that if I left school to be at Microsoft full-time, I would tell Paul I wanted an even bigger share of the company. I mulled both decisions after I returned to Harvard in January for the reading period ahead of finals. Steve Ballmer and I had stayed true to our plan to skip the ECON 2010 lectures. We spent the reading period teaching each other the material, working nearly nonstop trying to cram a semester's worth of knowledge into our brains. We were triumphant when we passed the one-page final.

On January 15 I wrote Harvard: "A friend and I have a partnership, Microsoft, which does consulting relating to microprocessor software. The new obligations we have just taken on require that I devote my full-time efforts to working at Microsoft." I said that I planned to return to school in the fall and graduate in June 1978.

My parents knew it would be pointless to tell me to stay in school. I was too independent. But my mom sometimes used subtle means to try to convince me. At some point, during either that year or the previous one, she arranged for me to meet a prominent Seattle businessman, Sam Stroum, who had built a big chain of electronics stores before acquiring and expanding a major regional auto-parts chain. He was also very active in nonprofits, a pillar of Seattle society. My mom got to know him through her work with the United Way. Over lunch I explained Microsoft and my plan to make software for every microprocessor we could and how that market would grow, and our company along with it. Whatever hope my mother may have had for that lunch, I don't think it was achieved. Instead of telling me to stay the course at Harvard, Sam was excited by what I was doing. His enthusiasm might have assuaged my mom's concerns a little but not fully. (Sam liked to joke years later that he regretted not writing me a check for part of the company at that lunch.)

"If Microsoft doesn't work out, I'll go back to school," I assured my parents.

Back in Albuquerque, I told Paul I wanted to make the split sixty-four–thirty-six. He pushed back. We argued, but eventually he gave in. I feel bad now that I pushed him, but at the time I felt that split accurately reflected the commitment Microsoft needed from each of us. We signed an agreement in early February and made it official. (A little over three years later, that slice of the company would come up again as I was trying to convince Steve Ballmer to quit business school to join Microsoft. As an incentive, I included that extra 4 percent as part of his package. He joined in 1980 and became the twenty-four-hour-a-day partner I needed.)

Despite our tension over ownership of the company and our perennial spats, Paul and I had a strong bond. We had already shared an incredible journey; now we were building something unique. And having a pretty good time at it too.

We had also figured out one way to help keep our friendship intact: don't live together. While I was in Boston, Paul had left our Portals apartment and rented a three-bedroom house in the suburbs with Ric and Marc McDonald. When I returned to Albuquerque, I moved into an apartment with Chris Larson. Chris had been coming and going from Albuquerque to work summers with us. Now in his senior year at Lakeside, he convinced his parents to let him join us at Microsoft, taking off a semester as I had done for the TRW job.

Living apart from Paul meant I no longer had access to the Death Trap Monza, so I bought my own car, a 1971 Porsche 911. Though used, it was a major expense for me, but I had always coveted Porsches and loved the raspy whistle sound of their six-cylinder engines. Still, even today I'm a little self-conscious admitting that I bought it.

Driving that Porsche became my escape, my time for thinking through the company's issues as I whipped around the Sandia Mountain roads well over the speed limit. Often Chris joined me. The previous year we had found a nice smooth road that wound up and up into the mountains, leading to a cement plant. After I got the Porsche, we took regular high-speed drives on Cement Plant Road, as we called it. Late one night we stopped at the plant and discovered they kept a couple of bulldozers with keys in the ignition. Chris and I spent more than a few nights at the top of that cement plant road teaching ourselves how to drive the massive earth movers.

Racing around in my car at night with Chris, seeing movies,

and hanging out with Paul and the rest of the Microsoft team was the extent of my non-work life in Albuquerque. Steve and Marla Wood, who as the only married couple in the group offered a dose of domesticity, would often host us for dinner, or we'd head to Paul's house to watch shows on his projection TV. We found ourselves obsessed with *The Pallisers,* a BBC production of Anthony Trollope's Palliser novels. We'd meet after work, settle on the couch and carpet, and get thoroughly sucked into twenty-two hours of the dukes and duchesses, love triangles, and money troubles of Victorian England.

As spring arrived in 1977, it was increasingly clear to me that MITS and Pertec had no intention of paying us back royalties or sublicensing 8080 BASIC to any other companies. In their eyes, they owned the software and we were a nuisance, a small wrench in their plan to buy the leading personal computer maker. Pertec had structured the acquisition as a merger between MITS and a new Pertec subsidiary created for the occasion. We thought it had done so in part to ensure that the rights MITS held to our BASIC would become part of the deal. Yet now I wondered if they had even read our contract. We didn't transfer ownership of the software to MITS. We licensed it to them. And MITS was obligated by the contract to make its best efforts to sublicense the software to other companies.

It all went back to the spring of 1975 and the weeks after Paul, Monte, and I wrote the 4K BASIC and delivered it to MITS. This is the period during which Ed had delayed signing the contract and I holed up in Seattle until he did.

In negotiating that contract, Ed had insisted that we give MITS a worldwide exclusive license to 8080 BASIC for ten years. I didn't want to agree to that, but I wanted to close the deal. And I wanted to make a good impression on our new partner.

I asked my dad if he could help us find a lawyer in New Mexico. That led him to a trial lawyer at his old firm, whose nephew, a man named Paull Mines, worked as an attorney in Albuquerque. I called Mines, and his firm, Poole, Tinnin & Martin, helped us draft the contract. In 1975, a contract to license software was still a very new thing. I'm sure this was probably the first time the firm had worked on one. They did a good job, and I made one important inclusion.

I don't know when I first heard the legal term "best efforts," but a good guess would be at the dinner table as my parents discussed my father's work. When a company agrees to make its best efforts, it agrees to do everything in its power to make good on whatever is stipulated in a contract. However the phrase had first lodged in my brain, it surfaced in those contract negotiations with MITS. I said we'd agree to the exclusive license if MITS agreed to make "best efforts" to license our source code. The MITS lawyers pushed back, saying that nobody agreed to best efforts. They'd consider "reasonable efforts," but I wouldn't agree. Best efforts it was.

Now, I went back and reread that clause again and again. Page 2, clause 5: "Company Effort. The Company [MITS] agrees to use its best efforts to license, promote, and commercialize the PROGRAM. The Company's failure to use its best efforts as aforesaid shall constitute sufficient grounds and reason for termination of this agreement by Licensors."

It all seemed so clear to me.

Over the past year I had become friends with Eddie Currie, general manager of MITS and our partner in trying to market BASIC to outside companies. Eddie had grown up in the same Florida community as Ed Roberts; the two had known each other since elementary school. But where Ed could be strident, Eddie was even-keeled and acted as the calm middleman between MITS and Microsoft. Eddie seemed very invested in helping both companies succeed. Together we pitched 8080 BASIC to outside companies, and when we landed one, Eddie worked with Ed Roberts to get the contract signed.

In his capacity as middleman, Eddie Currie had encouraged me several times to meet with the Pertec lawyers to see if we could work through the disagreement. I felt intimidated and hoped that we could instead hash out the whole thing directly with Ed. I also knew that Eddie was trying to persuade Ed to hold out for another suitor who might offer a higher price. When it was clear that wasn't going to happen, I agreed to meet with Pertec. Walking into a conference room at MITS, I found three Pertec lawyers. They asked Eddie to wait outside while we talked.

The lawyers told me that when Pertec closed its deal with MITS, it would take over the licensing agreement, and the contract would be "assigned" to Pertec. That wasn't going to happen, I said. Paul and I would have to agree to sign it over to Pertec, and we weren't going to do that. Page 7: "this agreement may not be assigned without the express written consent of the parties." Had they read that? None of that mattered, they responded.

I felt myself growing more frustrated. "You guys are totally wrong," I snapped. "The BASIC interpreter is not yours!"

The rest of the meeting devolved into a shouting match between me and the lawyers. At one point we reached a standstill, the argument simmering, when Eddie knocked on the door. There was a phone call for me. It was Paul. He said that Eddie had heard us yelling and had called him, thinking Paul should come and yank me out of the meeting. Should he run over? "No," I told Paul, in a voice loud enough for everyone to hear. "These guys are trying to screw us over, but I've got it under control." I hung up and went back to the lawyers. During our resumed argument, the lead Pertec lawyer laid out in stark terms what he would do if I continued to insist on holding on to our software and not agree to his terms. He "would destroy Microsoft's reputation." He informed me that I would be "personally liable for criminal fraud, and I will sue you for your entire personal wealth." Later, Eddie said he felt bad about arranging the meeting and that he thought the lawyers had ambushed me.

I called my father that night. He was appalled that the lawyers had met with just me, without a lawyer to represent Microsoft. The next day I visited Paull Mines. He reviewed our contract and confirmed we were in the right. The best-efforts clause was binding. And if it wasn't clear already, MITS was going out of its way to not make its best efforts. Within weeks, Ed Roberts sent ADDS a letter stating that MITS had determined that it should discontinue any efforts to license the BASIC software. He said Bill Gates might try to restart those discussions. "To avoid any embarrassment to any of us, you should be aware that MITS holds the exclusive rights to the BASIC software programs developed by Mr. Gates and his partners and that any commitments regarding the rights to the BASIC program, or any modified versions or portions of it, by anyone other than MITS personnel are not authorized."

In April, amid the standoff, I flew to San Francisco to attend the First West Coast Computer Faire. Walking into the Civic Auditorium, I was astounded. Thousands of people—all told, just under thirteen thousand attendees over two days—were pushing their way through the rows of booths of companies like ours, Processor Technology, IMS Associates, and Commodore, showing its PET. To a company, all focused on personal computers. In that moment, I felt that the industry had arrived.

On the first day I was talking to a crowd of people about our Extended BASIC when out of the corner of my eye I noticed a handsome guy around my age with long black hair, a tightly cropped beard, and a three-piece suit. He was a few booths away, holding court with his own gaggle of people. Even from a distance I could tell he had a certain aura about him. I said to myself, "Who is that guy?" That was the day I met Steve Jobs.

Apple, though smaller than many of the other companies, stood out. Even then the trademark design sense that would make Apple—and Jobs—so iconic in coming decades was on display. At the show they launched the Apple II, which in its sleek beige case looked more like a polished piece of consumer electronics than a personal computer. The company had decorated their booth with fancy Plexiglas signs, including an elegant logo of a bitten apple they'd commissioned from a marketing firm. They had a spot at the entrance to the event hall and were using a projector to cast the Apple II's color graphics onto a giant screen, ensuring that anyone walking in would immediately see their logo, signage, and new computer. "The Apple guys are getting a lot of attention," Paul said to me.

That first encounter in the spring of 1977 would mark the start of a long relationship between Steve Jobs and me, marked by cooperation and rivalry. At the Computer Faire, though, I mostly spoke with Steve Wozniak, who had designed and built the Apple II. Like Commodore's PET, the Apple II used MOS Technology's 6502 chip.

Wozniak at the time was one of a rare breed in our industry, someone who deeply understood both hardware and software. The BASIC he'd written, however, had a fundamental problem: it was a simple form of the language and could handle only integers—no floating-point math, which meant no decimal points or scientific notation, both of which are essential for any sophisticated software program. Apple needed a better BASIC and Wozniak knew it. Having already written a 6502 BASIC for Commodore, we had a head start on writing one for Apple. At the convention I talked up our work and emphasized that it would be cheaper and faster to license our software than to try to write it himself. I left San Francisco optimistic that we'd sign a deal.

Days later, back in Albuquerque, I got word from Texas Instruments that it had chosen us to write a version of BASIC for the personal computer it was designing. The company said it had envisioned the computer as an appliance for families to manage home finances, play games, and write school reports. I hoped this would be the computer that would break out into the mass market. Not just a few thousand customers but maybe tens of thousands.

We had beaten out at least two other bidders for the work. Getting the deal was a big confidence boost. I had wanted to charge TI a flat licensing fee of $100,000, but I chickened out. Fearful that the company would balk at six figures, I asked for $90,000, which was still the biggest deal we had signed aside from NCR, which we had to split with MITS. When TI visited Microsoft for the first time, our new office manager had to run out to buy extra chairs so there'd be a place for everyone to sit.

TI was using its own processor, which meant writing a new version of BASIC from scratch. That would be months of work for at least two people. Monte was again willing to spend the summer in Albuquerque, but with Ric leaving, we needed to hire another coder. After we signed the deal at TI, I called Bob Greenberg, who had been in a few math classes with me at Harvard and who I knew was weighing job offers at the time. "I'm your man," he told me.

Whether we had the cash to pay him was another question. MITS had come through with a small amount of royalties but had refused to pony up the full amount that it owed us, then over $100,000.

Paul and I had had enough. In late April, working with our lawyer Paull Mines, we sent Ed Roberts a two-page letter listing the ways MITS had breached our contract, including the unpaid back royalties and its refusal to use its best efforts to license 8080 BASIC to companies such as ADDS and Delta Data. If MITS didn't meet our conditions to pay the royalites and resume licensing our software within ten days, we wrote, we would terminate the contract.

The response was swift: within days Pertec and MITS filed for a restraining order to prevent us from licensing 8080 BASIC.

In June, as stipulated by our contract with MITS, our dispute moved to arbitration. Initially I was worried about our lawyer. Paull Mines had a manner that could make him appear disorganized as well as a tendency to lose his train of thought—a somewhat scattered demeanor that only bolstered what I perceived as the opposing lawyers' misplaced confidence. They seemed smug, convinced that their victory was inevitable. In fact, Mines was very sharp and thorough. Every night he had us in his office preparing for the next day, poring through the details of our contracts and every interaction with every company that had expressed an interest in BASIC.

The hearings with the arbitrator lasted about ten days. I sat in on all the testimony as Microsoft's representative. Eddie Currie played the same role for the MITS side. Ric, Paul, and I were deposed as well as Ed Roberts, Eddie, and various other people from the companies. The stakes for Microsoft aside, I found the proceedings fascinating. In full Kent fashion, I showed up every day with my own monstrosity of a briefcase stuffed with every document I would ever need. I'd rustle around in the briefcase and yank out paper after paper—to find a reference but also for the show of it. I was hoping for an effect opposite of the one I'd sought by not carrying books in high school: *Look at all those papers! They must be super-prepared!*

Some nights after the hearing ended, Paul, Eddie, and I would go out to dinner and compare notes, speculating about whose side the arbitrator seemed more favorably disposed toward on a given day. The arbitrator continually struggled to grasp the basics of the technology at the center of the dispute. We tried to help him by dubbing our 8080 BASIC source code "the Grand Source," to differentiate it from the other versions not covered by the contract.

We had called a witness from ADDS, hoping to prove that the terminal maker wanted to license BASIC but had been blocked by MITS. At dinner the night before the ADDS testimony, I told Eddie that the code name for the ADDS product was "Centurion." I didn't realize that Eddie would share that tidbit with anyone else. I also didn't realize that I got the name wrong.

Both facts hit me the next day when the Pertec lawyer confronted the ADDS witness about the secret project. "Tell us about Centurion," the lawyer said, seeming very sure that he was about to expose some gaping hole in in our defense.

"I have no idea," the ADDS guy answered.

"You must know about Centurion," the lawyer fired back, to which the witness answered, "I guess I do. I think it's a Roman legion or soldiers or something like that."

I don't remember what the accurate code name was. Eddie surely assumed I had intentionally misled him. I wish I had been that smart. From then on, I learned to be more careful.

Our central challenge was to convince the arbitrator that (1) many companies wanted to license 8080 BASIC, and (2) Pertec/MITS was blocking those licenses when they were contractually obligated to make their best efforts at facilitating them. Fortunately, Ric had detailed our communication with all these companies over the past year in his Microsoft journal. That record helped us make the case that the world wanted what we made.

The hearings ended in late June. Then we waited. And waited.

With our money from MITS on hold, Microsoft needed cash. In one of my many phone calls with my parents that summer, I broached the subject that I wanted to avoid: I might need to borrow some money to keep us going. At that point we owed Paull Mines about $30,000, we had employees to pay, and our cash flow had slowed to a trickle. Paul was worried enough one night to tell me we should consider settling with MITS. Both Paull Mines and my father had assured me that we would likely win the arbitration, I told him. We should trust them.

The day after our hearings ended, Paul and I took our Microsoft employees for a lunch of prime rib and salad bar at a chain called Big Valley Ranch, which for us was a fancy choice. There were about seven of us, including Ric, who was leaving the company the next day for good. What do the President and the Veep do when they're worried and want to boost morale? Feed your employees lunch and talk frankly about their worries. It was a moment to communicate the obvious: though we were confident that we'd win the arbitration, it wasn't guaranteed.

That afternoon, I paid Ric what we owed him. The next day,

July 1, he came by the office to see us before heading to his new job and life in California. Even then he had mixed emotions about leaving. My feelings weren't so complex; I was just sad to see him go. In a job recommendation I wrote for him a few weeks later, I was honest: "I feel that Ric's leaving was a great loss to Microsoft."

I don't know if our company lunch that week prompted what happened next, but Microsoft got a lucky break: Bob Greenberg, who had worked with us for less than a month, told me he would loan Microsoft $7,000, enough to help make our payroll. Years later, neither Bob nor I could remember whether I asked or he offered, but the loan transpired, with the agreement that Microsoft would pay him interest of eighty dollars a month. (When he learned of the loan, Bob's father chastised him. Already upset that he'd taken the job at Microsoft and not at a brand-name company, he said, "When you get a job, they pay you. You do know that, right?")

Hoping I could drum up more money, a day after receiving Bob's loan I wrote Apple:

Dear Mr. Wozniak:

Enclosed please find our standard licensing contract. I believe I already communicated the price for 6502 BASIC to you:
    OPTION1:
    $1,000.00 flat + $2,000.00 for source + ($35.00/copy to a max of $35,000.00)
    OPTION2:
    $21,000.00 flat: includes source and full distribution rights for object
    We could work out an option in between these if you are interested. Because of your inhouse software expertise and special hardware you will probably want the source . . .

. . . If you want another demo version or you have any questions, please don't hesitate to contact me. I look forward to our resolving a mutually beneficial licensing arrangement.

Bill

A few weeks later I got a phone call from Apple's president, Michael Scott, who said that his company liked the second option. Within a couple of days a check arrived for half the fee: $10,500. With that I paid more salaries and sent our lawyer another $1,000 nibble at our growing legal fees.

That same month, Tandy, known for its national chain of RadioShack electronics stores, announced the TRS-80 home computer, becoming the next major company to jump in the market. Within a month, RadioShack sold a surprising ten thousand TRS-80s, which made it a runaway hit. The RadioShack machine was a more complete system than the Altair and other hobbyist computers. Starting at $599.95, it came with a keyboard, a monitor, and a cassette recorder, and was ready to use out of the box. With the computer, Tandy included its own version of BASIC, which it had based on the free Tiny BASIC. Called Level 1 BASIC, it was so limited that Tandy quickly heard back from angry customers. Though we had missed the machine's debut, I hoped to persuade Tandy to buy our software. I set up a meeting at the company's headquarters for late September.

Right after Labor Day, I flew to Seattle for Kristi's wedding and made time to talk to my dad about my upcoming meeting with Tandy. I knew that the technical people at Tandy were fans of our BASIC, but I would have to convince the executive who headed the group of its value. Though I had never met John Roach, I had heard he was tough—a native Texan known to be gruff.

I knew that Tandy was a company that bought capacitors, resistors, and toggle switches by the ton. It employed specialist "buyers" whose sole job was to squeeze pennies from the Asian companies that supplied the thousands of products RadioShack sold in its stores. Tandy's low-cost culture meant that the computer division had developed the first TRS-80 for less than $150,000. It got a bargain on RCA TVs that it would sell as displays for the TRS-80s. Those TVs' outer shells happened to be gray, so to keep things cheap, the whole TRS-80 became gray.

My pitch, I told my dad, was that Microsoft could sell BASIC at a price far lower than Tandy could write a version on its own. I drafted two pages of talking points about how much better our product stacked up against anything else out there. My dad had advised me to simply be honest with Roach. If anything, he just gave me confidence. If I offered a great price and explained why it was a great price, Roach would probably listen. My dad said I could even go so far as to break down Microsoft's cost structure so he understood my thinking.

Walking into Tandy's Fort Worth headquarters, I was primed to confidently lay out the benefits of our BASIC and offer them a cut-rate deal. We had charged TI $90,000, but that required a new chip and a lot of custom work. For RadioShack, I decided we would ask for $50,000.

We all stood around a table: me, the company's software guy, a few others, and John Roach. I ran through my carefully crafted sales pitch.

As I talked, Roach stood there, his chin jutting out, not giving any indication of whether what I was saying had any effect. He might have said something, I don't remember, but I couldn't help feeling that he was resistant.

As I spoke, I found it difficult to contain my excitement. "You've got to do this!" I implored. "Without our BASIC your computer won't be able to do anything!" At this point, I was flying way off script. "With our BASIC you're golden!" I added.

This was more than bluster. The depth of thinking and the work we were putting into BASIC were leagues beyond any available. I really believed in our work. At that point, I had my palms flat on the table and was leaning across it toward Roach, whose face was a vivid shade of red.

He asked me how much it would cost.

"Fifty thousand dollars," I said. A flat fee.

Roach's response remains one of the most memorable moments from my early days of Microsoft. "Horseshit!" he growled. *Wow, that wasn't in the script.* It was also the kind of thing that I could have heard myself saying, though maybe without the barnyard color. I decided in that meeting that I liked John Roach. And I liked RadioShack. They were very good businesspeople. It helped too that despite his reaction that afternoon, Horseshit Roach, as we'd come to call him, agreed to our price.

By the time I visited RadioShack, we had heard from the arbitrator in the MITS case: He sided with Microsoft. He terminated our exclusive 8080 BASIC license with MITS, clarifying definitively that we owned our source code.

Much of the arbitrator's ruling focused on Pertec's attempts to stop MITS from licensing BASIC to competitors and the fact that it used our software in developing its own version of BASIC, which the arbitrator described as "an act of corporate piracy not permitted by either the language or any rational interpretation of the Contract."

We immediately called all the companies that had been waiting for the software. Within weeks we had money coming in from five or six clients, including ADDS and its "Centurion" Project, or whatever it was called. We would make our own best efforts to license our software, and with MITS out of the picture, we didn't have to split the revenue.

In late October I sent Paull Mines the outstanding balance we owed him, writing that "I hope I am not speaking too soon when

I say I feel like this marks the closing of our adventure with MITS. Not only was the outcome favorable but the experience was exciting and enjoyable, both of which you are largely responsible for." Paull would continue to be a trusted advisor for me and Microsoft for several years.

Pertec's deal to buy MITS had closed in late May. Ed came away from the merger with a few million dollars and a choice job running a lab at Pertec tasked with ginning up the next technology hit. But from the start, Eddie Currie and our other MITS friends said Pertec was a bad fit. MITS was scrappy and loose, innovative in its own way. Pertec was buttoned-down, and overconfident in its ability to navigate the fast-changing world of personal computers. It very quickly smothered the smaller company. Steadily the Altair lost market share. Ed proposed a plan to sell a laptop computer, but Pertec shot it down, unconvinced there was a market for such a thing.

When Ed was growing up in Florida, he had wanted to become a surgeon and carried around laminated human anatomy study cards; at one point he even did a stint in a hospital as a scrub tech. After a short period at Pertec, Ed quit and moved his family to the small town of Cochran, Georgia. He ran a farm for several years before following his childhood dream: at age forty-four he graduated from Mercer University with his medical degree. For the rest of his life, Ed operated a small clinic that served rural Georgians.

My relationship with Ed was complicated but also one of the most formative in my early career. Around the time Microsoft won the arbitration, I had stopped by to see him in his office at MITS. He said he felt burned by the decision and thought the arbitrator had misunderstood the situation. "Next time, I'll hire a hit man," he quipped. Without question he was joking, but he didn't laugh. As our paths diverged, we saw each other less and less. In 2009, when I heard that Ed was hospitalized with pneumonia, I called him. We hadn't talked in many years, but I knew he still felt some ill will. On the call, I told him that I wanted him to know that I learned a lot from him when we worked together, something I never would have said at the time. "I was very immature and a bit arrogant, but I've changed a lot since then," I told him. That seemed to break the ice, and we had a great talk. "We did a lot of good, important work," he said. I agreed: we really did.

A few months later, when Ed's condition worsened, I flew to Georgia to visit him. He was hardly conscious, but for a couple of hours I talked to him and with his son David, recounting the early days of the industry. He died not long after, in April 2010, at age sixty-eight. Beyond being the first to market a commercially successful personal computer, Ed Roberts wrote the blueprint for how the personal computer industry would develop. MITS's newsletter was the first magazine devoted to PCs. The company sponsored the first PC trade show. The first computer stores were Altair dealers, and user groups that sprung up around the machine catalyzed the founding of important companies—including Apple. Yet during our talk, David told me his dad felt that his achievements as a small-town doctor were as meaningful as all he had done to start a technology revolution.

By the end of 1977, the Commodore PET, Apple II, and RadioShack TRS-80 started to make their way into schools, offices, and homes, within a few years reaching hundreds of thousands of people, most of whom had never touched a computer. Unlike the first generation of hobbyist machines, all three computers were fully assembled and ready to use, no soldering iron required. The PET came with lots of features, including a built-in cassette recorder for storing data and programs, while its limited keyboard—with frustratingly tiny keys that reviewers compared to Chiclets chewing gum—didn't stand in the way of its success. Over the next year Tandy updated the TRS-80, adding new features and leveraging its five thousand RadioShack stores to reach customers at a scale that other companies could not. Sales of the Apple II grew quickly, propelled by smart marketing, ingenious design, and color graphics, which made it especially great for game playing.

Later known as the "1977 Trinity," those three machines introduced the personal computer revolution into the mainstream as others fell behind. (TI, the feared giant we had been so excited to work with, never succeeded in PCs.) Installed on each member of the Trinity was a version of our BASIC that we had tailored to the requirements of their maker. In RadioShack's machine it was Level II BASIC, on the Apple it was Applesoft—an amalgam of its name and ours—and the PET was simply Commodore BASIC. In a version for Commodore we squeezed a little surprise into the code: if a PET user happened to enter the command WAIT 6502,1, one word would appear on the upper left of their screen: MICROSOFT!

With Microsoft no longer dependent on MITS and Paul and me having trouble hiring programmers in Albuquerque, in the spring of 1978 I wrote a memo for our ten or so employees, listing possible options for Microsoft's permanent home. I included Seattle, Dallas–Fort Worth—which was close to our big customers Tandy and TI—and Silicon Valley, which had a critical mass of customers, people to hire, but also competitors. Paul felt the pull of our hometown. He was sick of the Albuquerque heat, craved Seattle's lakes and the Puget Sound, and wanted to be closer to his family. Most of our employees were open to any of our options (though a few wanted to stick in Albuquerque). After giving it a lot of thought, I concluded that Seattle ticked the most boxes: The University of Washington was a great source for programmers, and the distance from Silicon Valley afforded a higher degree of secrecy and a lower risk of losing employees to rivals. And, of course, that was my mom's preference as well. Once we decided on Seattle, she couldn't resist sending real estate listings she clipped from the paper, often adding her take ("this would be very convenient to the bridge—a good possibility I think").

In December 1978, our last full month in Albuquerque, Bob Greenberg won a contest prize of a free family portrait. He sent out a memo with the subject "Esprit de Corps," asking everyone to come to the photo studio behind Shanghai restaurant. The family he brought was eleven of our twelve employees (one was home that day). The picture we sat for would become an iconic photo of 1970s Microsoft, complete with wide collars, shaggy hair, and five bushy beards.

About a month later, I crammed what little I owned into my 911, inserted a cassette of *The War of the Worlds*—on loan from Paul—into the tape deck, and headed north through Nevada to Silicon Valley for a handful of meetings, then up to Seattle. I remember the trip for the three speeding tickets I got. I also remember thinking about how odd it was to be moving home. When I left for college, I'd told my parents that I would never live in Seattle again; it seemed a given that I would build my life out in the larger world. In my mind that would be the East Coast, the center of finance, politics, top universities, and—back then—the computer industry. Returning could be seen as a retreat.

But as I thought about it, I realized this was different. It wasn't just me moving back, it was Microsoft—the company that a friend and I had co-created, with that motley group of employees and a growing, profitable business, and which from that point on would be an integral part of who I was. My path was set. As I sped along I-5 at a hundred miles an hour, I could hardly imagine how far it would take me.

Epilogue

My mother and grandmother had always wanted us to have a place on Hood Canal where we could all fit as my sisters and I grew up and had our own families. Gami died in 1987, before they could see that plan through. On the day of her memorial service, my parents, Libby, Kristi, and I drove out to look at a parcel of land my grandmother had found for us. I bought the property and in the coming years we built a set of cottages. That family compound, which my mom dubbed "Gateaway," became my refuge through the ups and downs—though mostly ups—of Microsoft's early years. I got in the habit of setting aside a block of time for myself at Hood Canal that I called Think Week. Once or twice a year I'd drive or take a seaplane taxi out to spend seven uninterrupted days poring over books, articles, and papers—a crash course in whatever I felt I needed to learn. Then I would write long strategy memos about how Microsoft could stay in the lead in areas like internet security and natural language processing. And just as Gami and my mom had hoped, Gateaway became the base for our extended family to meet every July Fourth and Thanksgiving, and for other get-togethers throughout the year. As our family expanded, it became a place where my children and their cousins carried on the spirit of Cheerio.

Ahead of our Fourth of July gathering in 2012, the seaplane deposited me at a resort near our place. Stepping onto the dock, I heard someone call out, "Trey!" I looked up to see a lanky older man I instantly recognized as Kent's dad, Marvin Evans. It had been about twenty years since we had last met.

Marvin explained that he and Kent's younger brother, David, were on a short sailing trip and had docked at the resort for the night. We sat on the deck of their boat and caught up. Kent's mom had died years earlier after a long illness. Now in his eighties, Marvin spoke with his familiar, soothing Southern drawl, transporting me into the backseat of his '67 Dodge as he shuttled Kent and me around Seattle. He had been writing his memoirs in recent years, he said, and naturally included the stories of Kent and me and the Lakeside Programming Group. He laughed when I recited the Evans family phone number, forever inscribed in my memory. You boys shared an intellectual creativity that was remarkable, Marvin told me. Whatever you call it, I replied, would have likely continued had Kent not died: there's a good chance we would have gone to the same college and been partners in some kind of venture. Marvin said he thought so too.

One thing was for certain. Even Kent, so boldly optimistic about our futures, would have been astounded to witness the path our programming passion had taken. The kid who wondered if $15 million would even fit in a car would have loved knowing that, of everything we studied, it would be the skills we learned at Lakeside's terminal, honed at C-Cubed, and put into practice on the class schedule that would lead to one of the most successful companies in history. And that the product of such skills, software, would be woven into nearly every aspect of modern life.

I'm not prone to nostalgia, but there are days when I'd like to be thirteen again, making that bargain with the world that if you just go forward, learn more, understand better, you can make something truly useful and new.

—

Often success stories reduce people to stock characters: the boy wonder, the genius engineer, the iconoclastic designer, the paradoxical tycoon. In my case, I'm struck by the set of unique circumstances—mostly out of my control—that shaped both my character and my career. It's impossible to overstate the unearned privilege I enjoyed: to be born in the rich United States is a big part of a winning birth lottery ticket, as is being born white and male in a society that advantages white men.

Add to that my lucky timing. I was a rebellious toddler at Acorn Academy when engineers figured out how to integrate tiny circuits on a piece of silicon, giving birth to the semiconductor chip. I was shelving books in Mrs. Caffiere's library when another engineer predicted those circuits would grow smaller and smaller at an exponential rate for years into the future. By the time I started programming at age thirteen, chips were storing data inside the large computers to which we had uncommon access, and by the time I got my driver's license, the main functions of an entire computer could be fit onto a single chip.

Realizing early on that I had a head for math was a critical step in my story. In his terrific book *How Not to Be Wrong,* mathematician Jordan Ellenberg observes that "knowing mathematics is like wearing a pair of X-ray specs that reveal hidden structures underneath the messy and chaotic surface of the world." Those X-ray specs helped me identify the order underlying the chaos, and reinforced my sense that the correct answer was always out there—I just needed to find it. That insight came at one of the most formative times of a kid's life, when the brain is transforming into a more specialized and efficient tool. Facility with numbers gave me confidence, and even a sense of security.

I spent a rare vacation in my early thirties watching films of Richard Feynman teaching physics to university students. I was instantly captivated by the absolute mastery he had of his topic and the child-like wonder he showed in explaining it. I quickly read everything he wrote that I could find. I recognized the joy he derived from uncovering new knowledge and exploring the mysteries of the world—"the pleasure of finding things out," as he put it. "This is the gold. This is the excitement, the pay you get for all of the disciplined thinking and hard work," he explained in *The Meaning of It All.*

Feynman was a special case, a genius with a singular breadth and depth of understanding of the world and an ability to reason his way through puzzles in an array of fields. But he articulates so well the feeling that took root in me as a kid, when I started building mental models that helped me visualize how the pieces of the world fit together. As I accumulated more knowledge, the models grew more sophisticated. That was my path to software. Getting hooked on coding at Lakeside, and through all the steps that followed, from hacking at C-Cubed to the TRW job, I was intensely driven by the love of what I was learning, accruing expertise just when it was needed: at the dawn of the personal computer.

Curiosity can't be satisfied in a vacuum, of course. It requires nurturing, resources, guidance, support. When Dr. Cressey told me I was a lucky kid, I've no doubt that he was primarily thinking of my good fortune in being born to Bill and Mary Gates—parents who struggled with their complicated son but ultimately seemed to intuitively understand how to guide him.

If I were growing up today, I probably would be diagnosed on the autism spectrum. In the time of my childhood, the fact that some people's brains process information differently from others wasn't widely understood. (The term "neurodivergent" wouldn't be coined until the 1990s.) My parents had no guideposts or textbooks to help them grasp why their son became so obsessed with certain projects (tiny Delaware), missed social cues, and could be rude or inappropriate without seeming to notice his effect on others. There's no way for me to know if this was something Dr. Cressey recognized or mentioned.

What I do know is that my parents afforded me the precise blend of support and pressure I needed: they gave me room to grow emotionally, and they created opportunities for me to develop my social skills. Instead of allowing me to turn inward, they pushed me out into the world—to the baseball team, the Cub Scouts, and other Cheerio families' dinner tables. And they gave me constant exposure to adults, immersing me in the language and ideas of their friends and colleagues, which fed my curiosity about the world beyond school. Even with their influence, my social side would be slow to develop, as would my awareness of the impact I can have on other people. But that has come with age, with experience, with kids, and I'm better for it. I wish it had come sooner, even if I wouldn't trade the brain I was given for anything.

The "solid front" my parents maintained, laid out by my mom in the letter she wrote my father before they were married, never wavered, but also allowed for their differences to shape me. I will never have my father's calm bearing, but he instilled in me a fundamental sense of confidence and capability. My mother's influence was more complex. Internalized by me, her expectations bloomed into an even stronger ambition to succeed, to stand out, and do something important. It was as if I needed to clear my mom's bar by such a wide margin that there would be nothing left to say on the matter.

But, of course, there was always something to be said. It was my mother who regularly reminded me that I was merely a steward of any wealth I gained. With wealth came the responsibility to give it away, she would tell me. I regret that my mom didn't live long enough to see how fully I've tried to meet that expectation: she passed away in 1994, at age sixty-four, from breast cancer. It would be my father in the years after my mom died who would help get our foundation started and serve as a co-chair for years, bringing the same compassion and decency that had served so well in his law career.

For most of my life, I've been focused on what's ahead. Even now, most days I'm working on hoped-for breakthroughs that may not happen for years, if they happen at all. As I grow older, though, I find myself looking back more and more. Piecing together memories helps me better understand myself, it turns out. It's a marvel of adulthood to realize that when you strip away all the years and all the learning, much of who you are was there from the start. In many ways I'm still that eight-year-old sitting at Gami's dining room table as she deals the cards. I feel the same sense of anticipation, a kid alert and wanting to make sense of it all.

Acknowledgments

I've written several books, but diving into a memoir was a different experience for me. Revisiting the early part of my life and sifting through memories took on a life of its own. To my surprise, the deeper I got, the more I enjoyed parsing my past, and the places it took me intellectually and emotionally. I'm committed to continuing this journey and plan to write another memoir focused on my years running Microsoft and a third one on this current part of my life and my work with the Gates Foundation.

I want to thank the many people in my life who helped to make *Source Code* possible.

In writing this memoir, I have been lucky to have Rob Guth extracting, guiding, and giving form to my memories. For more than a decade he has delved deep, spoken with my friends and family, and become a living archive of my memories and experiences. His ability to see themes and help me craft a compelling narrative made this book so much more than a collection of anecdotes, and I could not have done it without him.

I'm indebted to Courtney Hodell, whose story sense and wise counsel have guided this book from its inception years ago. Susan Freinkel's experience as a writer and editor were invaluable in giving shape and clarity to my story. Thank you to researchers, writers, and experts, including Chris Quirk, David Pearlstein, Harry McCracken, Lucy Woods, Pablo Perez-Fernandez, Tedd Pitts, Tom Madams, Wayt Gibbs, and Yumiko Kono, who supported *Source Code* in ways large and small that gave the book a solid foundation.

I'm extremely grateful to the many friends who were willing to be interviewed and shared their stories and memories from the early years of my life.

For their memories of my early life and my parents, I want to thank Llew Pritchard, Jonie Pritchard, Marty Smith, Jim Irwin, Jeff Raikes, Tricia Raikes, Tom Fitzpatrick, Tren Griffin, Chris Bayley, Anne Winblad, and Bill Neukom, as well as schoolmates Stan "Boomer" Youngs, Kip Cramer, Chip Holland, Lollie Groth, and Dave Hennings.

My Lakeside friends Page Knudson Cowles, Paul Carlson, Tom Rona, and Vicki Weeks shared stories from our high school years, as did our teachers, including Bruce Bailey and Fred Wright. In our many talks Bernie Noe, friend and member of the Lakeside family, provided sage advice about this book—as he always does about life.

Special thanks to Connie Gordon for sharing her memories of her late husband, my friend Doug Gordon, one of the brilliant ones, who always pushed me intellectually and engaged the world with an openness I will forever admire.

Dan Sill opened the door to my memories of our time in the mountains, while Mike Collier shared stories and photos from those expeditions. Thanks also to Chip Kennaugh and the other friends from Troop 186.

David Evans was incredibly helpful, and along with his dad, Marvin Evans, was generous in sharing both the beauty and the pain of Kent's short life. Thanks to Norm Petersen for his memories and photos of Kent's final months.

I am grateful to my college friends Sam Znaimer, Jim Sethna, Andy Braiterman, Peter Galison, and Lloyd "Nick" Trefethen for inspiring me at Harvard and sharing their memories from those years. My Harvard professor Harry Lewis went the extra mile to help color in my memories of Aiken Lab and Harvard life in the early 1970s, and though it doesn't appear on these pages, I owe Harry for my introduction to the "pancake problem." (For the record, I wasn't the one who moved the classroom clock ahead by ten minutes when Harry wasn't looking.) Appreciation to Eric Roberts, whose kind help at Harvard I will never forget, and Ed Taft for his thoughtful contributions to this book. Thanks to Tom Cheatham III for the memories of his father.

And then there are members of the original Microsoft team. I'm particularly thankful to Monte Davidoff, Bob Greenberg, Chris Larson, Marc McDonald, Steve Wood, and Bob O'Rear, who all believed in Micro-Soft when it was just a tiny start-up and helped me tell our story here.

Eddie Currie patiently reviewed the ups and downs of Microsoft's time with MITS and graciously reconnected me with Ed Roberts after many years. I am grateful for the time I spent with David Roberts and his help in bringing his father to life in the pages of this book.

Thanks to Paul Gilbert, our partner at Traf-O-Data, and Mike Schaefer, whose guidance helped me recount Ric's life and contributions to Microsoft. Van Chandler and Randy Wigginton filled in memories of the dawn of the personal computer.

Having access to archival materials related to my life was an enormous help. I want to especially thank Joe Ross, Meg Tuomala, and Emily Jones at the Gates Archive, Patti Thibodeau at the Microsoft Archives, and Leslie Schuler at the Lakeside Archives, in addition to her colleagues in Lakeside's Science Department. Thanks to Josh Schneider, archivist at Stanford University, and the archivists at Harvard and the University of Washington for their research and guidance.

When you get around to telling a story after half a century, it's a big plus that talented writers have already covered some of the ground. Those whose work helped jog my memory and round out the story of the early PC industry include Paul Andrews, Paul Freiberger, Walter Isaacson, Steven Levy, Steve Lohr, Stephen Manes, John Markoff, and Michael Swaine.

Early readers of the manuscript included Paula Hurd, Marc St. John, and Sheila Gulati. The close read from dear and trusted friends provided much-needed thoughtful and insightful feedback at critical stages in the writing.

I owe a special thanks to the many people at Gates Ventures who helped make this book possible.

Larry Cohen is a bright light in all the work we do together and had wise counsel as I first considered the idea of a memoir.

Alex Reid and her communications team deftly managed the release of this memoir, navigating the media landscape to help me find its audience.

Andy Cook and his team found brilliant ways to bring the book to market across an ever-changing landscape of readers.

Ian Saunders and his creative team discovered inspiration in the words on the page and worked their magic to reach even wider audiences.

Jen Krajicek and Pia Dierking kept every part of the book production on track with precision and diplomacy.

Gregg Eskenazi, Hillary Bounds, and Laura Ayers navigated the seemingly never-ending contractual and legal aspects of releasing a book.

Many others played an essential role in the creation and release of this book over the years: Alicia Salmond, Anita Kissée, Anna Dahlquist, Anu Horsman, Aubree Bogdonovich, Bradley Castaneda, Bridgitt Arnold, Cailin Wyatt, Chloe Johnson, Darya Fenton, David Sanger, Dinali Weeraman, Donia Barani, Emily Warden, Emma McHugh, Emma Northup, Erin Rickard, Graham Gerrity, Jacqueline Smith, Joanna Fuller, John Murphy, John Pinette, Jordana Narin, Josh Daniel, Josh Friedman, Katie Rupp, Kerry McNellis,

Khiota Therrien, Kim McGee, Kimberly Lamar, Kristi Anthony, Lauren Jiloty, Mara MacLean, Margaret Holsinger, Mariah Young, Meghan Groob, Mike Immerwahr, Neil Shah, Sarah Fosmo, Sean Simons, Sean Williams, Sebastian Majewski, Stephanie Williams, Tom Black, Valerie Morones, Whitney Beatty, and Zach Finkelstein.

And I want to thank the rest of the incredible team at Gates Ventures: Aishwarya Sukumar, Alex Bertha, Alex Grinberg, Alexandra Crosby, Amy Mayberry, Andrea Vargas Guerra, Angelina Meadows Comb, Anna Devon-Sand, Anne Liu, Avery Bell, Becky Bartlein, Bennett Sherry, Brian Sanders, Brian Weiss, Bridgette O'Connor, Caitlin McHugh, Chelsea Katzenberg, Chevy Lazenby, Christopher Hughes, Courtney Voigt, Craig Miller, David Phillips, Dillon Mydland, Ebony McKiver, Emily Woolway, Erik Christensen, Farhad Imam, Gloria Ikilezi, Goutham Kandru, Graham Bearden, Greg Martinez, Gretchen Burk, Hannah Pratt, Heather Viola, Henry Moyers, Ilia Lopez, Jamal Yearwood, Jeanne Solsten, Jeff Huston, Jen Kidwell Drake, Jennie Lyman, Jonathan Shin, Jordan-Tate Thomas, Kate Reizner, Ken Caldeira, Kendra Fahrenbach, Kevin Smallwood, Kristina Malzbender, Kyle Nettelbladt, Linda Patterson, Lindsey Funari, Lisa Bishop, Lisa Perrone, Manny McBride, Matt Clement, Matt Tully, Meredith Kimball, Michael Peters, Mike Maguire, Molly Sinnott, Mukta Phatak, Naomi Zukor, Niranjan Bose, Patrick Owens, Prarthna Desai, Quinn Cornelius, Rachel Phillips, Ray Minchew, Rodi Guidero, Ryan Fitzgerald, Sonya Shekhar, Steve Springmeyer, Sunrise Swanson Williams, Sydney Garfinkel, Sydney Yang Hoffman, Teresa Matson, Tony Hoelscher, Tony Pound, Tricia Jester, Tyler Hughes, Tyler Wilson, Udita Persaud, Varsha Krish, Vijay Sureshkumar, Yasmine Diara, Will Wang, and Zach Hennenfent.

This book would not have been possible without the world-class team at Knopf. *Source Code* had three editors, starting with the legendary Bob Gottlieb. Bob had edited my last two books, and he was the earliest cheerleader for this one. Sadly, Bob passed away just

314 *Acknowledgments*

as the manuscript started to come together. The world of publishing lost a very bright light. I recommend the film *Turn Every Page* (directed by Bob's daughter Lizzie Gottlieb) for a sense of just how amazing Bob was. After Bob's death, I was lucky to be introduced to the extremely gifted Reagan Arthur, who saw the book take its early shape and begin to find its focus.

Source Code was brought to the finish line in the expert hands of Jennifer Barth, who was willing to take on the project and commit an extraordinary amount of time and energy to make this book the best it could be. I am deeply grateful for her strong direction, generosity, and unwavering calm, even in the depths of a complicated edit.

I also want to thank everyone at KDPG who supported this publication, starting with the far-sighted Maya Mavjee, who always believed in this book, and Jordan Pavlin, Knopf's whip-smart publisher and editor-in-chief, who has been unwavering in her commitment. Director of production editorial Ellen Feldman's contributions were nothing short of heroic. I am grateful to all their colleagues who worked on *Source Code,* including Anne Achenbaum, Michael Collica, Meredith Dros, Brian Etling, John Gall, Erinn Hartman, Kate Hughes, Oona Intemann, Laura Keefe, Linda Korn, Serena Lehman, Beth Meister, Lisa Montebello, Jessica Purcell, Sal Ruggiero, Suzanne Smith, and Ellen Whitaker. I also want to acknowledge the amazing contribution of the teams of Knopf Canada and Allen Lane/Penguin Press UK, who were a joy to work with.

My life would not have turned out the way it has if not for Paul Allen, my friend, my partner, and my goad. Paul died too young. Writing this book gave me a chance to relive those wonderful years when we were the closest—a time in which we created something truly remarkable. I am so thankful to Paul for his insight, wisdom, curiosity, and friendship, especially in the tough times.

Above all, my sisters Kristi and Libby deserve a special acknowledgment. They have patiently supported me my entire life, and their contributions to *Source Code* were essential. Early in the writing of this book, we all sat down on Hood Canal one summer afternoon and laughed our way through childhood memories, family stories, and the day-to-day details of growing up together, from molasses dots to pickleball. It was hours of fun for the three of us and a happy reminder that the passing years have brought us even closer. I am lucky you are my sisters, and I am immeasurably grateful for the love and understanding you have always given me.

Finally, I want to thank my children Jenn, Rory, and Phoebe. Being your father and watching you grow up has been the greatest joy of my life. As I wrote this book, I thought about how proud your grandparents and great-grandparents would be of the extraordinary people you've become.

Illustration Credits

Pages 8–9 (all photos except Bill Gates in scout uniform, Boy Scout registration card): Mike Collier

Pages 10–11 (young Kent Evans in profile): Evans Family Archive; (class photograph, school portraits of Paul Allen and Ric Weiland): Lakeside School Archives; (four photographs of boys in school with teletype computer): Bruce R. Burgess

Pages 12–13 (three school portraits of Bill Gates): Lakeside School Archives

Pages 14–15 (Bill Gates and Paul Allen): Barry Wong/*The Seattle Times;* (Bill Gates and Ric Weiland): Michael Schaefer; (Bill Gates behind desk): © Stephen Wood; (early Microsoft headquarters): Gates Notes, LLC

Endpapers from the author's personal collection

In honor of Bill Sr. and Mary Maxwell Gates's commitment to civic engagement and philanthropy, all profits from *Source Code* will be donated to United Way Worldwide. Mary Gates was the first woman to serve as president of United Way of King County and was later the first woman board chair of United Way International.

A NOTE ABOUT THE AUTHOR

Bill Gates is a technologist, business leader, and philanthropist. In 1975, he cofounded Microsoft with his childhood friend Paul Allen, and today he is chair of the Gates Foundation. Bill is the founder of Breakthrough Energy, an effort to commercialize clean energy and other climate-related technologies, and TerraPower, a company investing in developing groundbreaking nuclear technologies. He has three children.

A NOTE ON THE TYPE

This book was set in Adobe Garamond. Designed for the Adobe Corporation by Robert Slimbach, the fonts are based on types first cut by Claude Garamond (ca. 1480–1561).

Composed by North Market Street Graphics
Lancaster, Pennsylvania

Printed and bound by Berryville Graphics
Berryville, Virginia

Designed by Michael Collica

3615				52520	SUBTTL IF ... THE		
3616	004325'	001000	000315	52540	IF:	CALL	F
3617	004326'	000000	005336'				
3618	004327'	000000	004323'				
3619				52560	IFE	LENGTH,<	
3620				52580	IFN	STRING,<	
3621				52600		LDA	V
3622				52620		PUSH	P
3623	004330'	001000	000176	52640		MOV	A
3624				52660	IFE	LENGTH,<	
3625				52680		CALL	P
3626				52700		MVI	D
3627				52720			
3628				52740			
3629				52760			
3630				52780	LOOPIF:	SUI	G
3631				52800		JC	E
3632				52820	NUMREL=LESSTK-GRE		
3633				52840		CPI	N
3634				52860		JNC	E
3635				52880		CPI	1
3636				52900		RAL	
3637				52920		ORA	D
3638				52940		MOV	D
3639				52960		CHRGET	
3640				52980		JMP	L
3641				53000	ENDREL:	MOV	A
3642				53020		ORA	A
3643				53040		JZ	S
3644				53060		PUSH	F
3645				53080		CALL	F
3646				53100			
3647				53120			
3648	004331'	001000	000376	53140	IFE	LENGTH-2,	
3649	004332'	000000	000054				
3650	004333'	001000	000314	53160		CZ	C
3651	004334'	000000	003426'				
3652	004335'	000000	004326'				
3653				53180	IFN	LENGTH,<	
3654	004336'	001000	000376	53200		CPI	C
3655	004337'	000000	000210				
3656	004340'	001000	000312	53220		JZ	C
3657	004341'	000000	004346'				
3658	004342'	000000	004334'				
3659	004343'	001000	000317	53240		SYNCHK	
3660	004344'	000000	000245				
3661	004345'	001000	000053	53260		DCX	
3662	004346'			53280	OKGOTO:		
3663				53300	IFE	LENGTH,<	
3664				53320		POP	
3665				53340		POPR	
3666				53360	IFN	STRING,<	
3667				53380		XTHL>	